LETTERS

from

THE FRONT

LETTERS AND DIARIES
FROM THE BEF IN FLANDERS
AND FRANCE 1914–1918

KEVIN SMITH

Fonthill Media Limited
Fonthill Media LLC
www.fonthillmedia.com
office@fonthillmedia.com

First published in the United States of America and the United Kingdom 2013

ISBN 978-1-78155-338-1

Typeset in 10pt on 13pt Sabon LT
Printed and bound in England

Contents

Dedicated to my family—all of them.

Introduction

Another book on World War I? Why? Can there be any more to say?

I have taught history to high school and college students for over forty years. They enter the classroom commonly believing that the Great War was too long ago to matter, that nothing about it could still be important, and it is probably boring, anyway. I feel compelled and privileged to enlighten them.

On 12 June 2010, a warm day with a few puffy clouds scattered overhead, I got out of an air-conditioned car and walked a short distance to the Bayernwald trenches in Belgium. There are not many genuine Great War trenches available to tourists and historians nearly a hundred years after the event, and I had come a great distance to observe these. After just a moment or two, a mist of annoying gnats swirled around my head, and I began a retreat to the car. Only having taken a step or two toward the exit, the irony hit me like a sledgehammer. Here I was, a person who had chosen to come thousands of miles to be here, fleeing from a handful of insects, while hundreds, no, thousands of other men, who certainly had not chosen to be there, endured gnats, and rats, and rain, and wind, and cold, and mud, and bad food, and sickness, and artillery fire, and poison gas, and fear, and stench, and noise, and possible wounds, and the constant danger and frequent occurrence of death. All of that was while they were on the defensive. When ordered to attack, add "withering machine gun fire" to the litany of misery. Moreover, they endured these threats for days turning into months turning into years—and never fled to a car or to anywhere else. What put these men into this place and what kept them there?

There were a number of teenaged students and their teachers who left the trench just as I arrived. I wanted to tell them that just the day before, I had visited the nearby grave of British rifleman Valentine Joseph Strudwick, who died on 14 January 1916. Just one death among millions, of course, but he was only 15. Is a fifteen year old properly termed a rifle MAN? I wondered what his friends called him. Val? Joe? What is known is that he volunteered for the army in January, 1915, when still just 14. He was killed just a month shy of his 16th birthday, St Valentine's Day. Valentine Joseph Strudwick was certainly one of the youngest soldiers to die in this war.

I had been cautioned that the trenches would be muddy and slippery. Forewarned, I proceeded to slip in the mud, get mud on my dress slacks, bang my head on the remaining piece of corrugated metal roof, and feel humbled.

My purpose in writing this study is not to plow new ground nor report profound new insights. Rather, it is an attempt to record what happened in such a way as to engender an interest in mastering and retelling this most profoundly moving story by the next generation of learners, an attempt to let the soldiers speak for themselves. It is to build a bridge between those who knew "It's a Long Way to Tipperary" and those who do not, between those who seldom used a telephone and those who seldom are without one. It *is* a tale worth retelling.

A Note on the Sources

I have quoted from many papers in the collection of the Imperial War Museum, Lambeth Road, London, cited "IWM." Efforts have been made to contact the known copyright holders of those papers, and most have kindly given permission for me to publish. In cases where the copyright is owned by the IWM, the Trustees of the IMW have granted permission for their use, and I thank them. If I have violated any copyright, it is certainly unintentional, and I apologize.

There is an extraordinary variety of material in these files. It may be an actual hand-written diary or collection of letters. It may be photographs or medals or programs from events. It may be a handwritten copy of original letters written by a contemporary family member into a tablet. In a few cases, it may be an actual book in bound form, but of very limited circulation; there might be just that one copy. It may be a photocopy of an original document now in delicate condition or even lost to time. Sometimes it is difficult to know the exact date being referenced, and sometimes the date is clearly indicated or can be deduced. For all of these reasons, it may appear that the form of citation in the footnotes is not consistent. As far as makes sense, it is consistent. It is the data that is so varied. Of course it is possible that I have juxtaposed some entry or another, but I doubt I have ever violated the sense of the remarks. Reading enough of these cements certain key themes in the reader's mind, for example, as you will read, mud and stench.

As far as possible, I have tried to keep the original spelling and punctuation, tried to let the men speak for themselves, except when having to modify the original for clarity's sake. Very seldom did I find any error in spelling.

Notes of Appreciation

My deep gratitude to Colonel Walter William Sigg, U.S. Army (retired) whose careful attention has improved every page of this study. Thanks also to Simon Offord of the IWM for his valuable suggestions.

My thanks to the late Rev. Francis E. Fox of Cardinal Dougherty High School and Professor John P. Rossi of LaSalle University who demonstrated outstanding teaching every day in their classrooms.

Thanks to my wife Barbara Ann, for enduring it all.

Prelude

What a remarkable set of circumstances! A few deadly shots are fired by a teenager in central Europe in June, 1914, and a mere fifty days later, crack British troops have crossed the English Channel onto the continent and are exchanging gunfire with Germans, who are also exchanging fire with French and Belgians. How in the world did these events devolve?

Certainly the assassinations of an Austrian Archduke and his wife did not cause the Great War. Years ago, teachers would list remote and immediate causes for this event, still a useful construct. Remote causes would include such things as nationalism, which in its extreme form asserts the superiority of one culture over another. Compared to France and Great Britain, the German empire was a recent creation. Only in 1871 had the myriad German principalities finally been united by Prussian leadership into one nation. Rapid modernization ensued. One index of a modern economy, steel production, grew exponentially in Germany, soon overtaking both France and Great Britain, while swift progress followed in other areas. In optics and ophthalmology, Germany soon led the world, while thanks to their science simple aspirin became even more useful, Diesel engines were greatly improved, and high order physics was explored. While Karl Benz was improving motor cars, Emil von Behring was exploring antitoxins. Indeed, German science was world class. Towards the end of the nineteenth century,

> ...the industrious Germans made giant leaps in modern technology and economics: steel production, mining, chemicals, education, finance, transportation, electronics, and, of course, the most up-to-date military armaments, while much of continental Europe, especially France, seemed content to languish as agricultural nations.[1]

The government of the new Germany had some profound weaknesses. As one historian declared, "The unification of Germany in 1871 had created a nation that combined the most dynamic economy in Europe with a regime that in many respects had hardly emerged from feudalism."[2]

The process of creating that new state had left behind a fatal if unrecognized flaw, the annexation of Alsace and Lorraine. At the conclusion of the Franco-Prussian War in 1871, the German military had unwisely insisted that the two provinces become part of the new German Empire. "This humiliation galled the French down to the last peasant."[3] The German leaders failed to recognize that such a forced union would insure a permanent grievance between France and Germany, making a future friendship between them impossible. This enmity was tolerable as long as Germany's eastern neighbor, mighty Russia, was kept in check by the Reinsurance Treaty, a document that placed Germany and Russia in a loose alliance. The brilliant German Chancellor Prince Otto von Bismarck had seen the danger of allowing Russia to form unsupervised friendships. After all, although she might be slow to prepare, once the Russian bear began to move, her immense armies would be a very large factor in any future war. Bismarck engineered two treaties, one with Austria, the other with Russia. In essence, Germany became the pivot of a diplomatic seesaw, the Austrians in Vienna on one end, with the Russians in St Petersburg, the other. Thus, when either displeased Germany, Berlin was able by means of mere hints to either Austria or Russia to move the offender back toward the German point of view. This arrangement lasted until the elderly Bismarck was discharged by the young and quite inexperienced new Kaiser, William II, in 1894. Reading and recognizing that on the face of them the treaties were incompatible, the rookie Kaiser exercised the non-renewal clause in the Reinsurance Treaty—and cast Russia adrift.

The Kaiser's action left Russia suddenly isolated in the diplomatic world. The French were quick to exploit the situation. Massive French loans to modernize the Russian railroad system quickly followed, and the new friends instantly had Germany in an unenviable position. Simple geography and inept German diplomacy now dictated that any future war between France, Russia and Germany would have Germany splitting her might between her eastern and western borders. Germany would be compelled to fight a two front war.

Some historians have been severe critics of the Kaiser. One concluded:

...the personality of the Kaiser was of overwhelming importance, and it was the misfortune not only of Germany but the entire world that at this juncture the House of Hohenzollern should have produced, in William II, an individual who in his person embodied those qualities that may be said to have characterized the contemporary German ruling elite: archaic militarism, vaulting ambition, and neurotic insecurity.[4]

Another of the remote causes of the war grew out of the alliance system. Just as Germany cemented relations with the Austro-Hungarian Empire, the French and Russians looked to a friendly future. While these four nations were firmly in place, one other major power was loosely aligned with France, but with increasing intimacy. For centuries, Britain had exercised a balancing role on the continent, never allowing one nation to become excessively powerful, and certainly never allowing any one power to interfere with British trade with the continent. Indeed, Great Britain never lost sight of an obvious but paramount fact, her island geography. Alone among the great powers, Great Britain did not grow her own food. On the contrary, in 1914, nearly sixty percent of her food was imported in the thousands and thousands of ships from all over the globe clearing her harbors each day. Imported foodstuffs permitted survival, exported goods funded an enhanced lifestyle. For Britain, keeping command of the seas was the supreme military priority. To this end, the British maintained at no small expense the most modern and most expensive fleet afloat, fully aware that their national survival depended upon those buoyant steel castles.

Yet Britain's German cousins did not seem to grasp the sacrosanctity of this truth. The glorious age of fighting sail had concluded, the time of rather dirty coal-fired warships had just peaked, and the new darling of the age, the oil fired battleship, was arriving. With the launching of HMS *Queen Elizabeth* in 1912, the naval course was set. Henceforth, the Royal Navy would be oil-fired—despite the British Isles total lack of that resource, as the North Sea oil fields were not yet discovered.

A world-wide program of establishing petroleum supplies and refueling bases was begun, and Germany saw an opportunity. At the moment, the European playing field, as it were, was about as level as it could be expected to be. Germany resolved to build a powerful blue water fleet, to carry the German eagle by sea into the sunlight of world respect. Germany, too, could be a first class naval power and use that might as a platform with which to stake out a world-wide economic empire.

While Germany had the economic wherewithal to build such a fleet, she did not have the wisdom to forgo it. In the minds of the British, Germany was a land power, already having an extraordinarily powerful army. Why did she also need a navy? Against whom could it possibly be deployed? The British did not take comfort in the likely answers to these questions, and soon sent the first of several delegations to Berlin for discussions. Keeping in mind the expense and manpower involved in building these seagoing colossals, the British offered a number of proposals. Might each side agree to build just a certain number, with Britain always being preponderant, due to her dependence on the seas? Might each side declare a "Naval Holiday", that is, a year in which neither side built any ships? These and other British proposals were drowned in the sea of Germany's resurgent national pride. What London perceived as German intransience caused the British to move ever closer to France and with some British reluctance, closer to France's friend, Tsarist Russia, an oppressive monarchy which enjoyed little popularity in Britain. Oddly enough, there were strong family ties among the rulers of Britain, Germany and Russia: the two emperors and one king[5] were all cousins, addressing each other in much of their correspondence as "Dear Nicky" for the Tsar of All the Russias and "Dear Willy" for the All-Highest Emperor of Germany

While Britain and Germany drifted further apart, Britain and France moved closer. What might have been a nasty colonial incident at Fashoda in Africa was resolved with effective diplomacy. A French navy which had insufficient strength at sea to protect both the Atlantic and Mediterranean coasts, and insufficient strength in the French legislature to improve its funding, looked with longing at the British fleet—the massive, ever-increasing British fleet. As in the time of Napoleon, the French army came first, the navy, an afterthought. With the quiet approval of only the most senior leadership, British and French military personnel and their civilian masters conducted intensely detailed and intensely private conversations leading to an understanding, an "entente." Not rising to the category of a formal alliance, but an honor-binding gentlemen's agreement, these conversations detailed the placement of the British Expeditionary Force, the BEF, in France promptly upon an invasion of Belgium by Germany. In addition, the French fleet would be free to concentrate in the Mediterranean, as the British undertook responsibility for the English Channel and the entire Atlantic coast of France.

There were many reasons for keeping this understanding secret. Perhaps foremost for the British was that only Parliament could ratify such detailed promises. Such was not the mind of Parliament at the time. Prime Minister Herbert Henry Asquith deeply worried over the split in opinion within his own Cabinet. A few of the Ministers were profoundly and genuinely pacifists, believing that war was to be avoided at all costs. Others wanted a very clear *casus belli*, a manifestly evil move by an enemy which would clearly justify a declaration of war. Still others were quite ready for what they saw as an unavoidable showdown with the arrogant Germans. Asquith could not ask Parliament for war with such division in his own team. Thus, while believing that war was inevitable, he had to wait for events to mold public opinion.

Still another remote cause of the war was militarism. This might be described as a willingness to use force or the threat of force to pressure other nations to settle disagreements. Each of these nations lavished a great deal of the national treasure on military preparations, and felt they could reasonably expect that the military could and should serve as the enforcer of national policy. Social Darwinism, Nietzsche's "Will to Power", and self-centered cultural arrogance were very much a part of the European worldview in 1914. The leader of Germany in particular had a penchant for public appearances in uniform. "The Kaiser appeared always in uniform as the All Highest War Lord, surrounded by a military entourage."[6]

Germany was not alone in this parade of uniforms. The King of England was an honorary Admiral in the German fleet; the Kaiser was an honorary Admiral in the Royal Navy—along with the Tsar of all the Russias and the Emperor of Japan. Each of these would from time to time don the uniform of the other. There is a classic photograph of the Tsar and King of England facing the camera together, each wearing an Admiral's uniform of the other's nation.

Very few Europeans alive in 1914 could remember a major war. After all, the last war among the great powers, the Franco-Prussian War, had been two generations ago and had lasted less than ten months. That war had broken out in July of 1870 and by September Napoleon III and his entire army were prisoners. Tales of the glories of war, of heroic sacrifices, of patriotism remained in common memory. Facts about sickness and suffering and maiming and death and destruction had faded into the misty and hallowed background. The young British officer knew from Horace that it was "sweet to die for one's country", and from Homer that it was in battle that one demonstrates "one's virtue and worth."[7] "The combatants knew that much more was at stake than mere ground and human life: honor; reputation; culture, tradition; the future. It must be victory, or extinction"[8] Many saw war as noble, as glorious, as manly. Few had the sense to devote all their strength to avoiding it. There were more glorious martial monuments about than there were maimed victims of actual warfare. Yet as one thoughtful British observer noted in his diary on 14 August: "I wondered at the time how many of the men would come back with the Battalion. Little did I think that within four months, hardly any of them would still be present."[9] One of the more thoughtful men among those first sent to France in 1914 expressed it this way:

The strange thing about it all was that we knew we were going to the front to kill, die, or suffer terrible wounds, yet not one man was dispirited.[10]

CHAPTER 1

1914: Plans and Counterplans

...now it is possible to take away thousands of lives by one man working behind a gun from a hill. This is civilization....
Gandhi, *Indian Home Rule.*

That war broke out between France and Germany in 1914 surprised neither nation, and their various alliance systems drew in multiple other powers, too. Both militaries had ample time to prepare, and some highly intelligent officers spent entire careers thirsting for what some Germans called "Der Tag."

The French plan took shape almost as soon as the smoke cleared from the war in 1871. Her lost children, the provinces of Alsace and Lorraine, were to be brought back home with all dispatch. Therefore, French planners envisioned a quick punch into Alsace-Lorraine, and a quick end to the war. Yet the French also realized that the 65 million Germans greatly outnumbered the 35 million French. This weakness would be offset by "élan", a triumphant spiritual superiority whereby the jubilant French through force of will would overwhelm the inferior Germans, material differences notwithstanding. The French dwelt in a prewar illusion that morale and a determined will could win.[1]

Concordant with this belief, some units of the French army still wore the bright red trousers of a pre-camouflage era. As a cardinal stands out among the birds of the forest, so too did these troops, making themselves both pretty on parade and pretty good targets, brilliant red against the green and gold of the farm fields. Meanwhile, the French believed that a series of forts along the northern border with Germany would stop any invaders while decisive victory was achieved in the lost provinces.

Germany also had a plan, and had spent years constructing, refining, and revising it. Named for one of its primary architects, General von Schlieffen's plan had been under annual revision or at least annual tweaking by the general staff since its first formulation in 1906. The general staff was a German concept denoting a team of experts, each devoting attention to one aspect of military operations. Some worked on training the army, others on arming and resupplying it, still others on transporting it and so forth. In broad outline, the German war plan was not terribly complex. In the event of a two front war, having to fight far to the east and far to the west, the Germans believed that the threats from France and her ally Russia were uneven. Superior French railroads and more modern communications could put troops into the field much faster than huge but backward Russia. The Germans calculated that they could employ the bulk of their forces in the quick destruction of the French army and then within six weeks hustle the army onto trains, rush over to the eastern front, and then defeat the poorly armed and under equipped Russians. The Germans expected that Russia's ragged and poorly led armies, composed of many ethnicities and speaking many different languages, would still be struggling to mobilize. But Germany also realized with some unease that there were 165 million Russians.

In order to achieve a German victory, speed and timing were essential. The German troops must be ready on time, must advance on time, must score victories on time, and could not tolerate delay. Consequently, time could not be spent on battering a way through the prepared French fortifications. Since these could not be subdued in the time permitted, they must be circumvented. Therefore, the German plan called for a holding action to the south. This would allow, almost invite, a French attack into Alsace Lorraine, while a terrific German blow would swing down through northern France like the spokes of a giant wheel rotating towards Paris. Indeed, "Let the sleeve of the last man on the right brush the English channel" was the plan. The brilliant historian Barbara Tuchman summarized the German doctrine this way:

> There was not enough room for the huge German army to get around the French armies and still stay inside France. The Germans had done it in 1870 when both armies were small, but now it was a matter of moving an army of millions to outflank an army of millions. Space, roads and railroads were essential. The flat plains of Flanders had them.[2]

But the French alone did not occupy all the land against the North Sea. Part of this land is called Flanders, a part of the mini-nation, Belgium. While Belgians regarded international events with keen interest in June of 1914, their King Albert, uncertain as to what to expect, positioned his army to defend against any foreign danger. Actually, most in Belgium hoped to be spared from being involved in the imminent war. They placed their faith in the treaty signed in 1839 by France, Germany and Great Britain which proclaimed that

Belgium was to be permanently neutral, and that those nations would each guarantee that neutrality against the others. But the German plan's need for speed dictated that German forces must attack France by swinging through Belgium, a clear violation of the treaty.

The matter of violating Belgian neutrality had been carefully considered by the Germans. A swift attack against France through the side door represented by Belgium was considered an operational necessity. Some Germans believed that little Belgium would formally protest, but in the light of the massive German presence, would offer only *pro forma* resistance. Those better acquainted with the Belgian character expected a strong if forlorn and temporary resistance. If Belgium were to resist with her whole strength, minor though it was, it might be enough to delay the carefully crafted German timetable. Much more important, such an invasion of Belgium ran the risk of war with Great Britain.

Germany weighed the risk of British military intervention with great care. Surely, the mighty Royal Navy would impose a prompt blockade of Germany, but would not the war be long over before a blockade could become mortally effective? Many Germans considered Britain's standing army to be too small to present much of a threat to their finely crafted plan. After all, Britain had a population of only 40 million, and a small and reputedly inferior army.

The last campaign of the British Army, the effort to subdue the South African Boers, had been a public relations disaster. The army struggled to put down a band of farmer-fighters. However, its showing in that endeavor was so poor that a goodly number of reforms were begun and the fruits of those efforts, such as the reorganization of the reserve army, were realized just as this war began.

The leaders in Berlin were not impressed with the British Army. The Germans calculated that the speed of their attacking armies would make any British reaction quite ineffective whether at sea or on land. Then too, the traditional British contribution to continental wars had been as the financier, arms supplier, blockade enforcer and even cheerleader—but the tiny British Army, the British Expeditionary Force, was only "perfection in miniature"[3], having nowhere near the power of the German colossus. Generally, Great Britain did not supply large armies to continental wars. But as a further danger to the Triple Alliance of Germany, Austria, and Italy, Britain received an astonishing degree of support from her major former colonies, particularly Australia, New Zealand and Canada. Their armies, also underestimated by the Germans, would show a remarkable tenacity as they joined in battle, and as they too endured enormous casualties. Overall, the Germans elected to invade through Belgium despite their awareness of the likely consequences.

Like Germany and France, Britain also had a plan for the coming war.

Her military leaders including Sir John French, the Commander-in-Chief designate, spent many hours working out the details. When were the British to arrive, where would they concentrate, how long would it take them to be ready to take an active part in field operations? These were grand questions, yes, but British war plans also incorporated even the little yet crucial details such as what would the cavalry horses eat, for example, and where would the blacksmiths mend the equipment? The story of that little army and its enormous expansion forms the core of the story remembered in this study.

As July of 1914 unfolded, Germany supported her ally, Austria, when Austria delivered a harsh ultimatum to Serbia. Yet Serbia had some powerful friends as well, and the biggest, Russia, felt unable to back down again (as she had been forced to do a few years earlier) lest she lose credibility among her Balkan clients. When Russia began mobilizing on her western borders, including the one with Germany, Germany reacted with alarm. After all, mobilization was a very serious step. When declared by the German, French or Russian governments, it required all the trained men to report immediately to their local armories, where they exchanged civilian clothes for their uniforms and weapons, and then hurried to the nearby railway facilities where empty trains would soon be arriving to rush them to their assigned place in the grand design. Mobilization was quite expensive, ultra serious, and rarely only a bluff. An alarmed German General staff persuaded the Kaiser to send an urgent message to his cousin, the Tsar of Russia, demanding that Russia cease mobilizing, at least along the German border.

However, that was not enough. Germany needed to know whether this was the opening salvo of the long-awaited two front war. The Great Question: what would France do? Honor her commitment to her ally, Russia, or sit this out? Germany sent a note to France, asking just what France would do. That was a rather astonishing moment. If France were planning to attack, would she say so? If she said no, could her response be trusted? If France promised to stay out, Germany planned to insist on some guarantees, such as occupying some major French forts along their common border. However, that did not occur, as the French delivered the opaque reply that France "...would be guided by her own interests."

Now feeling the full burden of the failure of diplomacy to obviate a two front war, Germany acted. Having no satisfactory reply from her ultimatum to Russia, the German Empire declared war on the French at 3:55 p.m. on 3 August 1914. By happenstance, just five minutes later, the French declared war on Germany, and the house of cards fell.

But what about the British? A tortured British Cabinet agonized over what action to recommend to Parliament. Some thought that maintaining the peace was the supreme goal. Others felt that the march of events had demonstrated that now was the time to stand up to the Germans. Perhaps a word of warning now might make them rethink their strategy and back away from the impending conflagration. At the end of a tortuous day, the British adopted a wait and see policy. It all depended on Belgium, little Belgium. If the Germans respected Belgium's neutrality, then Prime Minister Herbert Asquith's government would not have a majority for war, and thus would have to leave the French to their own destiny.

Just as Julius Caesar declared his intention for war by crossing the Rubicon River toward Rome in his day, so too did the Germans declare a similar intent by crossing the Meuse River into Belgium on 4 August 1914. Now the vast detailed machinery of war kicked into full speed ahead. The French armies quickly moved to their assigned locations, and prepared to liberate Alsace-Lorraine. The Germans expected that, planned for that, nearly welcomed that, as they hoped the bulk of French strength would concentrate there. Slowly, deceptively, the Germans would fallback until the French were snuggly in the trap: then, with the French surrounded on three sides, allowing the classic envelopment maneuver, the Germans would pounce, cut the French off from their homeland and supplies, and force surrender, as they had in 1870. Yet while that victory was unfolding, von Schlieffen's plan also called for a powerful thrust into the northern part of France and into Belgium. The German dispositions resembled a clenched fist. Five armies lined along the border, but the oversized thumb, as it were, on the northern edge was to race through Belgium and smash its way to Paris. Paris taken? War over, Germany wins, German army off quickly by railroad express trains to defeat the Russians.

As the threat of war became more real with each passing moment, one Englishman did not hesitate to enhance Britain's military position. The First Lord of the Admiralty, the civilian politician in charge of the Royal Navy, was thirty-nine year old Winston Churchill.[4] The fleet was just finishing its summer maneuvers, an annual drill of all ships and all personnel. At the moment, the Royal Navy was in excellent shape with all ships manned, all ships at war stations. Churchill ordered that the fleet remain in that posture, postponing its return to a peacetime status. He believed that the fleet in obvious readiness might influence Germany to reconsider her aggressive position. Moreover, the fleet had an extraordinary duty in the opening days of the coming war: it had to transport the army to the continent. An army at sea is in a vulnerable state. Geared to fight on land, its weapons and tactics are not at all suited for sea battles. The Royal Navy had to embark the soldiers, transport them across the English Channel, protect them from submarines and battle fleets, and once safely across, guarantee delivery of the daily ration of tons and tons of food, ammunition, medicine, replacement parts, and so on.

Not many non-military personnel have a realistic perspective on the overall demands of a modern army. In short, a large number of soldiers are transported to a new place where there is little in the way of the complex infrastructure needed to sustain them. It is as though an entire city of men, overwhelmingly men but with some women, were plucked away from their base of operations and deposited in the middle of a farm field far away. While the support system might be displaced—food, water, shelter, medical attention, or more detailed needs such as shoe repair for men and mules and horses, and water and food for the horses, and a way to launder the men's clothing and to prepare their meals and to get them haircuts and to entertain them while off duty and a million other things: while the support system might no longer be there, it is still very much needed and must be constructed with all due dispatch.

Churchill's first duty was to get the army safely into France and then continue to keep it supplied with all it needed to fight and sustain itself. To combat the submarine menace, for example, the Royal Navy strung miles of underwater nets in the English Channel. These were designed to snare a submarine, perhaps to tangle its propeller so that it would have to come up for air and could be attacked. In the event, the fleet strung seventeen miles of nets in the Straits of Dover.[5]

The actual decision to enter the war and send the army was reached by the British Cabinet on 4 August after the German invasion of Belgium was clearly underway. None of the men sitting in the Cabinet room that fateful day could clearly foresee the events to come in the terrible, terrible time ahead. For instance, at that crucial meeting, Winston Churchill sat between Lord Lucas and Lord Kitchener: both died in the war, Lucas in the air and Kitchener at sea.[6] The British Expeditionary Force, the BEF, ordered to the continent that day, about 250,000 men, would ultimately prove to be just a down payment on the millions who were to follow. In addition, Britain never had even a million soldiers before, let alone sent such a huge force out of the country. In the meantime, the army transfer was accomplished flawlessly. The entire army crossed into France 12 August through 17 August with not a single casualty.[7]

All those careful hours of planning were rewarded with a smooth deployment to France. What happened after their arrival was less smooth. The British force moved toward its prearranged zones with vigor, intending to hold a position between the French to the south and the Belgians to the north. Those first moves on French soil toward the battlefields may have been the last moves to go according to plan. Very quickly, the exigencies of war forced changes in the BEF's location and mission. Whatever the master plan, the comprehensive grand design, the meticulously planned great offensive; as in all wars, the actual result came down to the individuals and their flexibility on the battlefield.

Even in these earliest days, matters large and small failed to go according to plan as is fully detailed in the soldier's diaries. For example, one noted on 27 August that "Hunger makes men cantankerous and intolerant" and that thirty-four men were issued one and a half loaves of bread—which they cut into thirty-four pieces.[8] He recorded that the next day's meal was boiled potatoes from the surrounding fields.

There were quite a few much more serious observations such as Sergeant Cubbon writing on 10 September: "The most awful day I have had... shells bursting on all sides, bullets within a foot. Before entering firing line prayed and had a look at Flo."[9] On 17 September he added: "Saw my face in a glass today, what a fright." And twelve days later:

Am in a terrible filthy state. Dirt is simply ground into my hands and face, hair all matted. These dugouts. We are all cramped up like sardines here. I am fairly well off as I have an overcoat, one that I picked up on the other side of the wood. It has the left sleeve blown off. Belonged to one of the wounded but it comes in handy at night.[10]

Sergeant Cubbon was certainly not alone in reusing equipment: "There was a serious shortage of good boots after the retreat and dead men's footwear was not wasted."[11]

Even the weather became an early obstacle. One soldier recorded that he: "...never felt so cold, wet and miserable in my life as I do now."[12] He was happy to get his allotment on 7 October of one blanket.

Bad as these conditions may have been, there was much worse to come. "I drag a body by the leg and pull the leg off."[13] "I was in charge of the burial party. Terrible sights. Jakes had to be picked up in pieces and buried in a ground sheet."[14]

H. T. Williams wrote how:

...we were sorry for our mates, for we could see mud, duckboards, flung into the air, and then a body would be flung out, and another until we could not look any more, that continued for some minutes. Then to our horror, we realized that the flashes of the guns were coming from behind us, on Jerries (the German) front all was still, as there were no gun flashes at all, and no sound of guns firing, as all seemed quiet in Jerries lines. That meant only one thing, that our own Artillery was shelling our front line, almost as soon as we realized the terrible mistake the guns stopped firing, someone had found out the error. But in those few minutes many of our mates had been killed and wounded. I expect that was only one of many such incidents in the war. But to bear witness to such a tragedy on your own friends is another sad memory for me.

A career soldier who was both a physician and a Colonel, Cyril Helm, made an early observation of what was to become a staggering problem, keeping track of the dead and their graves. On 21 October 1914, he wrote in his diary:

> The little back garden of the farm was now a mass of graves. Any man who died during the day was laid out there until he could be buried at night. That day there were at least ten, both German and British, these of course were only men who had died from wounds in my Dressing Station.

About a week later, Colonel Helm lost everything but his life in an attack:

> I had no kit (left) of any sort, nothing to sleep in, no razor, tooth brush, change of clothes or anything. The Quarter Master was my salvation. He gave me an old mail bag as a valise, a new supply of ration blankets, a pair of men's boots, and old Burberry, razor and brush, belonging to an officer who had been taken prisoner. The five remaining brother officers in the Mess each gave me some garment of underclothing. The result was that in a few days' time I was more or less set up again but on a very rough and ready fashion. My kit being enclosed in an old mail bag made everything but an elegant turnout.[16]

That October was not a good month for Colonel Helm. At one point, a shell exploded trapping him in a cellar where he remained until "After some time" when he was dug out by rescuers.[17] He was candid in in his opinion of the German artillery:

> The German gunners, at the beginning of the war, were perfectly marvelous. The rapidity with which they found a target and spotted our guns, was always a source of amazement for us.[18]

Colonel Helm's observation illustrates an important point. By the early years of the twentieth century, the weapons Napoleon once called his daughters had been vastly improved. Even as recently as the war between France and Germany in 1870, artillery had been steel breech-loaded devices with no recoil mechanism. When fired, the weapon bounced, and had to be carefully re-aimed. The new pieces had springs or gas shock absorbers, so moved out of aim much less, while also having a metal shield to protect the gunners. A gun with a three inch bore, firing a shell with a diameter of just under three inches could fire six shells a minute, or as many as twenty in an emergency.[19] On the other hand, the newer pieces were often heavier and harder to move, and definitely more prone to sink in mud, a fact which would greatly complicate the gunner's lives. To insure reasonable accuracy, a modern gun would require a wooden or metal platform, a "gun pit."

One hundred years made quite a difference. The field gun of 1814 fired perhaps one solid cannonball a minute. Its maximum range was not more than a kilometer, roughly a thousand yards. The guns of 1914, on the other hand, were actually termed "quick firing." The gunner opened the breech, or rear end of the weapon, and loaded it from that end. These newer weapons did not fire solid cannon balls, but had a variety of projectiles. Some carried poisonous gas while others were designed to penetrate concrete defenses. Still other were to maim and kill troops. Some shells burst in the air, others delayed their detonation. Even these lighter field pieces could strike targets up to three miles away.[20] Their big brothers, the much heavier "heavy artillery" could fire as far as twenty-five miles. A few specialized weapons could fire even farther than that.

Meanwhile, as the BEF arrived on the continent, it was organized into three corps, designated as I, II, and III. Each of those had two divisions, and there was a separate cavalry force of about division size. Each division contained a little more than 20,000 men when at full strength. Two of the army's better known generals were the Commander-in-Chief, Sir John French, and his eventual successor, General Douglas Haig. Originally, the British were to take their place between the French on the right and the Belgians on the left. But the speed of the German advance overwhelmed the defenders' plans. British troops marching rapidly forward to the attack suddenly found themselves under unexpectedly heavy shelling and soon were moving even more speedily in retreat. The original plan called for an advance to the area of Mons in Belgium, a town pretty much at the northern end of a straight line between the capital cities of Brussels and Paris. Holding Mons would help protect Paris by blocking a main highway between the two capitals.

As planned, the BEF moved through France and Belgium toward Mons to stop the German advance. An army is generally set up or "deployed" to attack or be attacked from one direction. This is a fundamental principle of military doctrine. Even this up-to-date British army still employed methods that would have been familiar to Napoleon, his great battles already ninety years past. The common use of radio for orders and commands was still in the future. Telegraph wires could be cut by shelling. Telephones were in their infancy. Messages were still carried by messenger, both human and carrier pigeon. Orders were commonly given in advance. Wrist and pocket watches gave the time, and whistles and arm waving signaled the moment for their execution. Generals in houses way behind the battlefield studied maps and picked targets, but at the moment of the actual fighting, command and leadership was in the hands of the junior officers, the lieutenants and captains who had to storm out of the trenches and cry "Follow me!" to men who were just as frightened but just as obedient as the officers.

In 1914, the primary weapon of the foot soldier was a rifle. The highly trained British riflemen were reputedly able to fire as many as fifteen well aimed shots per minute with a rifle accurate to about 1,600 feet, or about five times the length of a football field. His rifle was a Lee-Enfield 0.303 caliber bolt action shoulder fired weapon with a ten round magazine. That means his weapon's bullet had a .303 inch diameter. "Bolt action" meant that the lever on the side of the weapon had to be pulled up, back, forward, and down to its original position between each shot, a skilled maneuver learned through hours of practice. More commonly, soldiers fired perhaps eight rounds a minute with less than perfect accuracy.

It is easy to dismiss that rifle as old-fashioned. But one needs to remember that such a rifle could fire a bullet through eighteen inches of oak, or thirty-six inches of dirt sandbags or a double thickness of house bricks at 200 yards— twice the length of an American football field. Perhaps it was old, but it was still quite formidable, especially in the hands of well-trained troops.[21]

Newly arrived in the arsenal was the machine gun. This weapon was heavier and less portable than the rifle, but had the advantage of rapid fire. Barring a malfunction, as long as bullets were fed into it and the trigger was held back, it would fire continuously. Early models required a crew of two, one to aim and fire, the other to feed ammunition into its voracious slot. The barrel became so hot that many models incorporated a water-cooled barrel. The cooling water became so hot that it was sometimes used as a heat source for warming food or beverages. The BEF employed two types, the Lewis "light" machine gun weighed twenty-nine pounds and despite being "...prone to a bewildering number of stoppages (one manual lists 33), it was well liked."[22] There was also the Vickers machine gun which could fire 100,000 rounds. Some companies of soldiers fired a million rounds in twenty-four hours.[23]

How were they used? A machine gun could "beat"—fill with flying metal— an ellipse 2,500 yards long and 500 yards wide. One heavy machine gun could fire as many as sixty rounds a minute, the rough equivalent of forty riflemen.[24] A well-placed machine gun formed a miniature castle, defending a section of the line against all comers. They could be overcome, but certainly not easily. Often only artillery fire could dislodge them. More for defense than offense, the machine gun quickly became a major force in this war. Soldiers charging or fleeing an enemy position could neither outrun nor dodge its stream of metal. Unfortunately, the British had only a few of these most modern weapons on hand, far fewer than the Germans.

Behind the riflemen and machine gunners in the standard deployment were the crews who fired the artillery. These weapons were much heavier than machine guns, required horses or trucks to tow them, and had multi-man crews. Since artillery pieces could fire a greater distance and over the heads of the friendly troops in front of them, these could be kept in the rear of the battlefield. Ideally, they were located close enough to fire on the enemy troops, but far back enough as to be out of range of the enemy artillery. These weapons were manufactured in multiple sizes for multiple purposes. Some, for example, fired "high explosive" shells designed to explode in the air just above the ground. These shells were expected to kill and maim troops as well as destroy machinery and rip out defensive positions. Another was the "shrapnel" shell, which also exploded near ground level and launched small pieces of metal, often looking like metal marbles or very large "BB"s, which were expressly designed to mutilate human flesh. Another type of artillery shell carried poisonous gas while still another was designed to penetrate deep into its target—perhaps a house or a fortified position—before exploding. The amount of propellant could be adjusted by the artillerymen to adjust the distance the shell would travel.

Shells came in all sorts of sizes and weights. External painted bands of various colors and different dimensions indicated to the trained gunners just what was the purpose of each shell. As the war went on and the guns became heavier and more powerful, so too did the weight of the shells, thus intensifying another problem, that of transporting and storing large stocks of ammunition. Too many shells on hand in one location was a possible target for the enemy and an unintended explosion waiting to happen; too few and the battery could not support the infantry who defended it and depended on it.

Among and to the rear of all these fighters were the "combat support" and "service support" elements. These soldiers provided various special services that enabled those at the very front to do battle more effectively. Those in combat support would be delivering ammunition and fuel to the front lines, and perhaps carrying wounded men out on their way back. They might be interviewing captured enemy soldiers and sending any relevant "intelligence" to those who could best use it. Service support soldiers included those distributing letters from home for morale, providing direct medical and dental care, or perhaps the medical officer overseeing the location of the latrines. The cobblers repairing shoes and the quartermasters issuing new ones, the blacksmiths re-shoeing the horses and the bridle makers fixing the horses' saddles and bridles: these and countless other details were handled by the support services. Cook and cobbler, parson and porter, surgeon and strategist, each had his role.

In addition to these other important units, there were the various levels of headquarters. Closest to the very front were the small unit headquarters, where the lieutenants and captains collected information on the situation and passed it back to brigade or division headquarters, which collected data from a broader front and passed it still further to the rear of the battle zone where the senior commanders kept their offices. From the rear to the front went the orders for such important actions as when to attack, at what time and when to stop the artillery barrage. Often the men in the front lines firmly believed that the leaders in the rear were completely out of touch with the real situation, as this study will record.

So the position of each of these units was pretty well determined by the line of advance, the general direction in which the army was moving. Obviously, the commanding officers would like their fighting men in the front, closest to the enemy, and the cooks, for example, more toward the rear. Thus it becomes crucial to the fighting effectiveness of the army that it be properly organized. In fact, an army in disarray will often refuse battle and retreat, seeking more favorable circumstances. The ideal maneuver for an attacking army is to catch the enemy on the flank, or side. In simple terms, if most of the weapons are aimed forward, and cannot be turned sideways for fear of hitting its own men, then the side is the ideal place to attack, the only better target being the even less well defended rear, or back side of the army. With the size of armies ever increasing, chances of hitting the rear became more and more remote, but the glittering opportunity of a flank attack—such as the one the German army hoped to spring on the French army plunging into Alsace Lorraine—became the Holy Grail of the Great War strategists.

The French requested that the Commander-in-Chief of the BEF, Sir John French, position his army to hold the canal running through the Belgian town of Mons. By truck and by train, by horse and on foot, the British moved forward swiftly. As the British advanced toward Mons, they became the guardians of the left flank of the Fifth French army which was engaged against the Germans at the nearby town of Charleroi. In reality, eighty thousand British were preparing to stop an army of roughly 150,000 Germans. The enemy had brought more than three million men across the Rhine river in just three weeks by means of 11,000 trains running around the clock, a remarkable achievement.[25] No wonder the British commander could not believe what was in front of him.

The arriving British army was in nearly perfect order. What neither British nor French intelligence had yet realized was that the size of the advancing German force was twice or thrice what was expected. The Allies did not yet know that the Germans had managed to integrate reserve forces with active duty units to such an extent that the oncoming German army was perhaps six times bigger than the one that had forced the French to surrender in 1870.

Following their plan, on 4 August the Germans began their attack on the city of Liege.[26] Just inside Belgium, this city formed a cork in the German bottle: the million German soldiers in the vicinity could not easily go north into Holland, or south through the Ardennes forest, so they pushed with vigor against the 40,000 Belgian defenders of Liege. This modern fortress was expected to hold out for some time. But the Germans quickly brought forward some new very heavy guns, and began a slow but methodical bombardment using newly invented shells, ones specifically designed to penetrate brick, stone or concrete before exploding. By 16 August, the stunned defenders of Liege had fallen, and the German juggernaut continued its flood toward Mons. The British David was hurrying toward the German Goliath, with only a few hints as to the giant's size.

There were several ways the Allies might have discerned what was coming. Military aircraft were in their infancy, few in number, and under-appreciated, but they did sound the alarm. The Royal Flying Corps was set up in 1912 as a means of observing the enemies' positions. Planes rapidly became the "…new light cavalry of the air."[27] Although this was the first major war involving aircraft, what started with just 2,000 or so men in 1914 very rapidly grew to hundreds of aircraft and over 100,000 personnel by the war's end. From merely looking at the enemy to actively bombing the enemy and shooting down his planes: these became the mission of the Royal Air Force, a name which did not come into use until the spring of the last year of the war. But that is a tale for a different study.

Meanwhile, planes also parachuted homing pigeons behind the enemy lines with instructions for the French civilians to report what they saw of the Germans.[28] Curiously, the Carrier Pigeon Service included four hundred men and over 100,000 birds. Only two percent of the birds failed to return to their mobile lofts.[29] It is not clear how the British were to detect among the responses those that came from legitimate sources and those that were misleading replies from French-speaking Germans. There were also a few people who managed to get word out from behind the enemy lines by more conventional means. However, the French plans and the British plans were set, and inconvenient facts were ignored until all but too late. The French were pouring troops into Alsace Lorraine, seeming not to notice how soft the German resistance was.

The advancing Germans had two basic tactical choices at Mons, the same two choices they would have repeatedly in the next few weeks. They could send infantry, foot soldiers, to attack and overwhelm the British positions, or, if meeting substantial resistance, wait while heavier guns were summoned forward to destroy the defense. Speed being essential to the von Schlieffen plan, the Germans more often than not elected to spend lives instead of time, hurling wave after wave of irreplaceable infantry against the British sharpshooters.

At dawn on 23 August, German artillery rounds began falling on the BEF defenders of the four bridges over the Mons canal. German infantry moved forward at 9 a.m., but were beaten back. Undaunted, the Germans sent more and more forces against the BEF until by afternoon the British realized they were heavily outnumbered. Moreover, the French Fifth army on the British right was in retreat, thus opening the possibility of a disastrous German attack on the now undefended British flank. General Haig employed a modern convenience to distribute his urgent orders: "Thanks to the motor I was able to give personal orders to all the chief commanders concerned in the space of an hour...."[30] Accurately sensing the conditions, the BEF commanders executed a retreat across their entire front, a retreat which continued for almost two weeks.

That retreat was costly. Colonel Helm's unit began the retreat with eighteen officers and 700 men. When he had a chance to take roll, he found the unit down to seven officers and 150 men, all the rest killed, wounded or missing.[31] Another soldier recorded this observation about that retreat:

> ...there were cases every day when, through complete exhaustion, men could not put one foot before another if they were to be shot for it. We helped each other.[32]

However, the troops retired successfully, always leaving a "rear guard" whose mission it was to delay the advancing Germans so the main force might escape to fight another day.

The retreat did not stop until reaching the Marne River, the last major natural line of defense before reaching Paris. Ominously, the citizens of Paris could hear the booming of the guns along the Marne. By this point, the Allies plans were in shambles. The French thrust into Alsace had been halted. Heavy casualties weakened the French army on all fronts. Nowhere did the Allies hold the advantage.

On the other hand, the Germans too had problems. While their careful plans were closer to fruition than those of the Allies, they had left unexpectedly large numbers of men along the route to "mask" places from which flank attacks could develop. The distances already covered were so great that supplies just could not quite catch up. Sixty-five percent of the German supply trucks were broken.[33] In addition, the troops themselves were very tired. Long marches, day after day, in the heat and dust of a very dry August had caused widespread and severe fatigue among the attacking Germans. Then too, the French at last realized that the capital city was in grave peril. Germany had conquered Paris in 1870. No Frenchman wanted to endure that again. With an air of confidence, the French high command shifted units around, creating a new formation to defend Paris by stopping the Germans along the Marne. Meanwhile, the discouraged German commanders, tired and not thinking with perfect clarity, became grievously alarmed by the unexpectedly swift penetration of Eastern Prussia by the supposedly slow moving Russians. Fearing a powerful attack from the east, the German Commander in Chief unwisely weakened the First Army, the one supposed to "brush its sleeve" against the English Channel, by several divisions, leaving the army too weak to fully follow the von Schlieffen plan. With very little time or energy to spare, the weakened British and French held the exhausted Germans along the Marne river. It is true, for example, that some soldiers were rushed to their posts on the Marne in taxi cabs borrowed from the city of Paris—one of these is even today proudly on display in the Imperial War Museum in London.

It was along the Marne that perhaps the most famous characteristic of the Great War, the trench, may have first appeared. As individuals arrived on the riverbank, they became aware of soldiers on the other side firing at them. Alternately, one side arrived first, and began to prepare for the enemy to arrive. Against active fire, the common sense reaction was to drop to the ground and seek whatever shelter was available. "In the wood we keep building little huts with the branches of trees to shelter us a little from the wind and rain."[34] But often there was little nearby that could be used for shelter or protection considering that most of these early maneuvers took place in ripening farm fields, and these improvised shelters were hardly bullet proof. At first, troops would carve a "scrape": using a knife or better tool, if handy, the soldier would start at the rear, digging a hole for his feet.[35] But this rough slot was both uncomfortable and vulnerable to shrapnel, so soon the deeper foxholes began to take shape. In a short time, these developed into a series of connected holes, and over a longer time, an elaborate system of genuine trenches. The original British trenches were only to be temporary so as not to instill a defensive mentality. The goal, after all, was to drive out the Germans, not build defensive earthworks.[36]

Trenches were never intended to be the elaborate network they became. To his diary entry of 29 August 1914, Sergeant McIlwain added this in the 1930's:

> ...the free movement of the retreat and the partial re-advancement was to terminate within a month in the long boredom and agony of four years of trench warfare.

> By its apogee, a kilometre of trench would consume an incredible 900 metres of barbed wire, six million sandbags, more than 20,000 metres of timber, and 33,400 square metres of corrugated iron.[37]

Robert Graves remembered the early days in trenches this way:

When I came out here first, all we did in trenches was to paddle about like ducks and use our rifles. We didn't think of them as places to live in, they were just temporary inconveniences. Now we work here all the time, not only for safety but also for health. Night and day. First, at fire steps, then at building traverses, improving the communication trenches, and so on; last comes our personal comfort-shelters and dug-outs.[38]

Farthest forward was the "firing line" or front line trench. This was close to the enemy position, and at first well defended. Then a second trench was dug to the rear in case the first fell to the enemy. To connect the front line and the rear ran the communication trenches, used for bringing up food, water, ammunition and reinforcements. Straight lines in trenches were avoided. If an enemy managed to get into one's trench with a machine gun, he could kill many men, if the trenches were dug in a straight line. Photographs of the completed trenches were sometimes taken by airplane and by observation balloon. To the modern viewer, these trench photos resemble a retinal scan or perhaps a child's ant farm.

Quite a few of the long-remembered themes of this war were present in these early days. Churchill wrote after the war that "...mobilization schemes, railway graphics, time-tables, the organization of bases depots, supply arrangements, etc., filling many volumes, regulated and ensured a thorough and concerted execution."[39] Some of the soldiers found the real world conditions to be less sanguine. In August, Colonel Helm noted in his diary "The road was now in a most indescribable state of confusion; infantry, cavalry, guns, limbers,[40] wagons, ambulances, staff cars, and every other conceivable form of vehicle, all going as hard as they could and all mixed up together."[41] Colonel Helm made quite a few mundane observations in his diary, such as this one from August 24:

By this time we were brown as berries and well on the way to having quite respectable beards, as of course there were no opportunities for shaving. That night we spent in a field, in the most appalling rain and soaked to the skin, which did not help to make us feel any more cheerful.

The Colonel was also an early critic of the food supply, noting that on the way over to France, the food offered was "chiefly sardines and French bread." On a happier note, Colonel Helm recounted that when a particular group of British officers were taken prisoner, they were offered a chance to donate to the Red Cross while in the German prison camp. They agreed, providing they could subscribe by check, and ten officers signed the check. When it ultimately reached Cox's Bank, officials there were happy to report to the various families that their men were alive.

In his dissatisfaction with the supply chain, Colonel Helm had a great deal of company. Even when the army settled down into a static pattern of trench warfare, until it more or less remained in one place, the supply services did the best they could, but were far from perfect. With increasing time on their hands, the troops found plenty of ammunition for their grumbling. As early as 23 August Colonel Helm was already complaining about "the eternal bully-beef and biscuits eaten with the aid of a pocket knife."[42] Another soldier complained about meals:

> Our food at that time was badly cooked, and all the money we obtained we spent in the canteen. I was able to buy prunes and custard with a slice of bread and butter for fourpence, and that was my usual evening meal.[43]

Keeping in mind the British soldier's fondness for tea makes this complaint from Sergeant T. H. Cubbon all the more poignant: "Can't get a drop of water, it's terrible as there is nothing to drink, not even tea while we are in the wood."[44] This soldier was not very happy with that day's food ration, either: one quarter loaf of bread, a piece of cheese, and one pound of jam—to be shared among four men. On an earlier day, the same soldier noted "Have had nothing but a cup of tea since 9 a.m. yesterday."[45] Within a month, simple things had become treats: "Fried some bacon in canteen lid in end of dugout with paper, so as to have something respectable for Sunday's dinner. Had a bottle of water with it so enjoyed it immensely."[46]

Something as simple as seeking water near a battlefield could be fatal. Two men went to a village pump, where German artillery blew them and the pump to bits.[47]

Sometimes the available water was not fit to drink and so was used for washing instead.[48] Dr Helm tried to protect the soldiers from contaminated water: "It was sometimes a very difficult job to find water that was good, but in any case I always insisted on its being filtered and boiled."[49] It took some time, but by 1916 the army would have 300 trucks ferrying 550 gallon tanks of drinking water to "water points" close to the front.[50] T. C. Cubbon's diary frequently mentions the inclement weather: "Raining all the night thro. The roads in some places knee deep in mud. Soaked to the skin."[51]

Soldiers also found humor in unexpected places such as this note in a diary from 2 September 1914:

Men threw away army equipment and clothing. Men lost their caps and girls sun hats became quite a fashionable article of wear. These were looted from houses and shops. Special instructions were afterwards issued condemning this eccentricity of the British soldier.[52]

A commodity readily available in one location might be quite scarce just over the hill. T. H. Cubbon noted in his diary "Meals—terrible. Biscuits[53] and strong tea chiefly. Occasionally cheese, jam. Yesterday we were issued a hard bread which was green, moldy. No bread, cigarettes or matches to be had."[54] A month later the Sergeant bemoaned "...an issue of ½ cigarette a man."[55] H. T. Williams reported a well-received culinary experiment: "...the meal was nearly always stew, and sometimes followed with rice, in which we would mix our jam ration to give it some flavor."[56]

Shelters were also extremely and unpleasantly dissimilar from life back in garrison. The army had been sheltered, warmed, kept dry and generally healthy and out of danger in oversized dormitories called barracks. Outside of occasional field maneuvers or training exercises, the army had a place to call home, as it were. Few such comforts were available in the fields of soggy Flanders. Soon, other forms of life joined the soldiers, and they were most unwelcome. As early as 9 October 1914 Sergeant Cubbon noted in his diary "...billets here swarming with rats." Robert Graves experienced rats: "When he turned in that night, he heard a scuffling, shone his torch upon the bed, and found two rats on his blankets tussling for the possession of a severed hand."[57] Later he added "We always ate with revolvers about our plate, and punctuated our conversation with sudden volleys at a rat rummaging at someone's valise or crawling along the trench support above our head."[58] Another soldier observed:

> Then there were the rats of course, the rats. You could not kill rats for you had no means of getting rid of them, they would putrefy and it would be worse than if you left them alive. I think they lived in corpses, because they were huge, they were as big as cats, I am not exaggerating, some of them were as big as ordinary cats, horrible great things.[59]

In an interview long after the war, Private Thomas McIndoe clearly remembered the rats:

> Rats! Oh Crikey! If they were put in a harness they could have done a milk round, they were that big, yes, honest![60]

R. M. Luther recalled the rats quite clearly:

All around us were ditches filled with stinking water, and huge water rats would crawl out at night, in their search for food. Heaven help the soldier who had any food in his haversack: they would attack and crawl all over him.[61]

Some of the men engaged in what they termed "rat bashing":

We would creep out in the dark and surround the (trash pits) and switch on a torch while we killed them with pieces of wood and sticks.[62]

There was also a problem with lice. On 21 October Cubbon declared himself "Lousy" and went on: "Had my shirt off 3 times in ¼ hour. Doused it with Keating's Powder", a reputed remedy. Another soldier complained "All our garments, both outer and inner, were literally alive with the little devils and there was nothing we could do about it."[63] Robert Graves recorded this exchange:

We were just having a conversation as to whether it's best to kill the old ones or the young one, Sir. Morgan here says if you kill the old ones, the young ones die of grief. But Parry here, Sir, he says that the young ones are easier to kill, and you can catch the old ones when they go to the funeral.[64]

Ralph Smith described the battle against lice this way:

"Chatting" consisted of stripping to our waist then burning all the seams of our shirts etc. with a candle to kill the lice. If not candle it had to be a flat stone and beat it hard with another stone but we were as bad as ever a day of two afterwards. We were issued with a powder to smear on our bodies, but we all swore it only fed them.[65]

More seriously, the army dealt with lice by collecting the clothing and washing it in hot water in huge vats called "Foden Disinfectors." While this device often killed the active lice, it just as often did not kill the eggs, and they hatched again in just a few hours.[66] One private was disgusted by what he called fleas:

Fleas, yes. Every man in the front line was in a state of—men in the front line had fleas after two or three weeks. Fleas used to get into the seams of your underclothes, and the only way to get rid of them was to get a candle and go along the seams with the candle and you could hear the eggs cracking. And the extraordinary thing is that lice were so bad in places I've seen men taking their shirts off with the skin of their backs absolutely raw where they'd been scratching. And there was no way of getting rid of them at all. Lice were a curse, a real menace to us. For one thing, you had very little chance of getting a good sleep anyway, and when you had the lice with you there to irritate you, drive you into a sort of frenzy almost—the whole thing was that lice were in the dugouts.[67]

Another attempt to deal with lice involved haircuts.

> We soon discovered that we were all ridden with lice, and every man jack of us was ordered to have all his hair cut off by a machine which was used to clip the horses. We all looked very ugly sights indeed with our hats off, but we also found that we had body lice, and were forever scratching, but to no purpose.[68]

In the midst of serious problems, the army occasionally and inexplicably devoted energy to mundane matters. Captain Peel noted a complaint from headquarters that individuals were sending their uniform shirts home. The reason was not clear: perhaps to be laundered? But the memo was insistent: Captain Peel was to "...punish such thefts of public property."[69]

The army was going to have to pay attention to morale. The downward trend is evident in one soldier's diary. On 5 August 1914 he calls the reserve men "keen and alert." On 23 August, he refers to his fellows as having "plenty of enthusiasm." By 26 August, he is reporting "Then rain, the rain! And I, in the stress of the retreat, like many others who were trained by Kitchener to travel light, had thrown away my great-coat."[70] Throwing away equipment often was often regretted:

> We had no overcoats, as they were thrown away on going into action. The only protection we have is a 6 foot by 2 waterproof sheet which is useless after an hour's rain. All of our wounded are lying in cellars in the village because thro some bad arrangement there is no ambulance here.[71]

Sergeant Cubbon's Diary of 17 September includes this powerful summary:

> Am having a terrible time here. Have been in this wood since 10 a.m. Monday, under artillery fire all the time. Am wet through, feet particularly, can't get water. Feeding upon bread, biscuits, bully beef, fruit and occasionally a tin of jam between seven men. Troops are beginning to get downhearted here, as the Germans have proven themselves to be a better army than we thought.... We are not too badly off for food as our ration are brought here at dark, but

water is so scarce that we have not had a drink of tea since we came here, and of course not allowed to light fire.[72]

Sgt. John McIlwain's diary contains this almost poetic comment: "The period (17-21 September) was rather terrifying, wearying, wearing; with moods of anger, funk, despondency and disgust...." He also observed "We are into the wet, cold weather now; the heat of August is a mere memory."[73] These depressing thoughts can be found over and over again in the soldier's diaries such as that of H. T. Williams:

That is the Pattern, that makes the daily life of an infantryman, words cannot describe the intense misery that is caused to a man, having to live among mud, and filth, watching death reach out to your comrades, hearing their cries of anguish, seeing them die, one by one, and wondering, who will be next. These incidents cannot easily be forgotten.[74]

Another soldier could not forget what he saw, either. First, he "Had a look through the wood with Danny Gilmore and saw about twenty men of the Worcesters who had been shattered to bits by shell & had been lying there for about ten days. Terrible sights. . . .

Went through the packs of some dead Worcesters. Got new overcoat and bags of tobacco and book of fag papers.[75] Only comforts I have are locket, Flo's letters, tobacco and Service Prayer Book.[76] A few days before, he witnessed one of his trench mates named Swallow who "...shot himself in the foot, fed up."[77]

Swallow appears to have been seeking a "Blighty", a wound serious enough to earn one convalescent leave at home, far from the trenches, but not so bad as to be permanently debilitating. Ideally, such a wound would lead to extended duty behind the lines in a non-dangerous position, perhaps sorting mail or filling sandbags with sand—anything to avoid the front lines. Sometimes a soldier would expose his hand above the trench, hoping a German sharpshooter would notice and oblige. It soon became a very serious offense to wound one's self or to deliberately court a disabling wound. But some still tried. One army physician examined a wound and found it almost healed; the next day, "...inflamed and enlarged" which the doctor concluded was self-inflicted. This same doctor treated thirty men with wounds in the palm of their hands, again making him believe they were self-inflicted.[78]

While many soldiers may have wished for a "blighty", officers sometimes had the same thought. Colonel Helm admitted:

One night a bullet came into the ground practically between my legs. I cursed because it had not gone through my foot and given me a nice comfortable wound to go home with. Bullets which come close to one's head are the most unpleasant. If they are very close they almost deafen one. One feels naturally inclined to duck on hearing one, but of course if it is going to hit one it would be so long before one could get out of the way. All the same, shells are much worse than bullets. I do not think there can be any comparison. I suppose it is the deafening row that puts the wind up one.[79]

Robert Graves thought he had "cannily" figured it out:

My best way of lasting through to the end of the war would be to get wounded. The best time to get wounded would be at night and in the open, with rifle-fire more or less un-aimed and my whole body exposed. Best, also, to get wounded when there was no rush on the dressing-station services, and while the back areas were not being heavily shelled. Best to get wounded, therefore, on a night patrol in a quiet sector. One could usually mange to crawl into a shell-hole until help arrived.[80]

Soldiers carried out numerous sad missions, such as this one recorded by Henry T. Williams:

(My mate) asked me to help him look amongst these graves to see if we could locate one, that belonging to his brother, it was not a pleasant task, as the spot had been shelled for months, and these graves had been blown to pieces but there was still some intact, or almost intact. So we started our sad task, but it was not long before he called to me, he was standing looking down at a cross that plainly showed the name and rank of his brother. I felt very sorry for my friend standing, with tears welling in his eyes, the War had parted them, but not as it happened for long, for about a week later he had joined his brother in death, but he poor chap did not get a grave, as he was blown to pieces. How can I forget?[81]

Just about any soldier's diary contains such harrowing descriptions. Colonel Helm's diary is especially detailed:

(Near the village of Wulvergern) the churchyard was torn up by large shells and the graves in many cases were laid completely open revealing some ghastly sight.... Just outside the village were two dead horses which lay there for months. One became aware of their presence a great distance off. Eventually, they were covered with chloride of lime but we could never make out why they had not been buried long ago.[82]

Henry Williams tried to bring home his point by writing this in his diary, repeated here exactly as he wrote it:

MY WORDS ARE SO SMALL IN THIS GREAT BIG WORLD AND CANNOT COUNT FOR MUCH, BUT THEY ARE SINCERE, AND JUST BY WRITING THEM
<u>I AM REMEMBERING</u>.

Sergeant McIlwain's diary contains this eerie observation:

The scent of a million decaying scattered petals in an untended garden, mingling in recent memory with the fumes of the incinerator should suggest to the philosophers mind notions of death, destruction and decay. But the soldier on active service unconsciously protects himself from such reflections.[83]

In reading many of the soldier's diaries, one is struck by a particular omission: there is not much mention of God or prayer. Men may have talked about such things more than they wrote about them.

On the other hand, the soldiers wrote about some things that amused them. From time to time, absurd rumors flashed among the men. On 27 August, the rumor was that the Russians were so close to Berlin that they had given the Germans twenty-four hours notice before the Russians would begin a bombardment of the German capital city. In fact, of course, the Russians were many miles from Berlin.[84] More amusing was the movement of troops behind the front by London and Paris buses—still with the advertising on their sides from the plays of three months past.[85] And one soldier's personal chuckle: "Had my hair cut by Bennett and I cut his after a fashion. Step ladders all over his head."[86] Another soldier recorded that since uniforms were at first rather haphazard, one oddly dressed soldier was mistaken for a Belgian refugee.[87]

Sergeant Cubbon's diary is filled with both the mundane and the profound. On 19 September, he noted: "Saw a couple of English newspapers this week dated August 23. They say 2 oz. tobacco are issued weekly to every soldier. Have been here now five weeks received 3 oz." On the same day he recorded: "Am scraping the dust and crumbs out of my pockets for a smoke." Two days later he wrote: "Patrol sent out to find Lt. Horton who was shot and left there yesterday but no sign of him." And then some better news: "Issued a new pipe, shirt, sock, postcards and cigs, 4 envelopes and sheets of paper, government postcards and a pencil per man."[88] By 29 September, he was already feeling the approaching winter: "The nights here are cold especially about 1 to 5 a.m. You wake up stiff and cold as a block of ice, with feet practically dead from cold." On 8 October he complained that what the newspapers say he is issued and what he actually receives did not match. On 12 October he recorded these two items: the doctor inspected his feet, and that morning was the first frost of the season. By 8 November, he mused "While having dinner shell burst in next trench. Most marvelous escapes which make one realize the value of life and its uncertainty."

Life was no more certain for the German soldiers. Colonel Helm recorded:

I was kept very busy with the wounded prisoners who were extremely grateful for any attention they got. They were astonished when we did not take their watches and money.[89]

Sometimes feeling the lack of supplies, soldiers would loot shops they passed. "I changed the drawers I had brought from Newcastle nearly a month before for a fine new pair from stock."[90] On 15 September, the same soldier admitted:

We had been doing a bit of looting in the deserted shops and houses. Our fellows are passing bottles of rum, syrop [sic], aniseed (which I suspected of being a hair dressing). The regiment is retaining its reputation as capable of drinking anything liquid.

With the Germans halted at the Marne, a new phase of the campaign began. The Germans moved a bit further north in an effort to outflank the British, that is, to attack the British in their vulnerable side. The British moved to block this attempt and to move past the Germans in order to turn their flank. The Germans counter-moved. Swiftly, a crab-like sideways race began, each side scurrying to outflank the other, each day moving closer to the North Sea. This phase became known as the "Race to the Sea."

It is possible to recount the autumn battles of 1914 in great detail. Voluminous primary sources are available. Among those are handwritten diaries, often with self-deprecating introductions such as this: "It will be evident to anyone who may read this purely personal narrative of mine, that it is not, nor is it intended to be, of any serious military or historical value whatever...."[91] But such a source, such a window on the unfolding events, is in fact priceless. Daily newspapers, magazines, letters from soldiers and civilians, official documents, memoirs: all have survived to serve the historian's interest. Some scholars have devoted their entire professional careers to this topic. And yet no one can master it all. To recount what happened in one place and skip the events in another is not so much to value one life over another as it is to respect the limits of time and space in a study such as this. In a broad outline, then, this is what happened in the remainder of that bloody autumn of 1914.

The last city of size in the path of this race to the sea was Ypres, a town of about 17,500 which had long ago been a center of the textile industry and which still had a "cloth hall" dating from the 1200's. The bell tower of the Cloth Hall and the similar sized spire of the adjacent Saint Martin's Catholic Cathedral gave a commanding view of the very flat surrounding countryside. Even today, one can stand several miles outside the town and see the distinctive shape of those two structures.[92] In fact, each of the dozen or so villages in the vicinity has a distinctive church tower, so that it is possible to identify the town just from seeing the church tower.

Both sides recognized the importance of Ypres. It was less than thirty miles from the sea, close enough that it could become a major transit center for the Allies, shipping in men and supplies, evacuating wounded. The Germans wanted it just as badly, both to deny it as a base to the British and to occupy the coastline just beyond it as another place along the North Sea that the German navy could use to support a submarine campaign. Some German leaders recognized that if the war was not won quickly—and a lengthy war was appearing more likely each week that victory eluded them—then an economic blockade of Britain, an island that they knew did not even grow its own food, would become an extraordinarily powerful weapon. Thus, bases for submarines became a priority consideration. Consequently both sides committed plenty of troops to this First Battle of Ypres. And since the British had difficulty with the pronunciation of this town it quickly became known, for them at least, as "Wipers."

A number of smaller towns and villages form an arc to the east of Ypres. Starting to the north and just a bit east is Langemark-Poelkapelle. To the east and south of that town is Passchendaele,[93] and moving to the south one arrives at Zonnebeke, and following the arc, then at Gheluvelt, Zandvoorde, and Hollebeke. These villages are only two miles or so from the next, an easy bike ride. Men fought and died over each of these places as well as at many others. On 19 October, for example, General Rawlinson's seventh division struggled to capture the town of Menin whose modest ridge overlooked Ypres, but German artillery took a heavy toll. On 20 October General Haig attacked Passchendaele, a small town on a small ridge two-and-a-half miles east of Ypres. Plunging through the mist, the rain and the cold, his troops were outgunned and outnumbered. Even worse, the Germans had captured a copy of the attack plan and so were prepared.

By 22 October, King Albert of Belgium decided the time had come to open the floodgates of the Yser River, thus inundating all of the land as far south of the North Sea as the town of Dixmude. This was to prevent the Germans from being able to circle around the battle zone. On 23 October the Germans were beaten back at Langemarck. By the next day, the German held the high ground of Hollebeke. This meant they could observe the British activity and bombard the British at their convenience thus keeping the British in "...sheer and constant terror."[94] On 24 October, the Germans wiped out the defending British in Polygon Wood, but failed to exploit this hard-won gain. In the next few days, further battles were fought for Gheluvelt, Ploegsteert Wood, and Zandvoorde. Several of these were very near-run things, where the British margin of victory was perilously slight. On 20 October, Colonel Helm lamented: "There is nothing I know of more trying to the nerves than to sit listening to the shells and wondering how long there is before one comes and finds your hiding place." Two days later he observed, "We all of us knew that if the Germans could make another big attack it would be all up and we should either be laid out or go to the Fatherland."[95] Then on 29 October, Colonel Helm wrote exactly this in his diary: "The quartermaster and I were the only two (officers) remaining of those who had left Dublin."

Sergeant Cubbon picked up on a most important point when he observed:

(We) have lost a great number of officers... Captains Marshal, Potter, Feneran, Tanner, Grounds (and Lieutenants) Horton, Small, Phipps.[96]

Invaluable experienced officers were falling in droves. One officer reported another urgent problem to General Haig in person, that "Rifles (were) jammed owing to mud and soil and no opportunity for cleaning and oiling."[97]

There were moments when the whole force of war seemed to be right in front of an individual. T. H. Cubbon was trapped in such a moment:

Surprised at 9 a.m. German broke the Black Watch (an infantry unit) as they had been shelled in the trenches for 3 weeks until they numbered 1 officer and 200 men. Everybody in a panic, running away, leaving rifles equipment and everything, 15th Hussars (a cavalry unit) charged those who broke through and drove them back. We had no reinforcements. (Other soldiers) are being put in trenches with another line behind them to fire on them if they attempt to come out. Terrible night thunder and lightning bitter cold and wet all night. This is the worst night we have had.[98]

Were one group of British soldiers actually prepared to fire on another as a desperate disciplinary measure? Cubbon certainly believed so.

The fundamental truth was that both armies were nearly exhausted: the forced marches, the various supply snafus, the unexpectedly high casualty rates, the disappointment that the enemy was not already defeated: each side wanted to give just one more great push—but neither had the strength to do so. Colonel Helm diagnosed exhaustion in himself:

> I was told afterwards that the officers of the Ambulance, after coming to
> take the wounded went back and told their CO (commanding officer) that
> they thought the shelling had affected my brain as I simply sat down and
> refused to talk to anyone. I do not think that there was any foundation for
> this except that I was worn out.[99]

For the British soldier, even his accoutrements became a burden. The average
British recruit weighed about 132 pounds, but was tasked with between
sixty (summer) and seventy-seven pounds (winter) of load, far in excess of
the optimum one-third of body weight.[100] And when the outer uniform, the
"greatcoat" became water-logged and mud-splattered, it could weight over
thirty-seven pounds.[101] By comparison, a medieval suit of armor weighed
about 70 pounds.[102]

Comments about mud occur with great frequency in the soldiers diaries.
Mud became a constant obstacle to their advance and a constant annoyance
in their daily lives. Immutable mud became a constant source of complaint.
Just three months into this war, Ralph Smith reported:

> On this part of the line conditions were very bad with the mud. On going to
> relieve another regiment in the front line, almost at the dead of night, so far
> along the road we would fall out and take our boots off, Those [*sic*] coming
> from the trenches would fall out opposite us and take their rubber thigh
> boots off, we then had to cross over and get a pair of thigh Boots to wear. I
> wore a size 6 Boots but always found myself with a 9 or 10 of the Rubber
> Boots. Being in continued use for months you may be able to imagine the
> state of the insides.[103]

Not very surprisingly, the soldier's swollen feet often would not go back
into their boots, so they would stumble on for three or four miles with "...our
toes stuck in them."[104]

From mid-September until heavy rains of October and then the snows of
November ended the campaigning season, both sides contested for this area,
first one then the other temporarily triumphant. Many men died, many more
were injured trying to control this strategic town. The First Battle of Ypres
lasted for two months, and cost 55,000 British casualties, 50,000 French and
perhaps 130,000 German casualties.[105] No estimate is given of the Belgian
casualties, although certainly many of the soldiers as well as local families had
suffered. As one soldier wrote:

...(for) the first time I saw Ypres, and witnessed what modern artillery can do to a town. Even at that early time in this long war the place was in ruins. Immense piles of dislodged masonry lay balanced perilously about the streets. Continuous bombardments throughout subsequent years reduced these masses to powder.[106]

In not much more than six weeks, more than two hundred thousand men were killed or wounded fighting just for this one quite modest town, a bitter sample of the massive human slaughter to come.

The fact that so many men were packed into such a small area begs mention of another aspect of this massive endeavor, the unintentional damage done by millions of pairs of boots, let alone hooves and tires, to the fertile farm fields and towns. The destruction of one well was already mentioned. There was much more destruction, contemporarily termed both "friendly fire" and "collateral damage." In the earliest days of this war, a claims commission was set up in the town of Boulogne to hear civilian claims against the Army. Within a short time, it was hearing thousands of cases a month. After all "...the enormous British force in France and Flanders was one of the most docile and good natured armies in history, (but) widespread damage to property and massive inconvenience to civilians were the inescapable by-products of its having to fight a modern industrialized war in a heavily populated and civilized country."[107]

The bloody fighting around Ypres produced an urgent problem. What should be done with the bodies of the dead? It was impractical to ship them home, and often the remains were so mutilated as to be unfit for family viewing. Many were buried close to where they fell, or close to the field hospitals where they died. Yet often they did not remain undisturbed. Subsequent shelling of the same area would become commonplace, the interred bodies were further desecrated and the odors became all but intolerable. Just to mark each grave in some of the earliest cemeteries required ingenuity: short on wood for markers, short of anything for markers, at least a few places were marked by upside down glass bottles, the only useable item in sufficient supply. Today the town of Ypres remains ringed by a series of small villages, and each of them has at least one cemetery.

By the time the fighting died down in late 1914, the British were left with a number of very serious problems to resolve. Indeed, the entire outcome of the war would depend on finding solutions to these great challenges. The problems included those with a human dimension such as the welfare of the troops: living quarters, medical care, family considerations, food, rest and leave. There was also a material side, producing enough supplies such as weapons, ammunition, vehicles and so on to enable the army to get the job done.

Perhaps the most serious problem concerned manpower. Casualties on the western front were never less than 6,500 a month.[108] By the end of November 1914, one third of the men landed in August—89,969 men—were dead.[109] Dead soldiers, wounded soldiers had to be replaced, but replacements were in very short supply. By the end of September 1914, nearly 478,900 additional men had joined the army.[110] These men knew, of course, that "Men enlisting for the duration of the war will be able to claim their discharge with all convenient speed at the conclusion of the war."[111] Men with a college education, or part of one, were quickly commissioned as officers. These new officers believed that "...Germany had broken the code of European nations and deserved to be punished."[112] After all, it was Germany who had invaded Belgium, Germans who had shot Red Cross Nurse Edith Cavell, Germans who had burned the medieval library at Louvain.[113] "Naturally, each nation believed its soldiers possessed the better morale and determination needed to overmatch its opponents, an outlook fostered by the prevailing nationalistic, racist, Darwinian, and somewhat romantic climate of opinion."[114] Indeed, "No sombre thoughts of trenches and gas masks troubled the clerks and greengrocers, teachers and farmers, manufacturers and publicans who joined up by the thousand in the first months of the war."[115]

The Army also needed officers by the thousands. The traditional sources were the sons of the peerage, the gentry, military families, and to a lesser extent, the clergy and some professions. A small minority entered from business, commercial or industrial families.[116] However, these traditional sources could not supply anywhere near the numbers now required, and despite whatever social consequence might ensue, the Army would have to admit many more men from beyond this traditional pool. The culture of the officer's mess was going to become very different. But even if men were found, there were no weapons to issue them. As Churchill noted:

> The small scale of our military forces had led to equally small factories for war material. There were no rifles, there were no guns; and the modest supplies of shells and ammunition began immediately to flash away with what seemed appalling rapidity....We had nothing but staves to put in the hands of the eager men who thronged recruiting stations.[117]

Manpower alone was a massive and complex problem. The BEF of 1 September 1914 was a splendid little army. Splendid, because it had long-serving volunteer personnel, officers and men, who had adequate if not generous amounts of time to learn their skills. Little, because the hierarchy of British arms had always been Navy first, Army second.[118] If geographically possible, a naval blockade of a particular enemy was a given. But deployment of large numbers of troops into Europe was not the British custom. Given Britain's population of about 46 million, it may be surprising that the entire BEF only fielded about 400,000 men, half of whom were on colonial duty in the summer of 1914. Meanwhile, over 900,000 sailors kept the island safe from seaborne attack. Four hundred years earlier, Shakespeare had pointed out the English Channel as a "moat defensive", but he had not foreseen how utterly crucial sea power would become to the island nation.[119] While nearly 400,000 fresh men had volunteered for service since the August attack on Belgium, it was just impossible to gather them up, bring them to a training center, issue them equipment, hurry them through training, and race them into the front lines at a rate that would keep apace of the battlefield losses. Such a policy would have been unsustainable.

While it was true that many men volunteered, it was also shockingly true that many of them could not pass the physical exam. Physicians routinely checked for the obvious defects in such things as eyesight, teeth, and chest, but tuberculosis was still widespread among the working class. However, men turned down at one recruiting station could often find another with somewhat lower standards.[120]

The manpower problem was seemingly intractable. First, there was an acute shortage of men to do the actual training. The most skilled men were nearly all in France or Belgium, hoping to win the war before Christmas. There simply were not enough instructors to train the horde of recruits. As one recruit noted, most of the instructors were "...elderly regulars who had never heard a shot fired in anger."[121]

Then too, there were nowhere near enough places for this training to take place. Existing training facilities were hopelessly undersized for the arriving horde. In August 1914, the Army had accommodations for 174,800 single men. But 298,923 joined that month, and 30,000 more each week in September.[122] Sometimes new camps were hurriedly constructed in absurd places. For example, a new camp was erected for the Scottish Rifles at Codford—in a large field surrounded on three sides by streams, the whole field prone to flooding after rain.[123] Another unit actually had to put up tents inside their huts to keep dry.[124] Some localities welcomed a new army camp nearby, both as a patriotic reaction to the need and as a boost to the local economy as well. Others did not exactly welcome large numbers of young unattached men into the local social circle. Yet even if a camp could be quickly constructed, there were precious few weapons to put into the trainees' hands, even fewer uniforms to clothe them, and repeating the crucial point, far too few experienced soldiers to instruct them. At one point, recognizing the critical shortage of rifles, Winston Churchill, First Lord of the Admiralty, directed that a search be made throughout the navy for unused weapons. More than thirty thousand were located and turned over to the army—enough to arm an entire division![125]

Another part of the manpower problem was the shortage of skilled craftsmen. While an individual who worked in a munitions plant, a craftsman who could run the special tools needed to make high explosive shells, for example, might want to enlist in the army or navy, that individual could much better serve by continuing to produce munitions—and teaching others how to run the machinery as well. Yet some men who were not permitted to leave their civilian job to enlist managed to do so under an assumed name.[126] Very quickly, the army realized that its predicted consumption of munitions far outran production of shells. In some of the earliest days of battle, the gunners were actually limited to firing nine shells a day—there just were no more, and the plants at home were by no means set up to produce the shells in the vast numbers that were demanded.[127]

What the BEF most needed was time: time to recruit, time to train, time to reinforce and resupply the BEF; in short, time to field a much larger modern army, a task Britain had never before faced. This time had to be purchased in Flanders with soldiers' blood. The Germans could be delayed, but Britain did not yet have the strength to defeat them. Thus many men who wanted to join the armed forces had to be retained in their civilian occupations. Many of these men and often their friends and families did not realize that while working in a "reserved" occupation might seem like dodging the dangers of combat, factory service in fact was a highly patriotic calling. The army could take an under-educated farm boy and make him into a soldier much faster than it could train the same lad to be a tool and die maker.[128]

A second of these great challenges had to do with tactics. In the earliest days of battle, blood bought knowledge. What seemed satisfactory in peacetime just did not survive field service. Perhaps the best example of this was that new weapon, the machine gun. Formerly, to take a position, a group of soldiers moved forward, maintaining a steady rate of fire toward the enemy. Some of them were wounded, others killed. While the attackers lost a good number of men, if there were enough of them, they could eventually overwhelm the enemy and conquer the disputed position. If the enemy position was particularly strong, the attackers might summon supporting artillery fire to help take the position. Napoleonic tactics, standards set nearly one hundred years before, employed dense formations of troops in mass attacks, and this tactic was still used with some frequency in the early days of this war. Generally speaking, the offense and defense were similarly equipped. Victory usually crowned the side having the most skilled and motivated riflemen.

The machine gun changed all that by giving the defense a huge advantage on the battlefield. One machine gun could fire hundreds of bullets a minute.

It also could have a predetermined field of fire, so that it need not be aimed very well: its many bullets would cut an arc of destruction through large numbers of soldiers attacking it. To simply advance on foot over open ground into machine gun fire was suicidal. In addition, if the enemy force had held the position for very long, its artillery was "registered." This meant that the battery—a group of cannons are known as a "battery"— had fired practice shells, and were thus able to fire confidently into the most likely areas from which an attack would come. The pendulum had swung so far over to the defender's advantage that alternative methods of offense simply had to be developed.

A third great problem had to do with munitions and weapons. In all of 1914, the British produced only 91 new pieces of artillery and only 300 machine guns.[129] The peacetime estimates of how much ammunition would be consumed in operations were woefully low. There were very limited stockpiles on hand, and these were quickly exhausted. There were only a few modest sized factories, more properly termed "arsenals", which had the expertise to produce the explosives. This was not a task quickly turned over to rookies: mistakes here would kill the workers, bad enough, but also put the plant out of commission until repairs could be effected, while the supply officers at the battlefront clamored for more and more and more, lest the war be lost! Furthermore, the factories also suffered from a shortage of materials such as steel and brass needed to manufacture the tools of war.

Beyond all that, individual soldiers were sometimes quite extravagant in their use of ammunition. As mentioned earlier, some troops in the trenches discovered that while there might be a shortage of kindling to heat their cup of tea, a readily available substitute was a machine gun. If a few hundred rounds were fired in the general direction of the enemy, the casing of the machine gun barrel, which was cooled by water, would get hot enough to heat the tea. This is a good illustration of an important and as yet unmentioned military concept, the "field expedient." This refers to the ingenuity of soldiers who lacked a tool or device to solve a need, and fashioned it out of whatever was available, such as heating water with a machine gun. Just how much ammunition was expended in such ways is impossible to tell, and what the total impact was on ammunition supplies could have been significant. One can only imagine what the troops used for fuel in their tiny trench stoves when traditional fuel was in short supply and the temperature was below freezing. Robert Graves believed he knew the ultimate consequence: "You'd be surprised at the amount of waste that goes on in the trenches. The real charge will be on the income tax after the war."[130] One officer summed it up this way: "A great deal of equipment has 'gone west' during our travels."[131]

Pity the supply personnel trying to measure and then meet all these needs. And while the shell shortage persisted, the British did all they could to prevent the enemy from knowing about it for fear it would embolden his attacks, which were already so perilously close to success. However, what British propagandists pretended that the Kaiser had called "a contemptible little army" did indeed manage to hold on until weather ended the 1914 campaigning season.

That modern armies had campaigning seasons may seem to be a throwback to much older times. But Flanders's snow and slippery ice were just as much a hindrance for the army of 1914 as they had been a hundred years earlier for Napoleon, or two thousand years earlier for Caesar. Regardless of the temperature, armies must be fed and watered and rested and trained and cared for and kept from freezing, as must the animals, and if fighting can be postponed until the ground is more conducive to these maneuvers, all the better. If ice and snow during an attack could be avoided, then perhaps operations might have been conducted with only extreme rather than nightmarish degrees of danger, difficulty, and unpredictability.

There is also the matter of light: the long hours of winter darkness interfere with the attacker's ability to see the often misty targets. Certainly in the Great War there were campaigns undertaken during exceptionally harsh weather, but they were more the exception than the rule.

Still another of these great problems at the end of 1914 had to deal with the learning curve. Could the army commanders incorporate and apply the many lessons they were learning at the price of so much blood and treasure? Not having fought a major war in a hundred years, and never having fielded an army with as many as one million soldiers—soon to be twice and quadruple that size—the British had much to learn. Its most experienced leaders had never commanded such numbers of troops. At this time, mid-1914, two army leaders occupied center stage in the public mind.

The first of these was the Commander-in-Chief of the BEF, Sir John French. His name was constantly in the press, seemingly accomplishing much. What was less well known was something extreme stress revealed, that he had a dangerously inadequate understanding of the realities of the battlefield situation. Served by a staff which seems only to have told him what he wanted to hear, the commanding General frequently believed the German enemy was either so weak that his force would march over them—as he boasted during those first August days in France—or so strong as to be able to drive his forces into the sea—his conviction the very next month.

To strengthen General French, one of his repeated visitors at headquarters was the most popular soldier in the whole British Empire, Lord Kitchener. This tall, elegant military leader had first burst into the public eye when he led a relief force to the rescue of what he thought was a beleaguered British force on the upper Nile River. In fact, that force had already been slaughtered by a local uprising, but Lord Kitchener's heroic attempt at a rescue made him famous. Thus, when war broke out, Prime Minister Asquith appointed him War Minister with a seat in the Cabinet. This gave him extraordinary influence, both as an experienced officer and as a person with the ear of all those in high office. The famous and extremely successful recruiting poster featured not the King, not the Commander-in-chief: it starred Lord Kitchener.

Almost alone among the leaders of Britain, Kitchener foresaw that the British Empire was entering a new phase in its history. To carry on as before would fail. There simply were too many Germans and her Austrian allies for the French and Russians to defeat. While the Royal Navy would counter the German fleet and protect trade, including the crucial war material imports, the army would have to become something more akin to the continental model. Kitchener talked in terms of a million man army, of a war lasting four years or more. Only a few generals agreed. General Douglas Haig, for example, told the British War Council on 5 August that it should prepare for a "...*war of several years.*"[132]

Meanwhile King George V was telling his Army they would be home before the autumn leaves fell, while the Kaiser was promising his men they would be home by Christmas. Kitchener was predicting a war of years, not months, requiring soldiers by the millions, not the "splendid little army of 1914." Kitchener also realized that such an army would require weapons and uniforms and barracks and food and training, training, training. He insisted that many of the BEF personnel be returned to Britain to train these new "Kitchener armies" which he also realized would not be combat-proficient until 1916. He saw that the new army he was proposing would be just a group of assorted men until the junior officers had taught them their new craft, and soldiering is indeed a craft. Kitchener thus demanded that these veterans come home from Flanders and from France to become the instructors of the new and much larger armies. The Cabinet, primarily civilians, weighed Kitchener's advice with grand disbelief but growing attention.

Many disagreed with Kitchener. The common viewpoint was that the war would be quite short. Barclay Godfrey Buxton was among those who mocked Kitchener's call for volunteers for a term of "...three years or the duration." He joined in September 1914 "...for we believed that the war would be over quickly and I might not otherwise get into the war in time before it stopped." He also noted in his exit interview after the war that "We took it for granted that of course the Germans could not last longer than October and that we would be back at Cambridge on the 8th...."[133] Other soldiers at first shared Buxton's opinion, but soon came to a different point of view: "The men at first expected to be home in about 2 months but now—not by Xmas. The German army is exceptionally good."[134] Another enthusiastic new arrival put it this way:

> I had heard about the previous battles but I couldn't get there fast enough. We had been brought up on the history of the Boer War and patriotism and heroics and everything, and we thought the war was going to be over before we could get there. However, in about half a minute, all that had gone. I wondered what the devil I'd gotten into because it was nothing but mud and filth and all the chaps who were already there, well. They looked like tramps, all plastered with filth and dirt and unshaven.[135]

The second of the key British generals came to know firsthand just how good this German army was. General Sir Douglas Haig would spend the entire war combating it. Like General French, Haig was a man of long experience and quite well at home on a horse. He also had a habit that served him well: he kept a diary, and almost every day, he sent a copy to his wife, a former lady-in-waiting to the Queen. Lady Haig produced an edited copy of the diary which she then shared with the Queen, who then shared it with her husband, the King, with each person in this chain aware of all the other links. Haig expressed his doubts about his commander through this back channel. Haig had great confidence in his own abilities and devoutly believed he would be a better Commander-in-Chief than General French, and was ready to take on the post.

The end of the 1914 campaigning season also brought a deeper realization of the great British disadvantage in battlefield position. As the Germans came across the nearly level land of Flanders, they paid attention to the few natural elevations such as the ridge at Messines, not far from Ypres, and a slight natural hill, later known as "Hill 60." As they retreated from the Marne River, they carefully kept all the high points, modest though they were. This resulted in a bulge of the British line into German held lands, almost like a blister extending outwards from Ypres. Of course, the Germans could now shell the British on three sides, the classic form of a "salient" or reverse dent into the enemy territory. By retaining these modest heights, the Germans kept important advantages. Not only could they see just what the British were doing, but perhaps more importantly, the British had little direct observation of the German activity taking place on the higher ground. German artillery spotters, for example, could more easily select targets and "range" their guns. Ranging is a form of practice fire so that when a moving target came into a particular location, the "firing solution", the exact data given to each gun, was already calculated.

The solution to these salient problems was simple: withdraw to a more defensible line. That was the common sense military solution. But not for the only time in this war, politics intervened. It was not politically correct to surrender more of Belgium or more of France to the invaders.[136] So at what would be a very great cost, the British held these barely tenable places.

This is not to say that either side had mastered precision fire. After all, the exact point of impact depended on more factors than a pre-computer world could accommodate. Among them were the size of the weapon, the distance to the target, the type of shell, the degree of precision with which this particular barrel had been cast as well as how close to specifications the mass produced shell was. But these were not all. Other factors included the time of day, temperature of the barrel, number of rounds already fired, air temperature and humidity, skill of the particular gun crew, and the degree to which the gun had "walked" or moved slightly each time it was fired. Perhaps gunners were lucky to hit even reasonably close to the target.

Not the least of the unresolved problems was medical care. In the crassest light, the army simply could not afford that each wounded man be removed from the fight. The soldier had to return, combat ready, as quickly as possible. On the other hand, he had to heal, so far as possible, but physically and, as was being increasingly realized, mentally as well. Long before the current terminologies of "post-traumatic stress disorder" and "combat fatigue", men were manifesting these as yet under-recognized injuries. In historian Gerald De Groote's marvelous phrase, "Shells that left behind no physical scars still tore at the mind."[137] John Ellis put it this way: shell shock "...was an extreme point along a steady progression of emotional torment."[138] It was not easy, it was not at all easy, to explain the soldier's experience to the folks back home, either. Men simply did not talk about their horrific experiences with their families. "Either you had been at the front or you hadn't."[139] These men lived with extraordinary mental stress, such as a fear of failing to do their duty. "Each man struggled with his intense private fears and nearly all triumphed simply because they would rather be dead than revealed to their fellows as cowards."[140]

Medical care, just as manpower, was complicated. Just getting medical help was not guaranteed. As one colonel insisted to his officers, "If you stay behind to help wounded, you double your casualties."[141] The wounded man first had to attract the attention of would-be rescuers. Failing that, or being too exposed to enemy fire, he would die in place, sometimes taking much time to do so. Everyone wanted the wounded to get quick and effective care, but two or even four men carrying another on a stretcher not only took that number out of the firing line, but also set up multiple semi-exposed targets for German sharpshooters. The wounded had to be taken across ditches filled with rainwater, causing them to be jostled and perhaps further hurt before reaching care. In a conversation with King George V, General Douglas Haig reported that "...we have to take special precautions to prevent more unwounded men than are necessary from accompanying a wounded man back from the trenches."[142] However, even prompt attention was often fruitless, as Colonel Helm lamented:

The poor fellow was brought to me absolutely riddled. He lay in my arms until he died, shrieking in his agony and said he hoped I would excuse him for making such a noise as he really could not help it. Pitiful as nothing could be done for him except an injection of morphia. I always will remember that incident, particularly as he was such a fine looking boy certainly not more than nineteen.[143]

Colonel Helm had a great many very sad moments as the first physician many of the critically wounded saw:

That day I had several who had gone stark mad and it was awful to have those poor fellows among the wounded as they were screaming the whole time and crying out that there was no hope for us, that we should all be killed. I think we all agreed with them but we did not want reminding of the fact.[144]

Other soldiers bore similar witness:

I thought of the awful night; of the howling artillerymen and others getting shrapnel probed out of their shoulders and back by the wearied surgeon, the last doctor left, carrying on by himself day and night. I took my aching body up the hill again that morning determined to stick it out until I was carried away alive or dead.[145]

In an interview long after the war, former Sergeant Jack Dorgan's voice became quite emotional as he recalled a moment with a few of his pals in the first days of battle:

They had their legs blown off. All I could see when I got up to them was their thigh bones. I will always remember their white thighbones, the rest of their legs were gone.[146]

There are a number of oral interviews in the collections of the Imperial War Museum. Many of these are available on line. They are of unique value. While the printed word has impact, of course, the human voice can disclose a deep and powerful range of emotion, even years after the events described. To hear the memories of the participants in their own words is a rare privilege and represents another terrific resource for students of the Great War.

Those recorded interviews include eyewitness descriptions of horrific wounds. Men suffering head wounds rarely survived, due to massive internal injury.[147] The usual sequence of medical care involved first aid on the field, removal to a local "dressing station" located behind the rear or "reserve" trench, then to a more distant "casualty clearing station", on to a "field hospital" or to a "base hospital" and then home for convalescent leave, if warranted. When the patient healed, as most did, he then returned to the trenches, sometimes with the same unit, sometimes with another. Sadly, often the first unit no longer existed, and many units were essentially dissolved, the few remaining men sent as replacements into another understrength unit. Soldiers assigned to the first aid stations often had ugly experiences, such as the "old soldier" who noticed the "carnal odor" from the incinerator used to dispose of bloody bandages and amputated parts.[148]

There was also the recurring problem of what to do with the dead. Many were buried in a shallow grave, marked by helmet and rife. But many of these were lost in later fighting; many other bodies were never found, having been buried or vaporized. In many cemeteries in Belgium there is grave maker with multiple names inscribed and the words "believed to be buried in this cemetery." In another, a marker indicates that a named individual was buried in this cemetery, but a subsequent shelling has obliterated the specific plot. Oddly, when the war finally ended, there was a specialized business of locating a particular grave, exhuming the remains, and returning them to Great Britain for final interment. There are multiple monuments in Belgium today, each honoring many men. The Menin Gate Memorial in Ypres, for example, has 56,000 names inscribed on the walls. No identifiable remains of these individuals were ever found. There is a similar ossuary, a collection of unidentified but revered bones in a very large grave in the German cemetery, at Langemarck, Belgium. In Britain, the Graves Registration Commission began its work in 1915. Its successor agencies today maintain the Great War cemeteries with great care.

The bloody year of 1914 closed on a distinctly odd note. On Christmas Eve, hearing the other side singing Christmas carols, a few men from each side entered the "no man's land" between the trenches. In short order, handshakes and cigarettes were exchanged, a few kind words were uttered, even a few impromptu football games ensued. There were even moments of humor such as:

As a sign of their friendliness the Germans put up a sign saying 'Gott mit uns'. Which means 'God is with us' and so we put a sign in English saying 'We got mittens too'. I don't know if they enjoyed that joke.[149]

Recognizing each other's humanity, the troops spontaneously paused in the killing. As senior officers became aware of this, fearing the long-term consequences, they immediately and emphatically ordered an end to all such fraternization. Meanwhile, already having endured hardships, on Christmas Day twenty-two year old Lieutenant Henry Field wrote the last three lines of a poem he would never complete:

> Vouchsafe that we may see, dear Lord,
> Vouchsafe that we may see,
> Thy purpose through the aching days, [150]

Field would die on 1 July 1916 of combat injuries.

Despite such momentary aberrations from the war as the Christmas Truce, the random deaths continued:

(Two men) were killed by their folly; a German shell had not exploded, and they attempted to remove the fuse for a souvenir, with an entrenching tool. It exploded, and killed them both. [151]

T. C. Cubbon's diary for 1914 includes the observation on 18 November that it was "Snowing here today." On 3 December 1914 his unit was inspected by quite a high power team: the King, the Prince of Wales, and Lord Kitchener. On 21 December, he noted that it was both his birthday and a "…rotten time." He took some comfort when on 27 December he received "Princess Mary's Gift", a token present given to each person wearing the King's uniform. Smokers got a pipe and cigarettes; non-smokers received pencils and candy. [152]

With victory not even on the horizon, 1914 ended with an emerging awareness that this conflict was going to be won neither as quickly nor as easily as the combatants had initially expected. The British might have been brought up to believe that "…one Englishman was worth ten Germans", [153] but those Germans were proving more tenacious than expected. What the BEF most needed was time to solve the many problems it faced.

CHAPTER II

1915: Build and Train

"Tell Jim to learn bricklaying. There will be plenty of that
over here when it is all over."[1]

The first days of 1915 in Flanders were indistinguishable from the last days of 1914: all were cold, rainy—when it was not snowing—damp, dark, depressing. Letters home from the soldiers report all these conditions, but reading enough of them, one frequently finds an undercurrent of expectation. Somehow, all is going to work out in the end, and it is just a matter of endurance until then, with the "then" somewhere in the vague future. But in the meantime, Sergeant Cubbon found his new assignment was to "...rotten trenches terribly wet. Am wet up to the hips." Two days later he added: "The communication trenches are waist deep in water so instead of coming through them [we] are relieved by coming right over the top in the open", a very hazardous procedure.[2] Another soldier reported "...we could not dry our saturated clothing & the liquid mud just ran in at the open doorway."[3]

While the soldiers were enduring these conditions, the editors of *Debrett's Peerage* were facing an unprecedented problem. So many sons of the aristocracy were dead that the editors would need extra time to catch up with how the titles of nobility had devolved. Consequently, the spring edition would be published late.[4]

Little things were causes for joy in the trenches. Sergeant Cubbon was quite happy on New Year's Day to receive a parcel and some photos of his wife Flo and their baby. Another soldier recorded in his diary that "...here there is no room for a swelled head as the caps they send out are all one size, very small, and in the great scheme of things one is a mere atom."[5]

Senior military commanders believed that no grand success would be achieved on the battlefield in 1915. No, the primary task would not be military triumphs, but rather a year spent in achieving two goals. The first was keeping pressure on the enemy, essentially preventing the Germans from winning. Some form of attack must be maintained to stop the enemy from controlling the time and place of the next great battle. Britain's allies, Republican France and Tsarist Russia, had endured staggering losses, actually in the millions. Pressure must be kept on the Germans to prevent them from concentrating against the Russians, knocking them out of the war, and then turning Germany's full might against the western allies of Belgium, Britain, and France. While no great victories were anticipated, catastrophic loss had to be avoided

The second great goal would be preparation. Weapons would be redesigned, improved, manufactured. One example of an improved weapon is the Stokes mortar. By January 1915, Wilfred Stokes had designed a weapon consisting of a short tube and a baseplate. The plate kept the tube from sinking into the mud when fired. The soldier dropped the shell into the tube, and when it hit the bottom, an explosive charge shot the projectile high into the air but only a short distance. It could be fired from the shelter of a trench towards the enemies' trench. The projectiles came in various sizes and could carry an exploding shell as much as a thousand yards away.[6]

There was also a hand-thrown explosive called a "Mill's bomb" which would later be called a grenade. Sir John French wanted 4,000 of these in late 1914, an absurdly low number, and another demonstration of the fact that Sir John just did not get it, this time the "it" being the vastness of the war just beginning. By November 1914, only seventy grenades a week were arriving at the front. By the third week in that December, 2,500 were arriving weekly.[7] Ultimately, more than sixty-one million of these were produced,[8] although some officers when first seeing a Mill's bomb were unsure about its usefulness: "They appeared to be far more dangerous to the thrower than the Germans."[9]

Men would be trained, trained some more, and then trained beyond that. Lessons learned from the fall campaigns, such as to always precede infantry attacks with artillery barrages, would be more widely practiced. Since over one third of the original army was now beyond hearing all but the heavenly call to arms, the army had become deskilled. The tried and true little customs and mannerisms so valuable to the army, the day to day practical and empowering methods and shortcuts had to be relearned. The experienced junior leadership of the army had to quickly share their wealth of experience with youth from what was often a very different world.

The soldiers needed "…time to settle down & learn the many lessons & dodges of trench warfare."[10] They learned that mules did not want to go over bridges across trenches.[11] They learned not to go toward the gaps in the barbed wire, because "…that was a bad thing, really, because that was the point the German machine gunners were aiming at, you see."[12] Another wrote:

Gradually we learned that tree stumps are not necessarily an enemy patrol &
that it is better to remain motionless when a flare goes up; to move is to attract
the eye of the observer & produce the inevitable machine gun chatter.[13]

One soldier remembered how he had pinpointed some German guns for
his artillery to destroy: he took bearings on their location from three different
places in his own trenches at night and made the calculations.[14] Artillery
Captain Noel learned to sit in a front line hole and telephone target corrections
to his guns some miles away.[15] One soldier knew he was unfit for a special
duty, but did not think anyone else could do it, either:

> I had my usual misfortune to be detailed for gas-guard, my job being to
> strike with my bayonet the used shell casing hanging in the doorway of our
> and all other billets whenever or if we spotted any gas coming over & I leave
> you to imagine my feelings as I stepped out for that first spell of duty. How
> do I recognize whether it is gas or just smoke?[16]

The soldiers learned not to trust newspaper accounts. On the one hand,
"It is rather keenly interesting to get the news absolutely first hand and every
detail of the progress, otherwise you can take it from me that the accounts you
get are nothing like [*sic*]."[17] And on the other, "Reinforcements came out from
England, and were able to tell us more about the War than we knew. It seemed
they got the newspaper news in England, while we got the latrine news."[18]

That point of view is not surprising in light of the contemporary newspaper
reporting. The newspapers in these early days of the war were fountains of
patriotic distraction. Column after column of newsprint was devoted to such
topics as when and how "Roumania" (one of several common spellings) would
enter the war. *The Times* printed an appeal to major landowners to allow
their groundskeepers, woodsmen and gardeners to help with the harvest.[19]
Such an appeal rated space in a time of such more serious events? On the
same day, *The Times* published an advertisement for an illustrated history of
what it already termed "The Great War." The war was only twelve days old!
By October, that document was being offered in monthly installments. Major
news, such as the number of soldiers killed and wounded or battlefield reverses,
was seldom highlighted. Reading the newspapers of the day with the benefit
of hindsight makes it amply clear that the public, despite the appearance of
"full disclosure" was remarkably ill-informed. Trivia was celebrated; serious
topics were lovingly refashioned into marginalia. In truth, the public was just
not well informed.

The newspapers did not earn much respect from the men in the trenches. In
his papers, Ralph Smith wrote:

The daily papers at home I found always had the same quotation "All is quiet on the Western Front." I don't suppose they knew that our Artillery were only allowed to fire 12 shells a day owing to a shortage of ammunition....

Smith was not alone in his low opinion of the papers. In Reginald Haine's interview from 1974, he declared:

Newspapers talked the most awful ballyhoo you could possibly imagine. It was tripe that came from them. None of the reporters was allowed near the line you know. They were all back miles behind and they only sent back what they thought the people would like to know.

Meanwhile, the personnel problems continued. In addition to new soldiers, new officers, too, would have to be recruited and trained if they were to be effective. Not every member of the educated or upper classes wanted to be in the military. One individual wanted nothing to do with leading other men: being both underage and undersized, he did not want to be "...in charge of men much older than myself."[20] Robert Graves was quite frank: "What I most disliked about the army was never being alone, forced to live and sleep with men whose company, in many cases, I would have run miles to avoid."[21]

Where did these new soldiers come from? Why did men join the army in such record numbers? Some of the answers are surprising. First to the colors were those without strong commitments, while a second group were impelled by socio-economic factors.[22] A considerable number joined out of patriotism, of course, but others were attracted by the expectation of three square meals a day, a place to sleep, and pals to share it all with. Army food was more generous and more nutritious than many were used to, and the army also provided boots and clothing. Moreover, the army's crowded living conditions were seldom worse than those in so many homes.[23] Curiously, the wives and children left behind were often more healthy, because now the women controlled the household funds and used them to feed the family better.[24]

Some men who were trapped in daily grinding poverty saw the army as an opportunity. That the army was believed to be a healthier alternative to their previous lifestyle is remarkable. That thousands and thousands were declined enlistment due to sub-par physical development—in reputedly the most advanced nation on earth—was another eye opener. For still others, men trapped in dead-end jobs such as working in dangerous coal mines far underground, jobs that would have been familiar to Charles Dickens or Karl Marx: for some men, it was a chance to escape the monotony and drudgery of their drab lives.[25] After all, the army offered better food, a regular wage, companionship, promotion and perhaps some degree of travel, as well as the dark side: a real chance at death, disability, disease.

At first, the recruiting stations were swamped. Twenty-five stations were set up just in London, and most were packed.[26] For the first year of the war, volunteers were enough. One historian summarizes this very well:

> Unemployment did not fill the ranks of Kitchener's armies; popular sentiment did. The protection of "little Belgium", the defense of the empire, the need to be seen to be doing one's military duty alongside the men of one's district or village; these may sound like outworn clichés today, but in 1914 they had force and substance in the minds of ordinary people.[27]

A few joined in a patriotic outburst but soon learned to regret their impetuosity. "Foul language, night urinal buckets, unappetizing food and the personal habits of the lower working class put sensitive recruits through a purgatorial existence."[28] The continuing casualty lists certainly colored the young men's perception of the military option. Just as the other continental powers, Britain had to begin conscription in the fall of 1915, but, remarkably and unlike the other Powers, not until then.

Lord Kitchener encouraged men from the same locality or school or club to join as a group, anticipating a high degree of unit cohesion. This was commonly thought a splendid idea, and many joined as "pals", such as the "Accrington Pals." The cost of this system was not evident until the casualty lists began to cut great swathes through the army-age population of, for example, a small mining village in a remote corner of the country.

Even as the army moved ever deeper into its rebuild and retrain mode, all the other components of military life likewise labored to improve. One of these involved horses. A person standing on a street corner anywhere in London in 1914 would have been able to count more horses than automobiles and "lorries" or trucks. Horses were a part of the common culture. Rare is the modern reader who has a first-hand knowledge of horses. Occasionally driving by a few on a rural property or a mounted policeman in a parade: the average contemporary student has had minimal contact with horses, and so knows little of their types, their care, or their uses. One enlightening exhibit in the "In Flanders Fields Museum" in Ieper[29] incorporates a horse fitted with saddlebags. Sewn into the fabric are slots to accommodate three or four artillery shells on either side of the animal. The shells were simply too heavy for a man to carry for any distance through the mud of the trenches. The British actually built small new railroads to bring supplies from the seacoast to the rear supply bases. Then horses or mules brought them as close to the batteries as possible, and the troops manhandled them the last part of the journey. In a war in which shells were fired in the millions, the number of trips made and the number of horses and mules involved is staggering.

The Army had to introduce men to horses, horses to gun limbers and carriages, and both to new skills:

> ...an aged gentleman dressed in civilian clothes, wearing an arm-band, gathered us together, and told us he was in charge of us. We were about 150 strong, and would form a new battery of field artillery. Eventually, he became our Sergeant-Major. He had seen service as an artillery man in the Boer War. He was a fine type of man, about 50 years of age, small of stature, and had volunteered services to train men.[30]

The fact that this unit was to be trained by an elderly retired veteran was just another indication of the shortage of qualified instructors. No wonder Lord Kitchener was insisting that more of the experienced men be recalled from the continent.

Meanwhile, the Army trained new cavalrymen as well as they could. Beside the draft or working horses, there were still hundreds of thousands of cavalry horses on the Western Front. One estimate holds that altogether there were nearly 500,000 British horses. Many were held ready for the day of the big break-through, when it was supposed they would ride behind the enemy lines and disrupt his power to fight. But that was for the future. For now, all the horses had to be watered and fed and exercised and moved and provided whatever else was required to keep them healthy.

The BEF had far more horses than it had men trained to ride and care for and to work them. Thus a good number of fresh recruits suddenly found themselves learning all about horses. First, they had to learn not to fear a horse, and then to ride one. For the first time in their lives, some of these men had to wear spurs, metal attachments onto the heels of their shoes with which they learned to direct the horse. But first the soldiers had to master their spurs: "...men whose feet turned outward often got their spurs entangled."[31] Men learning to ride horses were often sore in unfamiliar places. "As they marched to their dinner of bully beef stew each felt as though he had a beer barrel between his legs; he certainly felt sore in the region of his posterior."[32] One soldier learned that "...we slept with our horses, the heat of their bodies keeping us warm, together with our blankets and greatcoats."[33] He also discovered that horses could be stubborn, and some would not go onto a ship. "The impossibles were slung up in a hammock, and dropped in the ship."[34] Most importantly, just as officers were taught to care for their men before themselves, so, too, for the horses. "We were taught that, after every job was done, the horse must be attended to first; they must be fed and groomed."[35]

Nearly sixty years after the war, Gunner Leonard Ounsworth was interviewed as part of an oral history project. To hear the tone of voice, the emotional content of their memories as these elderly men recalled a time from so long before created another valuable window on these events. Despite the passage of time, Ounsworth remembered a great deal about his time with horses. In early 1915, for example, the best horses already having been taken, the men coming together to form new artillery batteries were issued fresh horses from America. Many of the imported horses had never been ridden. Soldiers who hoped to form a battery of guns first had to learn to ride the horses which would pull the guns. He remembered many funny moments of how the rookies fell off the horse forwards, backwards and sideways, yet each day each man becoming a bit more proficient. The men were taught that having fallen off, if they lay still on the ground, the horses would not walk on them.

At first, the training regimen denied the new riders the use of saddles. They had to learn to ride bareback. They had to learn to turn the horse, not by jerking on the bit in its mouth, but by the contact of the reins on his neck. Soldiers had to master holding the reins in one hand only. Originally, the right-hand had been kept free to hold a sword. In this war, the right-hand would be used more often to hold such things as spools of wire so communication lines could be strung while mounted.

The gunners newly learned skills included the care of their horses. At first, Ounsworth's particular battery misunderstood its directions concerning feed rations and was feeding its horses fourteen pounds of corn a day, almost one-third too much. The horses did not complain. The diet for horses was a matter of some controversy. While grass was cheap and often plentiful, it was "… watery and innutritious" and needed to be supplemented with large portions of oats.[36] As a military consequence, horses had to be supplied with food, water and shelter, as well as skilled caregivers—still another drain on army resources, still another imperative need that had to be accommodated.

Soldiers also learned how to care for the horses and the horses' tack, which may be defined as the combination of leather and metal components that signal the rider's intentions to the horse. The piece that went into the mouth was made of steel: regular, not stainless steel. This piece was subject to rust and so had to be polished every day. The leather pieces would become wet from the horses' sweat and that too had to be cleaned every day. Ounsworth and his colleagues learned that proper care for just one horse could easily take an afternoon's labor.

Among all these new riders, the horses occasionally caused a bit of excitement and even harm:

One day…a thunderstorm broke out, and here I witnessed a most exciting event—about 2,000 horses broke lose, and galloped pell-mell, taking everything before them. A number of men were injured, and the scene was frightening—a veritable stampede.[37]

As the new soldiers soon learned, a horse requires a great deal of attention to be kept healthy and ready to work. For example, a stabled horse cannot be kept too long in the same area. The ground beneath him becomes unfit for him to stand in and must be "mucked out" and fresh straw spread. The manure must be removed. This is not just a matter of odor and human sensibilities; it also is required to prevent the horse getting a debilitating condition known as "wet foot." As Col. Helm noted in his diary, "I was Transport officer and as the horses were suffering from the wet and sodden ground I took them back to a place where they could be looked after better."[38] The doctor who treated the wounded soldiers thus shared responsibility for the health of horses as well. This curious relationship between men and horses was mentioned in J. Barclay's diary:

> The train stopped to allow the horses to be watered and the stationmaster realizing that the men also needed "watering" had provided a large kettle of tea flavored (very strongly) with rum. On a cold morning that was very acceptable indeed.[39]

Just as the men suffered from the elements, so too did the horses. Many of the men felt quite badly for the horses:

> In this cold and hunger, the horses now developed a new habit—they all started chewing—ropes, leather or even our tunics. While you were attending to one horse, the other would be chewing at you. So we resorted to chains, a big steel chain for pinioning down, another from the horses nose band, just like a heavy dog chain. The bags from which they were fed oats and corn had become sodden with rain, and when a harness man was placing this on his head, the horse would swing it up and sideways. Many a driver was hit senseless with such a blow.... The horse then turned to chewing at one another, and they soon became hairless, and a pitiful sight. This was war, however, and no inspector from the Society for the Prevention of Cruelty to Animals came that way.[40]

Protecting the horses from excessive rain was a frequent theme in soldier's diaries. Captain William Henry Bloor observed "The horse standings have gotten quite impossible owing to the constant rain, and it is hardly safe to go there without a lifeboat."[41] And how were all these horses employed? Captain Bloor noted later "Had 12 horses on one wagon and could not move it."[42]

There is an entire science devoted just to the care of horse's hooves. They require regular attention with specialized tools and skilled practitioners known as "farriers." A unique vocabulary deals with the care of horses, creatures which for example may be "quidding hay" (meaning to partially chew and then spit out, indicating a health problem) or may be suffering from pedal osteitis (an inflammation of the coffin bone in the hoof) or from laminitis (an inflammation of the hoof) or Thrush (a bacterial infection of the hoof) or something as simple as standing too long in snow. Sometimes a horse could be dangerous when being shoed, and so the horsemen might use "shackling", a method of tying all four hooves to a short wooden board so the horse could not kick but could be safely shoed.[43] The point is that the Army needed to maintain skilled personnel to ensure that the horses were properly cared for, capable of working, and making a genuine contribution to the war effort. An enormous number of horses both served in and were killed in the Great War. There is a sculptured monument to honor them in London today.

The care and training of horses is not a monolithic science. Various schools of thought emerged as to how a horse should be trained, what foodstuffs should be included and excluded in their diet, and so on. One example of this concerned riding the horse in rivers and streams. Horses have a natural tendency to move their heads up and back when finding themselves in water over their heads. Yet if they are carrying a rider at the same time, both will likely drown as the horse struggles. But there is a particular pull on the reins such that the horse will be able to swim through the deep part with his rider and emerge safely on the other side—all conditional upon holding the reins a certain way, and training the horse in advance for this eventuality.[44] Crossing deep water was just one of many skills that horses and riders needed to master.

Different respected individuals had precise views on how and when to train a horse:

> The horse should be accustomed to objects and noises. So that he may not be afraid of them. An army horse should be bold and ready to pass anything. To teach it to do so, all sorts of objects should be placed under his feet in the school. He can best be taught in the stable, at the time of feeding, to stand the noise of tambours, clarions, clashing of arms, firing, etc.[45]

There were even devotees of individual breeds of horse. Recalling a war from forty years earlier, James Fillis wrote in 1902:

> In the Crimea, the English lost the majority of their thoroughbreds, but the Normans, Percherons, Bretons and Auvergnans (breeds) held out

admirably. The war horse ought to remain serviceable under conditions of hunger, cold, rain, snow and nights without shelter or covering.... To make use of a thoroughbred, one must know more than ordinary cavalry men do about riding.[46]

Once the horses were fed and watered and once the men mastered riding them, then the training of the horses began. To move one gun took eight horses which were hitched to the gun in pairs. Thus four pairs of powerful horses stood in front of each gun. The problem? To get all eight to move as one. If the horses began at even slightly different moments, the strain on the apparatus could be such that it would break. In fact, it was easier to move a gun with fifty men than with eight horses, because the men could all be given an order to "forward march" and carry it out at once. Horses had to be taught such precision. The Royal Artillery horses were taught particular maneuvers. Horses were hitched in pairs side by side and then in teams of six or eight. The runners learned to control these teams:

We learned to use reins with the left hand, and always leave the right free for emergencies. Every driver had four reins in his hand at the same time, but used his knees to guide the horse ridden for direction. There were three drivers to each gun—lead driver, centre driver and wheel driver. ...after a few months, we had become proficient horsemen.[47]

Sometimes the soldier-drivers surprised themselves with what they learned:

I was the lead driver, and right by our team I could see the glitter of water. I enquired if it were a river or a canal, and kept edging away from it. It looked just like a big river at night. Later on, in daylight, I found that it was caused by pools of water on the wet ground. It had been raining very heavily and the pools were just about three inches deep, but the gun flashes made it look just like a big river at night.[48]

Some soldiers took great pride in caring for their horses. One soldier noticed that his horses were "...up to their fetlocks in muck..." so he arranged to collect bricks and stones from badly shelled nearby villages, bring that debris to the stable area, and construct a solid foundation for the horses to stand on.[49]

At quiet moments behind the lines there were even horse shows and riding competitions. Men challenged each other to tugs of war on horseback, even wrestling on horseback, and photographs of these competitions remain.[50] Robert Graves's classic memoir of the war recalled:

We used to boast that our transport animals were the best in France, and our transport men the best horse-thieves. No less than eighteen of our stable had been stolen from other units at one time or another for their good looks. We even "borrowed" a pair from the Scots Greys.[51]

It was not just horses who suffered in this war. Many soldiers noticed that:

...all about that part of Flanders, the terrified cattle go wild about the fields; roaring every night in their hunger and fright and desolation, wanting to be milked and yet running stupidly from our men who attempt to relieve them.[52]

On the other hand, "Many birds still remained and among them a nightingale which sang every night in spite of the incessant shellfire."[53]

While some soldiers concentrated on keeping the horses healthy and happy, others took a shot at keeping the Germans in their place. Enemy sharpshooters took a toll of British soldiers every day. The improbably named Hesketh Vernon Hesketh-Prichard, a big game hunter, set up a British sniper school. Among his techniques was to set up a dummy head that could be raised and lowered. German sharpshooters would fire at such a target. Their fire could be observed by the ambushing British sharpshooters, who would then try to eliminate them. Phony targets, moving targets, anything which would mislead the Germans into revealing themselves was fair in this deadly game.[54]

To repeat a key point, what the British most needed as 1915 began was time. Building additional factories, importing additional raw materials, recruiting and training soldiers, collecting manufactured goods and transporting them to the seacoast, crossing the English Channel, moving those men and materiel close to the battlefield depots, moving from the depot to the trench, all the while preventing the enemy from winning: all of this was to take time. The critical question was quite stark: would there be enough time to accomplish these massive tasks before Germany could defeat the allies? After all, Russia had already left one million men in fresh graves on the Eastern front while the French had lost a similar number. More than half of the original BEF was gone. Would there be enough time to fashion victory?

While the military command recognized the need for development in all these areas, the Army in the field could hardly stand idle in 1915. Quite to the contrary, there were immediate military and political considerations, especially the demands of Britain's bleeding allies, that pressure be kept on the Germans to prevent them from concentrating all of their strength either on Russia or France. Yet the ghastly casualties of trench warfare, the realization that Germany could produce so many more bullets than Britain could produce soldiers, led some to challenge the strategy of attacking well defended trenches. Churchill, for one, condemned further attacks on trenches, calling them "chewing barbed wire in Flanders."[55] In his book written after the war, he lamented the continuing frontal attacks as a "forlorn expedient."[56]

A new school of thought proposed a new target. Could the north coast of Germany be attacked from the sea, thus bypassing the trenches? Admiral Sir John Fisher, Churchill's flamboyant senior associate at the Admiralty, advocated this approach, but extensive studies concluded that such an attack was impractical and had a high likelihood of failure.

A second approach looked to the south of Europe, focusing on the Dardanelles, a narrow strait connecting the Aegean Sea with the Sea of Marmara. This would allow a connection between the Mediterranean and the Black Seas. In 1915, this area was under the control of Turkey, which had already joined the German side. Invading there would divert German troops from both the existing Western and Eastern fronts. Much more importantly, it would open additional supply routes to Russia and expedite the placement of French and British munitions into the hands of millions of the Czar's soldiers. The British and French were fully aware that every German taken off the battlefield by a Russian soldier was one less fighting them on the Western front. Therefore, in its most crass equation, the more bullets sent to Russia, the less cost in blood to Britain and France. Consequently a plan vigorously spearheaded by First Lord of the Admiralty Winston Churchill envisioned a naval attack using expendable older ships. Advocates of bringing the battle to Turkey became known as the "Easterners" while those who remained convinced the war could only be fought and only be won in Belgium and France were the "Westerners."

The Easterners had a point. Thus far, no battle on the Western front could be called a success for the Allies. Quite the contrary, as already noted, the British army was losing a minimum of 6,500 men a month, even when there was no "big push" going on.[57] Random enemy artillery fire, a moment's inattention to cover while within range of enemy sharpshooters, accidental friendly fire, smothering under a collapsed trench: the list of pointless or at least non-productive ways to die was endless. Nor did there seem to be a way around the obstacles. By early 1915, the trench warfare system was pretty well... well... entrenched.

The trench line ran from the North Sea to the slopes of the Swiss mountains. There was a general pattern with many local variations. First came the firing trench, up front, closest to the enemy. This might be anywhere from just a few dozen yards—just about within earshot—to as much as half a mile apart from the enemy. Behind that was a second trench far enough back that a shell aimed at the first trench ought not to be able to also damage the second trench. Often there was a third and sometimes even a fourth trench. Connecting these were "communication" trenches. These provided a route for the daily delivery of water, food, supplies, replacement soldiers, perhaps mail, and so forth. In some places, the water table was so high that digging holes just a foot or two into the earth would quickly fill with water. In such places, the trench had to be built up above ground level. Sandbags were used to form parapets, and holes were fashioned into the wall to allow observation of the enemy. Looking over the top was extremely dangerous. Sharpshooters on the other side were seemingly always looking for the unwary. Soldiers learned to use a periscope, a tube containing a mirror at the top and bottom allowing a peek over the top. Sometimes even these were targeted, sometimes resulting in horrific eye wounds.

It was not possible to construct an unbroken line of trenches. Various natural obstacles such as a river made that impractical. In some locations, "strong points" were constructed such as a concrete "pillbox", a small but thick walled little fort often sheltering a machine gun, which then could defend a large swathe in front. One can drive through Belgium today and see many such pillboxes sitting alone in the middle of a farm field. They are of no great use today, but are too expensive to remove. Both grazing cattle and contemporary farmers seem to ignore them.

Soldiers attempted to make the best of life in the trenches. As mentioned earlier, the British did not want them to become too comfortable, always keeping in mind that these were temporary shelters on the way to defeating Germany, always wary of creating a defensive rather than an offensive mindset. But they still had to be livable. A typical British pattern in early 1915 was to have "stand-to" at 4:10 a.m. This meant all the soldiers were on alert in case the enemy planned an attack for dawn. Breakfast was at eight, lunch at noon, and dinner at six.[58] Needless to say, these were all target times, hardly fixed in stone. Any of a thousand reasons might upset the schedule: a lucky enemy artillery round landing in the kitchen area, or perhaps delayed supply delivery, or simply bad weather.

The daylight hours were the least active in the trench. Since the Germans usually held the high ground and had pretty good visibility as to what the British were up to in their trenches, daylight was reserved for sleeping, or trying to. Even on the otherwise most quiet day, quite deliberately, random shells would be fired just to prevent the British from enjoying the quiet. When evening came, the day's chores began. One third of the men would remain on sentry duty, guarding against sneak attack. On third would hustle down the communications trench, bringing back rations and stores. The last third would be divided among sleeping, or work details such as repairing a spot of the trench weakened by shellfire or undermined by water, while the final contingent went out on patrol, silently entering no-man's-land, the area between British and German trenches.

Sometimes new sections of trench were added or others extended or repaired. Sometimes a curved piece of corrugated metal was placed over a trench, sort of a miniature covered bridge. As more of these pieces became available, they were installed as quickly as possible. They provided some shelter from shrapnel and some shelter from German sharpshooters. A few sections of such protected trenches survive today, such as on Hill 60 outside Ieper.

Trenches are perhaps the most remembered feature of the Great War, but the common memory is much more sanitized than the reality. The most consistent theme in the firsthand accounts of the Great War is the intensely miserable life in the trenches. This was an imposed, never selected, lifestyle. Trenches deserve extended attention.

To begin with the obvious, no one wanted to be there. Pre-war professional soldiers expected a few pitched battles, a triumphant parade through the enemies' capital, a joyous reunion at home among duly grateful family and friends. Instead, they were living like moles in holes in the ground, a veritable subterranean world unlike anything in their experience. Nor did there seem to any end in sight. Men who later volunteered may have had more realistic expectations, but such made their lives no less miserable.

Examining the obvious about the trenches, there was the fact that these men lived in the field, that is, exposed to the elements—all the elements. Over and over again is the complaint about rain. This was not just an exaggeration of tired men. From 25 October 1914 to 10 March 1915, there were only eighteen dry days in Flanders, with eleven days below freezing.[59] The trenches were holes in the ground into which rain poured directly from the sky. But also being the lowest points, much of the adjacent area drained into them as well. There was just no other place for this water to go. Even in places where a pump system was installed, much of the evacuated water shortly found its way back into the trench again. While the windmills of Flanders might decorate a lovely postcard, they actually served a critical function, that of pumping water out of the farm fields into the draining streams. The bottom of the trench in many places was lined with duckboard, a walkway made of boards. Men were known to drown in trenches, especially when encumbered with all the equipment they were expected to carry when making an assault on the enemy. The problem just seemed intractable: "There is more water in the trenches every time I go in."[60]

The trenches were also a problem for animals. Mules sometimes had to cross them on makeshift little bridges, and they did not want to do that—ever. One soldier recorded:

One night, a particularly filthy night made worse by the enemy shelling, one mule slipped from the bridge into the trench below & stuck there upside down completely blocking the trench. A party of fifty men with ropes failed to move it & accordingly it had to be shot & the battalion butcher then carved it up into sizable chunks & that night a working party removed them & buried them in dead ground at the rear, thus removing the fear of getting stewed mule for dinner one day.[61]

A few more fortunate soldiers took shelter in the rare remaining farmhouses with not much better results, as Harold Brooks described:

It is chill [*sic*], wet and cold, cold and wet. Unfortunately the rain has a nasty habit of finding the weak spots in the roof (and there are many) and maliciously percolating through the plaster above one's head or immediately over one's face.[62]

Since the water really had no place to go, the soldier's feet were constantly wet. This resulted in a serious problem grandly summed up as "trench foot" which was actually a combination of unpleasant conditions. To prevent this condition, soldiers were supplied with a grease made from whale oil. Men carried up to three pairs of socks with them, and were ordered to change these once or twice a day. Despite these efforts, nearly 75,000 soldiers were admitted to hospitals with trench foot.[63] In an interview recorded nearly sixty-five years after the war, Thomas McIndoe clearly remembered the grease as "…horrible smelling stuff."[64]

Wartime physicians were faced with whole new diseases. Since these farm fields were so rich in manure, they were also rich in a bacillus usually found in horse intestines. A bullet entering the body often brought in a piece of infected uniform fabric as well, beginning an infection called "gas gangrene", which often caused swelling. It was treated by "debridement", removing all tissue from around the wound and irrigating with saline solution.[65]

Water was not the only discomfort. Occupants of the trenches were exposed to the ambient temperature as well. The soldiers endured the bone-chilling snows in winter and the sweltering heat of summer and all the variations in between. That first fall may have been the worst, as the army began its campaign in summer weight uniforms. No one expected to need heavier clothing since no expected to still be at war in the autumn. Nor was it easy to maintain a heat source. Stoves and trenches just didn't go well together, not to mention the problem of finding a fuel for whatever stoves there may have been.

Another complaint was quite understandable. These men suffered sleep deprivation to the highest degree. A good spot was a "funk hole", a one man slot dug into the side of the trench. Its greatest danger: being buried alive in a shelling. But even if one could lie down, the noise never stopped. Men passing, men working, men talking, men just living, all made noise, not to mention the war sounds such as exploding shells. One of the greatest joys of being on leave was just simple, undisturbed sleep.

Trenches were seldom designed to be where they were; they grew by happenstance and circumstance. In some places, they were a modest hike apart; in others, such as a few places near the Belgian town of Zonnebeke, they were only seven or eight yards apart.[66] Enemy conversations could easily be overheard.

Among the foremost complaints about trench life was just how awful the trenches smelled. This occurs time and time again in the soldier's diaries. The sources of unpleasant and persistent odors were legion. To begin, there were the men themselves: bereft of any sort of bathing facilities, soldiers often spent weeks at a time in the same trench in the same clothes. Their clothes were often wet as well, since there were but minimal opportunities to dry. They relieved themselves in latrines, holes dug into the wall of the trench or perhaps a very small niche cut into the side of the main trenches. While officers and physicians tried to control where these were located and how they were cleaned, the standards were of necessity quite varied and often quite low. Such sanitation did little for the general health of troops, either. Being advised to take a journey to a latrine some dangerous distance away—or a quick surreptitious relieving on the spot—no doubt at least some of the later occurred.

There were other obnoxious odors that were ordinary consequences of a modern battlefield. Smoke from burning buildings and supply dumps, smoke from cooking and heating, smoke from fired cannon all contributed to the acrid air. The air quality index must have been at the extreme end of the scale. One soldier decided to use the latrine as a defense against a gas attack:

> We'd been tipped off that the only way to protect ourselves was by urinating on either our handkerchiefs or soft caps and covering our mouths with them. …Personally I wasn't satisfied with these measures, I didn't think it sufficient protection. So I went into one of the trench latrines, which was just a bucket stuck in a hole, and put my head in the bucket. I stopped [*sic*] down long enough until I couldn't hold my breath anymore, then came up, took a good breath of air and went down again.[67]

Then there was the stench of the unburied dead. Not only was the field often strewn with dead soldiers, but also with parts of dead soldiers, large parts and little parts, parts too small to gather for burial but parts big enough to decompose pungently. Nor were human remains all there were. There was also a huge number of putrefying animals: sheep and mules and cows and horses, to list the larger. Robert Graves remembered the odor quite well: "The trenches stank with a gas-blood-lydlite-latrine smell."[68] He also recalled the death of a man named Sampson who:

> ... lay groaning about twenty yards beyond the front trench. Several attempts were made to rescue him. He had been very badly hit. Three men got killed in these attempts: two officers and two men, wounded. In the end his own orderly managed to crawl out to him. Sampson sent him back, saying that he was riddled through and not worth rescuing; he sent his apologies to the Company for making such a noise.... At dusk we all went out to rescue the wounded, leaving only sentries in the line. The first dead body I came upon was Sampson's, hit in seventeen places. I found that he had forced his knuckles into his mouth to stop himself crying out and attracting any more men to their death.[69]

Lieutenant George Crake remembered his service to the dead this way: "the corpses were dragged to the nearest depression, there lightly covered in dirt while their identify disk was removed. To stand while doing this was to risk death by sniper fire."[70] More permanent graves came later, sometimes much later.

Not all the bodies remaining on the battlefields were of the dead:

> If you can imagine a flock of sheep lying down sleeping in a field, the bodies as thick as that. Some of them were still alive, and they were crying out, begging for water and plucking our legs as we went by.[71]

Another of the difficulties of trench life concerned food. Soldiers objected to the quantity, quality, variety, and preparation of what they were offered. Barclay's diary of May, 1915 notes: "It was now that we were served with bread for the first time, but—one small loaf for five, six or seven is not much and left us absolutely dependent upon the parcels of food that were shipped from home."[72] Barclay added that his diet was supplemented "...with the help of parcels (our own and those of missing pals) & eggs bread and milk purchased at the farm...."[73] A rather odd feature of this war was that soldiers could write home asking for specific items such as a "torch" or flashlight, a pair of gloves, a home-town newspaper. Often in less than a week, the requested items would be delivered to the front line trenches. Harrods's department store even had sales on the items most requested by the trench-dwellers. In one of the oddest quirks of this war, soldiers often purchased wire cutters from home: the army issue item just was not strong enough to cut the improved German wire.[74]

When a parcel did arrive from home, it was quickly "shared out" and consumed. No edible could be kept:

It was useless to try to keep [parcels], as the rats were ready to pounce on any food on a man's person. It was a case of: If you can't eat it, give it away, or face the rats, and wrestle with them. They had a keen sense of smell.[75]

Other than waiting for the next shelling, the soldier's main concern was food. The official daily rations included a half pound of fresh or a pound of salted meat, one pound of biscuit or flour, four ounces of bacon and three ounces of tea, three ounces of sugar, two ounces of tobacco and half a "gill" of rum a day (about two ounces). So much for the rule. In fact, the front line troops were often hungry as the rations failed to "come up." Almost always on hand, however, were the tins of biscuits which have been described as resembling dog biscuits.[76]

There were many problems involved in feeding the army. Men living in holes in the ground did not have abundant nearby kitchen facilities. Food was prepared well behind the lines and brought by wagon or truck as close as possible to the front. Then it was manhandled through the supply trenches for the last part of the journey. By the time it arrived at its destination whatever warmth and flavor it may have once had was seriously compromised. Even on the best of days, it was institutionalized nutrition, hardly a culinary delight. The soldiers sorely missed home cooking.

The amount of food provided to the BEF by the end of the war was 3,240,948 tons. Rather, that is the amount shipped over. A good bit was lost, pilfered, thrown away or otherwise improperly consumed. The closer to the front line trenches, the more likely that one's rations consisted of biscuits, bread and bully beef. During a "push", cooks often had extra difficulty getting food forward, and often it just did not arrive. Thus troops were issued with emergency rations of bully beef, biscuits, tea and sugar, and what they reported as often moldy cheese.[77]

Even supplying the men with water was fraught with difficulty. Nearby streams were generally polluted with sewage, war debris, dead animals, expended munitions, and the like. Water was purified in rear bases and sent forward to the trenches, sometimes in freshly laid pipes and sometimes in tanks mounted on trucks. It was for the soldiers, of course, but the Army's many horses also had daily water rations. In response to the author's question, in 2013, a Columbus Ohio mounted policeman estimated that his horse drank about twenty gallons of water on a hot day. That is only anecdotal evidence, but recall that the army had as many as half a million horses. By that rule of thumb, something on the order of ten million gallons would be required—daily.

To maintain this supply, to keep so vital a resource as simple drinking water available, took a great deal of effort and a good number of men. Some of the troops became quite frugal with water:

...I indulged in a shave (first for exactly a week). For water I used the remaining drops in the bottom of my bottle which scarcely filled my shaving soap can but provided sufficient for both shave and a "lather brush" wash.[78]

One soldier was delighted at an opportunity to bathe:

One morning it was arranged that we should have a bath and a change of our lousy clothing, and we were marched down to a village called Sailly-La-Lys, to the rear of us. There was a laundry in the place, and small tubs were provided, with hot water. We stripped off everything except our identity disks, and any private belongings were put into a separate bag with name rank and number attached. As we stood there in our nakedness, awaiting our turn, a heavy shell came along and blew part of the building to smithereens. The strange fact was that no-one was hurt, and we all dashed out of the building onto the street, in our "birthday suits." No wonder the French think we are mad.[79]

Recognizing the enormous stress of life in the trenches, the Army evolved a rotation scheme. A unit of men might serve in the front trench for two weeks, be rotated into a middle trench for two weeks, and then be rotated behind the combat area for two weeks. The time spent in each of these was highly flexible, influenced in part by the current intensity of combat operations. During a lull more men could be rested.

To be rotated to the rear was the soldier's second greatest desire, only leave at home being more popular. While in the rear, the soldiers often spoke of feeling almost human again. They had an opportunity to bathe and to launder or replace their uniforms. Even to just stand up straight without fear of being the target of a German marksman was a treat. One soldier recalled taking a bath in what had been a beer vat while the temperance members of his unit were amused by this paraphrase of Scripture: "They shall turn thy vats into baths."[80] Bathing at a brewery appears to have become rather common: "...we had a bath in a brewery in a nearby village, six of us at a time in a large vat...."[81]

There were various policies regulating leave. For example, General Haig ordered "Leave to private soldiers, to the extent of 50 per Corps per day, has been approved for seven days to England. Only those of good character who have been in the field three months can obtain leave...."[82] General Haig may have believed that his men received such leave, but according to one study, it was actually only about once a year.[83]

Soldiers living in the trenches had plenty of living company. The stagnant water was a reproductive bonanza for mosquitoes and other annoying insects, and there was very little that could be done about that other than simply enduring the irritation. More serious was the rat infestation. There is little doubt that the number of rats ran into the millions. Men tried shooting, trapping, poisoning, beating, and even drowning these vermin. One soldier recorded overhearing another soldier boasting "Why, boys, they're as big as donkeys: I've shod one, and I'm having a saddle on 'im tomorrow and going for a ride."[84] Most soldiers were not amused by rats and believed they carried disease, ate prodigious amount of the soldiers' food and dehumanized the men. Barclay remembered that soldiers used to put their bayonets on their rifle tips and then put cheese on the blade. When a rat came for the cheese, goodbye one rat and one bullet.[85] Oddly enough, the rats, perhaps because they were lower to the ground, seemed more susceptible to gas attacks than the troops.

A still lengthy list of trench life disadvantages remains. The lack of privacy, the extended living in close quarters, the lack of choice even among the most simple things such as food: all of these drained the spirit. To counter some of these disadvantages, soldiers frequently played games such as "House", a forerunner of Bingo. But they did not do much reading: many of them were barely literate.[86] And while they may have bet on various card games and the like, there was not much exchange of cash. In fact, there was not much cash in the trench at all. First, there was not much use for it there, and perhaps more interestingly, most of the soldier's wages were paid to their wives or parents: they just did not have much with them.[87] Not that the pay was all that lavish: many lower ranking soldiers earned less than the poorest agricultural laborer in mainland Britain.[88] Furthermore, one can hardly consider their housing as anything but substandard.

One service for the men in the trenches grew up with little official supervision. A soldier who was off duty but not on leave had few places to go. "Estaminets", buildings providing wine and beer and women quickly appeared. Sergeant Alfred West recorded:

Out of the line, the boys were all wanting women. And the women, knowing that, used to put a sign in the window saying 'Washing done here for soldiers'. I've seen up to twenty men waiting in a room, and there were probably others upstairs. Afterwards these women used to sit on the edge of the bed, open their legs and flick this brownish stuff around their privates, ready for the next man.[89]

One soldier recalled being followed by little children chanting the only English they seemed to know: "Anglais soldat... my sister 2 Francs... follow me."[90]

Robert Graves recalled:

The Red Lamp, the army brothel, was around the corner in the main street. I had seen a queue of a hundred and fifty men waiting outside the door, each to have his short time with one of the women in the house.... Each woman served nearly a battalion of men every week for as long as she lasted.... three weeks was the usual limit: 'after which she retired on her earnings, pale but proud.'[91]

After the pleasures of leave, the soldiers' minds returned to duty. The worst aspect of the time spent behind the lines was the certain knowledge that a return to the front lines was inevitable. The psychological cost of returning to the front was extreme, and experience taught the men that conditions were unlikely to have improved. Sergeant Cubbon returned on 6 January 1915 to find "The worst trenches ever in. Knee deep mud. Front all falling in. Raining cats and dogs. The worst 24 hours ever experienced."

Soldiers' diaries for any month in 1915 repeat the same themes as in 1914. One soldier had multiple complaints: "Our food here only consisted of biscuits and 'bullie' jam, butter and cheese supplemented by a few potatoes found [where they had probably never been lost] in a barn."[92] Barclay also made this gruesome entry on 25 April 1915:

Men were killed and wounded on all sides but one of the most ghastly sights was when a "coal bucket" burst among a party of Canadians & after the black smoke had somewhat cleared a shower of arms and legs etc. became visible.

Again his complaint about: "Water here was very scarce—so that the pump water was to be used for drinking (after being boiled) while washing was to be done in the river. This of course we all set out to find and were amused but disappointed when it proved to be a stream only one foot wide." On 10 May he added:

Shells fell in all directions and a description is absolutely impossible. "Hell with the lid off" being much to [*sic*] mild. Many dougouts were blown to pieces & the occupants buried but comparatively few were wounded. The ground simply shook as we laid each expecting his turn to come next. From one shell a large piece of shrapnel burst through the roof of our dugout and hit my ankle. It was only a bruise but it caused considerable pain both at the time and during our marches for the next few weeks.

Robert Graves witnessed a man who "...took three hours to die after the top part of his head had been taken off by a bullet fired at twenty yard's range."[93]

Sometimes there were horrific accidents, what are now termed "friendly fire" casualties. Whether caused by inaccurate maps or poor observation conditions, on more than one occasion, the British artillery accidently fired on its own trenches with heavy casualties.

And always, always, the complaints about the rain:

...now we were beset with rain, continuous rain & soon the trenches were filled with water to our knees, the trench sides caved in & no hope of any kind of shelter whatsoever. Trench feet, a new phenomenon [*sic*] became very bad indeed & a number of more serious cases being sent out to hospital. The only prospect of warmth was when the rum ration was issued....[94]

Long after the war, Captain Graves remembered this time very clearly:

We had no blankets, greatcoats or waterproof sheets, nor any time or material to build new shelters. The rain continued. Every night we went out to fetch in the dead of the other battalions. The Germans continued indulgent and we had very few casualties. After the first day or two, the corpses swelled and stank. I vomited more than once while superintending the carrying. Those we could not get in from the German wire continued to swell until the wall of the stomach collapsed, either naturally or when punctured by a bullet; a disgusting smell would float across. The colour of the dead faces changed from white to yellow-grey, to red, to purple, to green to black, to slimy.[95]

While the BEF struggled through all of these problems, the senior military commanders were aware of another that they very much wanted to keep secret. There simply was not enough ammunition. Lord Kitchener told the War Cabinet on 14 May 1915 that "The army in France was firing away shells at a rate which no military administration had ever been asked to sustain." And worse, "The orders which had been placed for ammunition of every kind were being completed late."[96] Pre-war stocks had long since been consumed by the ravenous guns. Keeping that shortage a secret was not going to be easy. Obviously, the troops knew there was not enough, and while their letters home were censored, no doubt some references would be missed, not to mention the tales they could tell while home on leave. Then too, there was the power of the press.

While Sir John French had managed to keep most reporters out of the war zone, there was one quite well-known former soldier there with the General's blessing, his old friend retired Colonel Charles Repington. Under

Sir John's protection, as it were, Repington was permitted to go everywhere, see everything, with the understanding that his patriotism and discretion would infuse all he wrote. In a candid interview with General Haig on 22 January 1915, Repington asked if Haig could advance from where he was. Haig replied that:

> ...as soon as we were supplied with ample artillery ammunition of High Explosive, I thought we could walk through the German lines at several places. In my opinion the reason we were here was primarily due to want of artillery ammunition and then to our small numbers last November.[97]

General Haig's mention of an ammunition shortage put a hidden match to a long-smoldering fuse. Six months later, it would explode and shock the nation.

The never publically discussed problem was this: by the end of 1915, there were thirty-six British divisions on the continent, more than six times the original force. Because of the widespread use of machine guns, a war that all sides had expected to be decided quickly by offensive action had morphed into a defensive stalemate. Steady and heavy use of artillery, especially in attempts to "break through", resulted in a severe ammunition shortage, ammunition that simply did not exist and could not be produced quickly. Even if sufficient quantities had been available, the existing supply system was incapable of delivering them to the front. Because a long war had never been contemplated, the now-necessary rail lines across Belgium and France had never been constructed and were only now being hastily laid. These soldiers needed munitions that the nation just did not have.

Had the British ample supplies of ammunition, would anything have been different? The historians Richard Prior and Trevor Wilson believe that:

> The German defenses had not, at that time, reached such sophistication that they could ward off assault by a large accumulation of high explosive shells. The problem, of course, was that such an accumulation of shells happened not to exist. But then, their absence would have been equally an obstacle to British military operations in any other region.[98]

Heroic efforts were underway to increase production in Britain and to buy supplies overseas, especially from the United States and Canada. Sometimes safety was sacrificed to speed. At least one kind of fuse was manufactured that had no external indicator of its status, "hot" or not? Many of these exploded prematurely, causing considerable loss of life.[99]

Munitions production required that which was in shortest supply, time.

Meanwhile, as already noted, the Army felt compelled to plan offenses to prevent Germany from concentrating her strength with fatal results against either France or Russia. Germany must not be permitted to restart the von Schlieffen plan. Further, if Britain were to maintain her position as a full partner in this war with her allies, she must carry a goodly share of the land portion of the war.

Continuing lack of progress on the Western front gave impetus to the Easterners' argument. Easterners argued that their proposed attack on Turkey would require only older ships to reduce the Turkish forts with naval gunfire and then only a modest number of soldiers to land and occupy them. The Royal Navy planned a campaign along such lines. A fleet of aging battleships, powerful in their own right but no longer capable of standing up to the German High Seas Fleet was assembled. Both British and French battleships participated. The Admiralty included the modern HMS *Queen Elizabeth*. Bombardment of the Turkish forts began on 19 February 1915. The Turks returned fire, but unknown to the British, were critically short of ammunition. Quickly and dishearteningly, several of the attacking ships were seriously damaged by mines laid by the Turks. Mines were attached by long chains to the seabed or different types were allowed to float on the current toward enemy vessels. The main countermeasure was the minesweeper. This specialized vessel used a paravane, an underwater device designed to either detonate the mine where it was or to cut the chain and to bring the mine to the surface where it could be safely detonated by gunfire before it damaged a friendly ship. While the fleet had a few minesweepers available, intense fire from the shore prevented them from completing their task. Consequently the naval commander was reluctant to proceed, given the losses his fleet was enduring. His orders may not have made it sufficiently clear that the success of this mission would justify a considerable price in the form of sunken or disabled warships.

After a disappointing beginning, the Navy withdrew to allow the minesweepers to clear the area. It was also decided to land troops to support the mission. At the time, soldiers from Australia and New Zealand were training in Egypt. Those men and a division of the new Kitchener armies formed the invasion force. However, the delay in assembling this force gave the Turkish army and the German officers advising them almost six weeks to strengthen their defenses. The element of surprise had been lost from the moment of the first bombardment.

It is easy to summarize the Dardanelles campaign. Soldiers were landed on beaches. Despite their best efforts, they were pinned down by the defenders. In a short time, the trenches of Gallipoli were every bit as dangerous and as unyielding as those in Flanders. Repeated attempts were made to "push on." Illness was rampant. Repeated break-out attempts failed. Casualties were high. Gains were minimal. Reputations of senior commanders were destroyed. By January 1916 the last remaining forces were withdrawn and the word "Gallipoli" became synonymous for a bloody failure.

It is easy to summarize the Dardanelles campaign. Yet while it was going on, of course, some of the Allies had high hopes that the Turkish campaign would become the primary battlefield and shorten the war, bringing Britain and France a great victory.

While the Easterners did their best in the Dardanelles, the Westerners intensified their efforts against the German trenches. The British planned a March attack to capture the French city of Neuve-Chapelle. This town was in an area opposite General Haig's forces, and is located about twenty miles south southwest of Ypres. One reason for choosing this area was a matter of tactical advantage. Neuve-Chapelle was within a German salient bulging into the British lines. An attack here would allow shelling the Germans from three sides. But even as the plans were made for this battle, BEF headquarters realized that existing supplies would have to be shared with the new expeditions being sent to protect Egypt and to attack Turkey. While engaged in planning this attack, General Haig wrote in his diary on 11 February 1915: "The 4.5 howitzer, which is our best gun, is reduced to less than five rounds a day.... the output of ammunition in January was only half of what was expected."

General Haig knew that the howitzer was designed to fire a high trajectory shell which would come plunging into the enemy lines close enough for its impact to be observed by those firing, thus allowing for adjustment, all with the hope of hitting a reasonably precise point held by the enemy. But no matter how effective the weapon, too few shells for it certainly would hamper its effectiveness.

The General believed he knew why output was so dangerously low: "This is doubtless due to the New Year holidays which our unpatriotic workman at home insisted on taking!"[100] He added this entry on 16 March 1915:

...but there was no ammunition at present, as the expedition to the Dardanelles had to be supplied! It would be necessary to wait a fortnight. This lack of ammunition seems serious.... It effectively prevents us from profiting by our recent success and pressing the Enemy before he can reorganize and strengthen his position.

As General Haig's staff was preparing their plan to attack Neuve-Chapelle, his officers proposed four days of shelling. Knowing the status of his ammunition, General Haig ordered them to compress the shelling into a "terrific outburst" for three hours and thus to maintain the element of surprise.[101]

This mention of surprise highlights another point of disagreement among the senior British commanders. Some believed in an extensive bombardment, hoping to destroy the barbed wire and collapse the front trenches of the enemy. But that would also make the freshly overturned terrain more difficult for the attackers to cross. Others believed that an extended bombardment alerted the enemy as to where to expect the next attack and allowed him to summon reserves into the area so that if his lines were penetrated, these fresh reserves would be able to plug the gap and prevent a British victory. Both sides learned pretty quickly to have only minimal numbers of soldiers in the front lines in order to hold down casualties. When a heavy bombardment began, soldiers retreated into their deeper trenches or even underground bunkers and waited for the shelling to stop. Hearing the silence, the defenders hurried back to their front trenches hoping and expecting to arrive there in time to prevent the first wave of attackers from overrunning the positions. If the front line were overrun, the defenders would man their second or third row of trenches thus limiting the attacker's gains to what was often a small piece of dirt for a very large number of lives.

More than 50,000 British troops surged out of their trenches toward Neuve-Chapelle on 10 March. In some places they were able to overrun four lines of trenches. But headquarters was unaware of the success and was unable to bring forward enough reserves to exploit this achievement. Indeed, the Germans were able to seal both sides of this penetration and bring their own reserves forward in time to prevent a significant British victory. By the time the battle wound down three days later, more than 11,000 of the attackers had been killed or wounded. It is so easy to write that number, a few soft strokes on a keyboard, just a few dashes of ink on paper. Yet that number represents actual human beings who became dead or disabled, men who were dear to their parents, spouses, children, relatives, friends, colleagues and neighbors. True, many would heal and return to fight again. Some were found dead but whole and then buried. Pieces of others were found and buried. Many were sent home incomplete—minus an arm or arms, a leg or legs, an eye or eyes, or with other deformities. Still others went home mentally disabled. Some of these wounds healed rapidly. Many of them never healed, especially the subtle indefinable mental disabilities. Somehow, this does not seem well encapsulated in these few dashes of ink, the simple number: 11,000.

To what end? After this three day battle, after these men had paid the various prices, what had changed? The line of demarcation between the two sides had moved a few feet here and a few feet there. Perhaps the greatest result of the battle of Neuve-Chapelle and the very many battles like it was to generate a resolve that those who died in these obscure places could not be permitted to have died in vain. The war simply must go on until victory.

General Haig was disappointed with the results, but he was convinced that given sufficient ammunition, his men would triumph. As one historian has noted, "The command seemed chronically unable to calculate exactly how much artillery was needed to capture particular objectives.... the general modus operandi seems to be to assemble as many guns as possible and hope for the best."[102] Meanwhile, General Haig heard from his commander, General French that "...owing to a shortage of ammunition active operations could not be resumed for two or three weeks, [so he suggested] that I should run over to England for a few days."[103]

It is not hard to find criticism of the British generals in the literature of the Great War. Yet for every seemingly foolish remark a senior officer made, one can find others seeming more prescient. General Haig himself had considerable experience as a cavalry officer, certainly an old-fashioned skill, yet he sometimes seemed quite open to change. He had, for example, an appreciation of the new airplane, as in this observation from 22 February 1915: "Thanks to the wonderful map of the Enemies' trenches which we now had as a result of the airoplane [sic] reconnaissance it was now possible to make our plans very carefully beforehand...." On the other hand, one historian surmised that "Haig could envision cavalry sweeps and decisive battles more in keeping with Napoleonic conceptions than with industrial war."[104]

One of the most senior generals was Lord Kitchener. After inspecting the front, he concluded that Germany had established a "fortress" and so the British for the time being ought to consider "operations elsewhere."[105] On the other hand, his immediate subordinate, Sir John French, told General Haig in January 1915 that the New Armies of Lord Kitchener would not be ready before June—by which time Sir John thought the war would be over, a remarkably shortsighted prediction.[106] The British generals as foresighted or shortsighted: there is evidence on both sides.

With the big push of March over, the month of April was devoted to rebuilding. One soldier, J. Barclay, saw much to record in that month. First, he came to the front via the Menin road, and so marched right through the town of Ypres which he first saw at night:

In spite of (the darkness) we saw more than enough—ruined houses, dead horses & men(soldiers & civilians) homeless women & children clearing out & occasionally shells....[107]

His understanding of his circumstances grew rapidly:

Red cross cars came to the dressing station regularly & men wounded in the arms, etc. walked in. At that time we did not know that they meant that the no. of wounded was too large for the Red [*sic*] & vans to cope with.[108]

As his unit moved around in Flanders, he was not supplied very well:

Food was very scarce indeed and water could hardly be had at all we paid fruitless visits to all farms near in search of a pump in working order.[109]

At one point while moving toward his assigned position, Barclay had a harrowing experience:

I was with a party of about 35 moving along the road until surprised by a party of Germans who approached from the right shouting "hands up" & firing. To offer resistance was useless as many men were without arms & I am afraid many of these were captured. The idea of standing to be shot or captured did not appeal to me so tired as I was I decided to run for it. My example was followed by others—four I think—the last I saw of these Germans was the whole party on their knees firing at us.[110]

Barclay was not the only soldier who was moved by the shelling damage done to Ypres. Colonel Helm recorded:

Never shall I forget my first sight of the place. There was not a house that had not been hit and the majority of them were level with the ground. There was a horrible musty, mouldy, damp smell that depressed one beyond words. The Cloth Hall and Cathedral were of course mere skeletons.[111]

At the same time, just as the British were preparing for a 1915 campaign, so too were the Germans. Having failed to punch through the Allied lines in the fall of 1914, the new German commander, General Eric von Falkenhayn, resolved to try again. This series of battles became known collectively as the Second Battle of Ypres.

The Germans began the campaign with a new weapon. German superiority in the chemicals industry put them ahead in the development of poison gas.[112] Heavy metal cylinders filled with chlorine gas were brought to the front line trenches near Ypres, trenches defended by French Algerian troops. There the cylinders waited until a gentle breeze began blowing toward the Allied line.

On dawn on 22 April, a new horror was unleashed for the first time on the Western front. Men already living in holes in the ground, men already living among the mud and rats, the depredations were not yet complete. Now began a new manner of dehumanizing warfare, the use of poison gas. The gas drifted over some French trenches, killing nearly half of them by asphyxiation and opening a hole in the line almost four miles wide. Tentative German soldiers came along behind, allowing time for the gas to dissipate, since they themselves had only primitive protection from their own weapon. Had there been ample reserves available to exploit this success, the war might have taken a very different course, might even have been lost that day. But the British under General Smith-Dorrien hustled to throw every available man into the breach, and the hole was plugged.

The British were not prepared for gas attacks. One of the first defenses against gas called for the soldiers to urinate on their handkerchiefs and hold that over their noses.[113] Actually, despite how unpleasant and unprofessional that sounded, it did make sense chemically. The ammonia in urine helped reduce the effect of chlorine. Colonel Helm wrote that:

> ...the Germans launched their first gas attack on our lines north of Ypres. The gas was chlorine and at that time we had no protection from it and in some cases treatment was of no avail. Dozens of cases lay choking and dying.[114]

Barclay's diary records a similar sight: "...a weird scene presented itself— we were moving along a road now & to either side lay dead and dying in all positions mostly Canadian Highlanders who had suffered in the Gas attack."[115]

Despite the terror aspect of a gas attack—being fully conscious but unable to breathe as one choked to death—gas attacks were "...surprisingly non-lethal." While one-third of the men hit by shells or bullets were killed, fewer than one in twenty gas casualties died. In fact 93 percent of gas casualties returned to duty within a few weeks.[116]

As the war went on, various gases and gas combinations were tried. Chlorine gas was described as a combination of pineapple and pepper odors; mustard gas resembled a rich bon-bon filled with perfume; phosgene gas, rotten fish. How they harmed varied. Mustard gas, for example, caused nausea and vomiting as it stripped the mucous membranes of the bronchial tubes.[117]

One soldier remembered these gas attacks for the rest of his life, punctuated here as he wrote it:

> I call this incident, the memory of a folly, that was to make its mark, and remain with me for the rest of my life, I do not blame anybody, excepting myself for what happened, except the powers that make the wars, for without the war this could not have happened,
>
> My battalion was in the line, and I as the company runner, had to take messages to, and from our trench to the Headquarters of the Battalion which

was about half a mile to the rear, to make this journey, and I had to several times a day, I had to pass near what was left of a gasometer, and then through a small valley,

Jerry knew that this gasometer was used as an observation post, and shelled it continually, mostly with mustard gas, all around that place used to reek of the deadly gas, as did the valley, in there the fumes was as thick as a fog,

I was forced to use that route, for it was the only part that Jerry snipers could not get at, but there was always gas shells falling around, so for most of the journey, I had to wear my gas mask,

Wearing a mask is a must in this situation, but it has to be worn while you climb up a bank, or jump over some obstacle, and then it is not so comfortable, and then when you begin to perspire, and the eyepieces get steamed up, it could cause you to trip, and it is always difficult to breathe in a mask,

So I decided to try, and make the journey without wearing the mask, when I was nearing the valley I took in a deep breath, and held it until I had cleared that part that was so thick with the fumes, then carry on as usual,

I found that I was in better shape at the end of my trips, so from then on that is what happened, since those days I have found out a great deal about mustard gas, that a slight whiff of it now and again will build up in your lungs until it weakens them, and causes many ailments,

As I was to discover later in life, and which has resulted in my early retirement through ill health, with the loss of a good job,

And the memory of a folly that will live on as long as I do. [*sic*][118]

On 24 April the Germans tried gas again, this time against the untested Canadian troops holding the line to the north-east of Ypres. The Canadians suffered terribly, but held, and so anchored a reputation as formidable opponents. Today a very large stone soldier stands eternal watch over a large Canadian cemetery on that spot.

The gas attacks were not terribly effective as a weapon. In fact, they may have been counter-productive in that since the Germans were the first to use poison gas as a weapon in this war, their action "...added to the German record of barbarism and added propaganda value...." In the long run, it "...probably lost more than it gained."[119]

After these attacks, General Smith-Dorian took the opportunity of making the eminently sensible recommendation that the British pull back from the salient. He wanted to move back from being such a tempting target, surrounded on three sides by the Germans. Not wishing to set such a precedent, not wishing to appear to be retreating again, Sir John French not only refused to sanction this move, but relieved General Smith-Dorian of his command and sent him home. Yet when the incoming commander, General Herbert Plumer, made the same suggestion, it was accepted.

Meanwhile, the German General von Falkenhayn decided to return to the defensive in Flanders, to hold onto his strong positions, while shifting the main strength of his army to the eastern front. He reversed the concept of defeating the French first in favor of a new series of battles with the Russians, hoping to drive Russia out of the war and then return to Flanders and finish with the British and French.

In these battles around Ypres, not only had the Canadian troops proved themselves valiant soldiers, but one of their number, Major John McCrae, gathered impressions for what became a famous poem. On 2 May 1915, Dr McCrae was attending the wounded and dying in a shelter along the banks of the Ypres-Yser canal. This shelter consisted of a very small low ceilinged room, all made of concrete. Enclosed on three sides, the rear allowed entry. It resembles a small garage dug into the side of a hill. On top, grass remained, and today cattle graze on that roof. One account has it that Major McCrae lost numerous patients that day, and stepped out for a moment's respite. He happened to glance at the poppies blooming in the nearby grass. According to this account, he quickly composed "In Flanders Fields":

> In Flanders fields the poppies blow
> Between the crosses, row on row
> That mark our place; and in the sky
> The larks, still bravely singing, fly
> Scarce heard amid the guns below.
> We are the dead. Short days ago
> We lived, felt dawn, saw sunset glow
> Loved and were loved, and now we lie
> In Flanders fields.
> Take up our quarrel with the foe:
> To you from falling hands we throw
> The torch: Be yours to hold it high
> If ye break faith with those who die
> We shall not sleep, though poppies grow
> In Flanders fields.[120]

While many consider this to be a masterwork, others believed it hardened the public mind against a negotiated peace and thus actually extended the war—which certainly was not the Doctor's intention. Today in Belgium it is unlawful to cut the wild roadside poppies in the spring until after they have bloomed. This ensures that the plant has time to produce the seeds for next year's crop. This is an effort to keep them abundantly visible.

Major McCrae was not the only combat physician to write hauntingly about his experiences. Colonel Helm recorded one terrible stretch:

> For two days and three nights I was without any sleep in fact without lying down at all. Our bearers were bringing the wounded down by the hundred. We had no shelter for them and as shells were raining all around us many of the wounded were hit again…. The corner where we loaded was a sight, packed with wounded, ambulances stretcher bearers, wagon, etc., shells coming into the middle of the mass every few seconds.[121]

The utter pointlessness of one particular death is captured in Robert Graves' droll description: "A corpse is lying on the fire step waiting to be taken down to the cemetery tonight; a sanitary–man, killed last night in the open while burying lavatory stuff between our front and support lines."[122] Graves also describes this practice of some of his men:

> Before a show [battle], the platoon pools all its available cash and the survivors divide it up afterwards. Those who are killed can't complain, the wounded would have given far more than that to escape as they have, and the unwounded regard the money as a consolation prize for still being here.[123]

By the end of Second Ypres, the Germans still held the high ground, and they had taken a series of small villages: Ploegsteert, Steenstraat, Langemarck, Gravenstafel, St Julian, Zonnebek, Westhoek, Pilckem and Frezenberg. These were often costly little battles. Second Ypres cost the Allies 70,000 men for less than three miles gain.[124] "Our transport column lying at St Jean had also suffered heavily (only seven horses and mules remaining out of 70 or 80)."[125] Barclay remembered in his diary: "Major Ritson spent hours censoring letters. He seemed to realize as no one else did how many men were writing for the last time."[126] One historian summed up the May battles this way: "And having forfeited sixty thousand men for the privilege of acting as a midwife, the British were then left to hold the most uncomfortably arranged new salient, or target, at continued expense for over two years."[127] Winston Churchill was quite open in his criticism of the way the war was being fought, telling the House of Commons on 23 May 1915:

> I say to myself every day, what is going on while we sit here, while we go to dinner or home to bed? Nearly a thousand men—Englishmen, Britishers, men of our race—are knocked into bundles of bloody rags every twenty-four hours, and carried away to hasty graves or to field ambulances.[128]

There were two other blockbuster events in May. The first had to do with another new weapon, the submarine. The German government had proclaimed a "war zone" around the British Isles in January, and announced it would sink any merchant vessels trading in that area. There was not much result at first. But on 7 May, a German submarine sank the British passenger liner RMS *Lusitania*. This large modern passenger liner had been *en route* from New York to Liverpool, and was sunk just off the Irish coast in broad daylight. Going under in just eighteen minutes, the loss of life was severe: 1,201 persons including 128 United States citizens. Cunard Line advertised the *Lusitania's* speedy voyage in some newspapers. Beside that advertisement for the voyage in many newspapers ran this message from the German embassy:

Notice!

TRAVELERS intending to embark on the Atlantic voyage are reminded that a state of war exists between Germany and her allies and Great Britain and her allies; that the zone of war includes the waters adjacent to the British Isles; that, in accordance with formal notice given by the Imperial German Government, vessels flying the flag of Great Britain, or any of her allies, are liable to destruction in those waters and that travelers sailing in the war zone on the ships of Great Britain or her allies do so at their own risk.

IMPERIAL GERMAN EMBASSY

Washington, D.C. 22nd April 1915 [129]

Americans everywhere including, reputedly, President Wilson, were furious at the loss of civilian lives. The Germans could claim all they wanted that there were munitions in the *Lusitania's* hold, thus making it a legitimate target, but no one outside Germany was listening. *The Times* presented it this way: "The purpose of the German Kaiser, the German Government and the German people—for in this matter there can be no division of guilt—was wholesale murder and nothing else." It also attacked what it called the "...culminating crime of the German war on peaceful merchant shipping...." [130]

The British propaganda machine went into overdrive, portraying the Germans as barbarians. Posters of drowning mothers with infants in their arms flooded the newspapers, and Germany suffered a huge loss in public opinion. The Kaiser did not help matters by having the submarine's crew rewarded with a special commemorative medal of the event. Event? Disaster.

One British officer had a most unique take on the *Lusitania*. In a letter to his parents, Captain Bert Noel observed:

...I suppose England is frantic over the Lusitania, but as they were mostly a non-fighting crowd that went down it is not half so important as one of our Casualty lists, which seem to leave our people unperturbed. I hope it wakes America up.[131]

The Captain refers to the Casualty lists. The War Office provided lists of those believed killed, wounded, missing and taken prisoner. Many newspapers published these under such heading as "Our Role of Honor." Sometimes the lists were many columns long of rather small type. While they were printed every day, they did not seem to have much public impact.

Returning to the submarine campaign, the rest of it at this time was not a success. Too few submarines were at sea to be effective, and Britain's First Sea Lord was able to write after the war that "By May their premature and feeble campaign had been completely broken, and for nearly eighteen months, in spite of tragic incidents, we suffered no appreciable inconvenience."[132] That would change considerably later in the war when Germany returned to the seas with more numerous and more powerful submarines.

The second blockbuster event of that May was a simple newspaper story. Based on interviews with Sir John French, war correspondent Colonel Charles Repington published his account of the shell shortage. The staid old *Times* published the story but was soon overtaken by the sensationalized version of the same facts as decried by the *Daily Mail* whose editor happened to be a strong political opponent of the incumbent government. This set off a crisis of public confidence which brought down Prime Minister Asquith's Liberal Party government. He quickly reorganized his team, bringing in a number of Conservative party members. Asquith saddled David Lloyd George, a most outspoken member of his Cabinet, with a new position as "Minister of Munitions", and charged him with getting the problem solved. Asquith would strive and struggle, but he was perceived as being insufficiently energetic to continue in office. Despite the public furor over ammunition shortages, it was still some time before the vast quantities of ammunition demanded by the generals were forthcoming.

The public had little understanding of the causes of the shell shortage. The impression given by the press was that it was just an example of government bungling. The truth was much harder:

Shells were ...complex to manufacture; even the apparently straightforward outer case could cause problems. Make the case too thin and the shell might burst prematurely, potentially as it was being fired; make it from cheap steel and it could be too brittle—with equally fatal results.[133]

While all these events were going on, General Haig's men kept up their attacks at various places with little success. Haig lists "conclusions" in his diary two days after the attack on Aubers Ridge of 9 May. He believed that henceforth there should be a long and methodical bombardment, with accurate observation of where the shells fell and how much damage they did. Then too, he observed that the bombardment should occur at night in order to "...shatter the nerves of the men who work his machine guns...." Five days later he reported a different stratagem: three minutes of intense shell and rifle fire, followed by two minutes of dead silence, then again an intense two minutes of concentrated fire. The hope was that the enemy would man their trenches fully during the lull—and then be cut down in droves. His diary does not report the result. However, by 22 June, he wrote:

> The Enemy's defenses are now so strong that they can only be taken by siege methods—by using bombs, and by hand to hand fighting in the trenches— the ground above is so swept by gun and machine gun and rifle fire that an advance in the open, except by night, is impossible.

Not having to react to German offensives threw the initiative back into Sir John French's hands. This time the British moved toward Loos, a town roughly thirty miles south of Ypres. The French command asked the British to take over more of the trenches, twenty miles more of the trenches. This would free French soldiers to prepare for a new attack on the Germans. While this study has mentioned the French efforts only in passing, it should be noted that they too were suffering great losses, and that much of the fighting and destruction of infrastructure was taking place in their country. French efforts were "...large, devoted and sacrificial" but did not prosper.[134] They were highly motivated to push the Germans back. So for political reasons more than military considerations, Sir John was committed to battle with fewer soldiers than he wanted, less ammunition than he desired, on land not of his choosing.

What made this a poor battlefield for the British? Although for the most part rather flat, it was also a major coal producing area, and was speckled with very large slag heaps. These were easily fortified into formidable defensive positions with cleverly hidden machine guns sprinkled among the rubble.

The battle plan called for a four day bombardment of the front trenches. This was unsatisfactory in three ways. First, visibility was so poor that the British observers could not see if their shelling was in fact destroying the barbed wire in front of the trenches. In fact, it was not. There was much thunder and light, but not much actual wire cutting. Secondly, the artillery could not target the first and second lines of trenches at the same time. They were too far apart. Thus, when it was time to shift targeting to the second line, there would be a delay while the British guns were brought closer. During that delay, the Germans would obviously have time to recover as well. Arial reconnaissance also showed that there was now even more barbed wire in front of the second trench than the first, and that it was often constructed on the far side of whatever modest slope was available, making it even harder to observe. Was the wire being degraded by the British artillery fire? It could not even be seen, let alone seen well enough to judge. Third, the artillery did manage to chew the land in front of the German trenches well enough to make it an enormous obstacle for the attackers.

The battle plan also called for an attack on a wider front. If many men tried to break though along a narrow front, it made them too easy a target for the defenders. Instead, a simultaneous attack would be made on a front miles wide by six full divisions of troops.

To further aid the attackers, the British planned to use poison gas for the first time, so thousands of cylinders of gas were laboriously hauled to the front lines. "Each heavy cylinder was suspended fore & aft to a wooden spar & carried on the shoulders of two men with two reliefs behind, all the party wearing gas helmets."[135]

As yet, the only way to employ the gas was to squirt it toward the enemy. Later artillery shells would carry it behind the enemy lines but those were not yet in common use. At one point, General Haig had become personally involved in obtaining the gas:

Hearing that the gas cylinders were not coming forward as rapidly as expected, I wrote... asking [General Robertson] to send a special officer to London to A) insist on gas factory working NIGHT and day—at present only working 8 hours daily and B) make SPECIAL arrangements to get the gas brought out and sent up to the troops.[136]

In fairness to the supply officers, it should be pointed out that maintaining all the needed and wanted supplies was a monumental undertaking, and likely to be disrupted by the most unlikely events, such as this one:

Both [the ports of] Boulogne and Calais are closed today on account of mines. This has caused us trouble—we expected more gas cylinders to arrive. We have urged that a special boat be sent to Dieppe and a special train onwards from there.[137]

One can only imagine how often supply officers were beseeched to accommodate this or that special need. Each may have been worthy in itself, but it was impossible to satisfy the myriad demands.

To summarize, the British were preparing to fight at Loos, with too few men, too little ammunition, over poorly chosen ground, all in the name of supporting their ally, France. A heavily burdened Lord Kitchener knew what he was asking and why he was asking:

> After washing his hands, Lord Kitchener came into my writing-room upstairs, saying he was anxious to have a few minutes talk with me. The Russians, he said, had been severely handled and it was doubtful how much longer their Army could withstand the German blows. Up to the present, he had favored a policy of active defense in France until such time as all our forces were ready to strike. The situation which had arisen in Russia caused him to modify these views. He now felt the Allies must act vigorously in order to take some of the pressure off Russia, if possible.[138]

As the British took stock in June, they still had only seventy-one heavy guns and 1,406 field guns while the munitions factories were turning out only 22,000 shells a day.[139] By comparison, intelligence estimates reported the German side was churning out 250,000 shells a day.[140]

The results of the attack are astonishing. In the first two hours of the Battle of Loos, the British lost more men than the Allies lost on all of D-Day, 1945.[141] In some places, the British did break through the German lines, sometimes well through the German lines, but spent their strength in doing so. At one point, General Rawlinson complained to another officer that the men were not advancing as they should. "This is most unsatisfactory. Where are the Sherwood Foresters? Where are the East Lancashire's on the right?" General Oxley replied "They are laying out in no man's land, sir, and most of them will never stand again."[142]

Lack of ammunition contributed to the lack of success. A letter from Arthur Cornfoot, a soldier in those trenches, declares:

> I must say that it brings to my mind how important it is for the Artillery to have plenty of ammunition to blow the enemies defenses down, such as barbed wire, entrenchments for the murderous machine guns and fortified positions which unless blown down, would not give our brave lads a bit of chance, for even such lads as we have got, for man cannot fight against machine and that has to be destroyed before our brave lads can give them the bayonet.[143]

The following troops, the reserves, were supposed to take over the task and push on. At Loos, however, by order of General French, the reserves were sixteen miles away, much too far away to arrive in under twelve hours—by which time the Germans had managed to seal the breach with their own reserves.[144] General Haig blamed General French. General Haig believed his men had "opened the door" but the delay in bring up the reserves ruined what would have been a major victory for the British.

Loos was not a victory. It was another bloodbath for little gain. General Haig wanted to go on, but "Happily, Generals Winter and Weather intervened."[145] In the meantime, the army itself had a new leader.

In December, Sir John French was relieved. This event was a long time in coming. While he was no doubt doing his best, his best was not producing victories. Only Sir John still seemed to have faith in his ability to lead. Back when the war was less than two weeks old, his subordinate, General Douglas Haig, had written to the King: "In my own heart, I know that French is quite unfit for the great Command at a time of crisis in our Nation's History."[146]

The spotlight of the top command was passed to General Douglas Haig, a son of the Haig whisky distillers. From this point on, this Scotsman became primarily responsible for all British efforts on the western front. Douglas Haig was a career soldier with a broad range of experience. He had led men in battle. He had served in various staff capacities. He had political as well as cavalry combat experience. He had married a Lady-in-Waiting to Queen Mary. He had visited the United States, served in the Sudan, the Boer War, and extensively in India. He was known to his own staff as "The Chief." He was styled the "Commander-in-Chief" and a year later would be promoted "Field Marshal", afterwards often signing documents "D Haig FM." One last but certainly positive factor in his selection: in the phrase of the day, Haig "looked the part." Just in his mid-fifties, he had the health, experience, good fortune and perhaps most important of all, the self-confidence to take command of his nation's forces.

Among his earliest orders as the new Commander-in-Chief was one to manufacture 1,000 units of a new weapon, the "land ship" or "tank."[147] These would soon have an important role to play.

Once again, a year that had started with high hopes for rapid and decisive victory was grinding to an end amid frustration, regret, and heavy loss of life and treasure. In this atmosphere, it was quite easy to find critics of the army. As in any large bureaucracy, it had its rules and procedures, many of which appear to be of little importance, except to those directly involved. Robert Graves made no secret of his feelings in his highly articulate post-war memoir:

...the usual inappropriate messages came to us from Division. Division could always be trusted to send a warning about verdigris on vermorel-sprayers, or the keeping of pets in trenches, or being polite to our allies, or some other triviality, exactly when an attack was in progress.[148]

The same headquarters wanted daily reports or "returns" on such topics as the weather, casualties, intelligence, stores required and so on, each due at a particular time between 5:15 a.m. and 9 p.m.[149]

The general public did not seem to understand just how things were in the trenches as this demonstrates: "Unit commanders received a never-ending stream of requests from dead men's relatives tartly demanding to know what had happened to their watches, money, etc."[150] An army that often could not find a body was to find a much smaller watch? Clearly the public did not understand, was kept from understanding, such things as a Parson burying a sandbag with a funeral service. Its contents were all that was left of eleven men.[151] For the sake of morale, the awful truths were sanitized. Only the lengthy casualty lists and the lengthy trains full of wounded crossing the nation gave evidence of the real peril. Less well recognized was the fact that some forty-nine percent of all pre-war trained staff officers were killed or died of wounds, well over a third of them by the end of 1915.[152]

Yet this same army could manage to deliver over twelve million letters per week to the trenches, only two or three days in transit.[153] This same army could deliver parcels containing underwear and tobacco and books and other small items.[154] The army could accommodate the astonishing growth from one which needed 2,500 shovels and spades in 1914 to issuing more than ten million of them by the end of the war.[155] The army could introduce a new helmet that was held in place by a strap connected to rivets. The rivets were cleverly designed to break under a certain amount of pressure, to prevent garroting or breaking the neck of the wearer.[156] A little of everything from the simple to the sophisticated was accomplished.

Once again plans were made for the next year. Conservative Party Leader Arthur Balfour told the War Cabinet that there should be a delay until a mid-year offensive in 1916, since by then the new armies of Lord Kitchener and the massive quantities of ammunition would be fully at hand.[157] In retrospect, it was clear that only trivial gains had been realized in the west, and the eastern campaigns had not done any better. The Army managed to hold on in 1915, but consideration was being given to new ways to break the deadlock.[158]

Looking forward, the major Allies including Russia, France, Great Britain, and Italy met at Chantilly in December and agreed that they would try to coordinate large scale offensives as simultaneous as possible in 1916. The goal was to keep the Germans from concentrating against any one of them.[159]

While the High Command made its decisions, while nations planned with nations, one soldier's diary in early December noted: "Rain all day and every day"[160] and then reported on the day after Christmas that:

> I was in Hebuterne today. This is one of those villages which is right
> on the line of trenches, and it has been knocked about frightfully. It
> presents a scene of absolute desolation and ruin. There is not one house
> unscarred. Roofs are off, walls blown in, trees and every sort of debris
> scattered about—it must be a horrible sight to a Frenchman.

Soldier Ralph Smith summed it all up in a few words: "We spent Christmas
Day 1915 in that same front line, amongst all that bloody mud with a cup of
cold stew for our Xmas dinner."[161]

But everybody knew: 1916 would be different, very different.

CHAPTER III

1916: The Big Push

What passing-bells for those who die as cattle?
Wilfred Owen, *Anthem for Doomed Youth*[1]

No doubt about it, 1916 was going to be the year of the great British victory. The enormous efforts of the past seventeen months were unquestionably coming together at last, and all that good effort was about to be rewarded. Titanic exertions in uncountable ways just had to guarantee victory. Everybody knew that. One need only look around, see all that was going on. Such is the sense of numerous soldiers' diaries.

The year opened with little visible change along the front lines. The trenches still stank, men still died, wicked wounds still hurt, home folks still feared telegrams. But oh, the sense of hope! So many things were promising. At last, the Kitchener armies were arriving in great numbers. Shell production was up and steadily rising. Heavier cannon were en route. The nation, no, the whole British Empire was now fully engaged, and there was just so much material on hand and imminently expected that this time it would happen. Victory, and victory soon!

And then, the nasty reality.

The new Commander-in-Chief, Sir Douglas Haig, enacting the agreements of the previous December, prepared an enormous attack on the Germans. The French, Russians and Italians were all keen to attack at the same time, thus preventing Germany from concentrating against any one of them. But as Haig planned his advance, the Germans, too, planned. In a renewed effort to force France out of the war, the German command committed to a sustained conflict over the series of French forts around the city of Verdun. General Eric von Falkenhayn believed that the French could not afford to lose this strongpoint, which was a French salient into the German line, and thus open to attack on three sides. As the snows of February drew to an end, Falkenhayn hurled his troops toward Verdun. For a long time, historians have believed that he was hoping to bleed the French army to death in this campaign, and thus hasten the end of the war. But perhaps that was just the point of view Falkenhayn chose to express after the war.

In any event, the battle over Verdun became a terrific drain on French resources. The French high command was forced to request that the British take over more miles of the trenches, so those Frenchmen would become available to fight at Verdun. General Haig was fully aware of how "precarious" the French position was becoming, and so to assist his principle ally, did as requested.[2]

In March, Lord Kitchener conferred with General Haig on a number of points. Kitchener warned Haig to "husband" the strength of the army in France since the war might not end this year. Haig replied that he:

> ...never had any intention of attacking with all available troops except in an emergency to save the French, and perhaps Paris from capture. Meantime, I am strengthening the long line which I have recently taken over, and training the troops. I have not got an army in France really, but a collection of divisions untrained for the field.[3]

This meeting between Kitchener and Haig must have been among their last. Lord Kitchener sailed aboard a Royal Navy warship on a diplomatic mission to Russia. In a grand irony, that ship was sunk by a German mine on June 5, 1916, and Lord Kitchener and nearly all on board drowned.

Meanwhile, taking over more miles of trench was a significant commitment. According to one study, each mile of trench required 675 tons of supplies per day. By October, 1916, 195,000 tons of stores were crossing the English Channel each week. The British 4th Army, all by itself, employed 4,671 trucks, 1,145 cars and 1,636 motorcycles.[4] Taking over more trench relieved French soldiers, surely, but also imposed new burdens on the British supply system.

Moving those supplies once they arrived took the efforts of 76,000 troops used to build, repair and run the light railway system. Rail was the most efficient way to move all this material, but there were just not enough railways. So, the Army built them where and as needed. Railways carried the bulk of the war material from the seacoast ports to the big supply depots near, but behind the battlefield. After that, it was carried onward by trucks, horses and mules, and men. In an interview recorded in 1984, Edwin Rance remembered walking four miles round trip guiding the mules who carried the ammunition over the muddy fields.[5] Some of the soldiers thought that supply system was pretty poor. One complained: "...we only get a two pound loaf (of bread) between five men and that is only enough for breakfast the remainder of the day we have to do with biscuits."[6]

More than a few British soldiers complained about their leaders. Colonel Packer wrote to his mother that:

...I took an old general all around my lines... and of course they were in an awful state as a result of the thaw after the snow, he was a rather old fashioned type of general (Brigadiers nowadays are old dodders of 35 or so!) and fat....[7]

This soldier had the opposite complaint:

I never saw one brass hat of the division or corps staff anywhere in or near the trenches & yet they were setting out to move thousands of guns and transport & even more of men into & through terrain the condition of which they themselves had no personal knowledge whatsoever.[8]

The French request for action complicated General Haig's own plans for an attack. In order to support the French even further, he agreed to an offensive along the Somme River. An attack there he believed would surely force the Germans to divert some of their strength from Verdun to this new danger. From mid-January on, Haig planned for his "decisive attack."[9]

A great share of the economic output of a major modern industrialized nation was now devoted to this battle along the Somme River. The British had been chronically short on ammunition, especially for their artillery, but by March 1916, substantial stockpiles were accumulating behind the lines in Belgium and France. Several vexing problems had been alleviated. New facilities to produce shells had been constructed. Fresh orders had been placed with foreign suppliers, particularly the United States and Canada. More streamlined methods of production had been incorporated. Production was way, way up. The numbers were impressive. What had been a Tiny Tim style supply had become a Daddy Warbucks production. By June 1916, the Army was receiving 140 to 150 heavy field guns per month. General Haig could expend 300,000 shells a week.[10] In fact, the guns could fire so much now that when the barrels became distorted from too much heat, they could be replaced—spare barrels were on hand now, too. A total of 7,908 guns had been ordered for 1916, and by years end 4,314 had arrived at the front.[11] Not the full order, obviously, but far ahead of the previous year. By late June, Captain Bloor's battery was firing "...about 5,000 shells per diem ... on a front of about 500 yards", a rather intense shelling.[12] To jump ahead a bit, later in the year General Haig would note:

A great artillery concentration was effected; that is to say, about the same number of guns were firing today on the spurs around Beaumont Hamel as we had firing on our whole front on July 1! By noon [General] Gough's 18 pounders had fired 240,000 rounds![13]

The guns themselves were improved and improving. Long range artillery was now constructed of high tensile steel, allowing larger guns. Accuracy was improving by better use of trigonometry and better training of gunners. Pre-registration also helped hit the actual targets.[14] The motorized transport supporting all these preparations consumed two million gallons of gasoline a month.[15]

The individual soldiers were far better equipped. In fact, they now had so much to carry that the load had become not only unreasonable, but so encumbering as to be just plain dangerous. One sergeant tried to make his general see the problem:

I asked the Brigadier if it is possible for his brigade major to put our equipment on, and he said certainly. So I got two privates, Lewis gunners, to put everything on him—bombs in the pockets, sandbags, spade, kit, rations, extra ammunition round the neck—all of it. Then I said 'How do you feel, Sir?' and the brigade major said 'It is a hell of a weight.' So I said 'you haven't started yet! You forgot your rifle, you've got to put that up, and how are you going to carry it, slung over your shoulders? You can't, because you have to have it in your hand ready, but you can't take it in your left hand because in that you've got a pannier which weighs 46 pounds....'[16]

There was a downside to all this preparation. As Henry Whiteman noted in his diary, the "Germans knew by ammo buildup, transport and troop movements of an upcoming attack."[17]

Moving all these shells from the factories to the gun pits was another grand undertaking. To transport the shells as well as food, fodder and all the other needs of the army required the construction of still more miles of light railroad. The muddy roads of Belgium and France could not accommodate the traffic, and trucks were proving to be less useful than horses, anyway, as the trucks were "expensive, scarce, and unreliable."[18]

By the end of 1916, over fifty million shells were delivered.[19] Haig's gunners would actually fire an astonishing nineteen million shells in this spring offensive.[20] In just a week, General Rawlinson's gunners would fire 188,000 shells at their assigned section of enemy trench.[21] On the morning of the attack, the British would fire nearly 250,000 shells in one hour, 3,500 a minute.[22] So much for the shell shortage.

Delivering those shells to the guns was extraordinarily difficult, as one soldier detailed:

> The worst part was that for the last mile or two, everything had to be carried by hand—somehow or another you had to get up all the food, drinking water, and necessary equipment. This included rifle ammunition, machine gun ammunition, and trench mortar ammunition, which was very clumsy, awkward stuff to handle. Then you had to carry enormous bundles of sandbags, bales of timber, planks, ready made-up duckboards, and, worst of all, coils of barbed wire. Barbed wire is the most damnable stuff to handle. It was made up in coils that weighed half a hundredweight that we carried on a stick over two men's shoulders. You were very likely to cut your hands to ribbons before you got it there.[23]

Mounted men had their unique problems:

> ...we horsemen had to make a bolt, under fire, driving straight into a heavy shell crater filled with stinking water. Our horses were up to their bellies in mud and water, and even higher, and how we ever got them out was a mystery. If they had received shell fragments, we cut their traces, and many received a bullet to end their suffering and agony. Limbers of gun carriages were no good here. We turned into pack horses, i.e. a fixture was placed on the saddle, with pockets of four each side, and two horses were handled by one man, with eight eighteen pounders per horse. The riders would ride one horse, and lead the other, sitting on top of the saddle, with eight shells, four each side, leading the off-horse, similarly placed.
>
> The continual order was: Feed the guns. Here we were, on horseback, sitting right on powder and shell, which, if ignited, could blow us to bits or hell. Rain and rain and more mud, and now getting colder.[24]

How effective was all this shelling? Anti-personnel rounds were not effective against the trenches because the Germans had mostly retreated from there. Precise targets, such as a specific machine gun nest, were easily missed. The only way to be sure to hit a specific target was to "register" it. This meant to fire at it in advance, to take, as it were, practice shots at it. However, if the British registered a target, they gave notice to the Germans of that fact, and then the Germans could and often did move whatever it was to a new location.[25]

The British also used high explosive shells. These were designed to tear out chunks of the trench like an "iron hand."[26] There was also the matter of fuses. Sometimes the shell was designed to explode on contact. Sometimes it was delayed until it had penetrated more deeply into the target and then exploded. Still others were designed to explode later, perhaps when the defenders had returned to the area. The Royal Artillery was still developing and testing various fuses at this time.

Sometimes urgency outweighed safety, and corners were cut. Some shells were produced without safety devices, such as an external indicator of the shell's fuse status: "hot" or not? This increased the chance of a premature firing in the gun barrel with a serious loss of life.[27] Furthermore, less rigorous quality control was allowing an increased number of defective shells out into the combat zone. These defective shells were indiscriminate killers, sometimes exploding prematurely, killing or injuring the gun crew: "...the last round of the day, which was a premature, burst within four yards of the gun, a piece of the shell flying back and hitting (a soldier) in the right groin causing a severe wound...he died."[28]

Royal artillery units prepared extensively for this campaign. First, they set up "gun pits", positions behind their own lines where the guns were located. Large holes were dug of various shapes. Then the bottom was lined as far as possible with lumber. When the guns fired, the recoil had a tendency to push the gun into the ground. The wood flooring was to minimize this action, not to mention keeping the crew out of the water that collected in the low points all over this countryside. A storage area for shells was also nearby. The men serving the guns worked hard, and they too were rotated out of the line just as the infantry was. But relieving a battery had its own rules and procedures. The major rule was to never weaken the battery's ability to fire:

> Despite the change which is taking place, there must not be a diminution of efficiency for a moment, nor must there be the least lessening of the ability of the unit to fire immediately if necessary, or attack, or meet any attack, or do anything else which it could do if not being relieved. [29]

Stocking those magazines was a backbreaking task. British munitions factories, not to mention those in Canada and the United States, were now manufacturing shells in the hundreds of thousands. Then they were shipped across English Chanel to the Belgian and French seacoasts. From there they went by rail or wagon or truck to a "depot" or supply center. To order these supplies, to move these supplies, to inventory these supplies, to protect these supplies and to deliver them to their end user required another whole group of personnel. "By 1916, paper was the nourishment of the military: the unsung machines of the First World War were the typewriter, the Roneo duplicating machine and the printing press...."[30] Without computers, clerks had to keep paper records of all that information: what was needed, where, when, in what quantity, by when, by what route:

> the challenge was mammoth, yet was managed, by most accounts, rather
> well. To offer just two examples, the Army issued 45,351,488 pairs of boots
> and 137,224,141 pairs of socks in the course of the war.[31]

From the supply depots items moved closer to the front line, again by
truck or wagon or horse or even mule. The last half mile or so was often on
the backs of individual soldiers, through crowded supply trenches, sharing
the journey with food, water and other needed items. That only men were
surefooted enough and small enough to lug the shells across that last bit of
rough ground is remarkable.

A "ready" supply of ammunition was close at hand for immediate use, while
a "magazine", usually dug into the earth, was within easy reach for quick
resupply during times of heavy firing. The weakness of this layout, of course,
is that with so much highly explosive material in a limited space, setting off
one explosion, whether by accident or by enemy fire, could be catastrophic.

Near the gun pit were horse standings, both for the horses bringing up
supplies and for those that would be hitched to the guns to move them to
another position. Then there were quarters for the gun crews. Seldom fancy,
they at least provided some shelter from the weather and enemy fire.

As the men suffered from being in the elements, so did the horses. Many
who cared for the horses regretted that they could do no better than they did.
Many became very fond of their horses, treating them as oversize pets:

> Our poor animals, which we had placed on a hill just above Carnoy were
> now sinking into the mud. True, we had been given a coat covering for the
> animals, but the cold and rain was getting worse. The horses, however thirsty,
> would not touch shell water. The ration of oats and hay were very poor, and
> the poor devils with the mud on their legs and bellies now developed balls of
> mud which froze on their limbs. It was impossible to release them from these
> balls of mud, which stuck to their hair and skin.[32]

Not infrequently the Germans were able to spot the British horses and
guns and to target them with their artillery. Consequently, the British devoted
a good deal of effort to "counter-battery fire", attempting to calculate
the specific location of a German battery by observation, including from
balloon or aircraft. They also employed direct observation, sound ranging
and mathematical computation. To avoid retaliatory fire, the gun pit would
sometimes be abandoned and the guns quickly moved to a fresh location,
often to a previously prepared gun pit. On Christmas Day, 1916, Captain

Bloor noted in his diary that his men had to move snow around to cover the "blast marks" his guns had made so as not to give away the position of his battery to the Germans.

There were several types of guns, and several types of shells. In simple terms, heavy guns fired powerful shells longer distances, while lighter guns fired less powerful shells shorter distances. Field guns were close to the trenches, could fire up to five miles or so, and were used in direct support of the infantry. Heavy artillery was farther back, able to fire up to twenty-five miles or so, but with less accuracy. Even so, there was disagreement as to just what the mission of the guns was, and consequently, over which guns should have priority. Each division should have some long range guns, surely, some shorter range, certainly, but in what proportion, in what production priority?

Part of that question turned on the role of the guns. Essentially, there were two objectives for the artillery. They could be used to target the thicket of barbed wire that protected the enemy trench. That wire could be five or six feet high, and in bands as deep as thirty feet or more. Sometimes paths through it were left open, but these funneled the attackers into the point of greatest danger, the machine guns' killing zone.

It was very soon learned that soldiers could not readily capture a trench defended with barbed wire, because while they were trying to cut their way through it or find a way around it, they were easily mowed down by small arms fire. So, one goal was to destroy the barbed wire.

That does not sound particularly hard: blow up the barbed wire. But in practice, when a shell explodes when hitting the ground beneath barbed wire, the wire is generally lifted up and then dropped to the ground again, essentially undamaged.[33] When a different type of shell is employed, one that blows up just above the ground, it often rips or shreds the barbed wire—but into an even a more formidable obstacle rather than eliminating it.

There was an alternative strategy. Ignore the barbed wire. Bombard the trenches with high explosives. The flying dirt and debris would bury the defenders, their machine guns, and hopefully some of the barbed wire so that the attacking foot soldiers could rush in and take over the position.

Yet like so many instances in this war, there was a countermeasure to trench bombardment. This war so often resembled a massive chess game, although unlike any mere game, with very real and very painful consequences. As soon as the bombardment began, the bulk of the defenders would retreat to their prepared bunkers. Some of these were as much as thirty feet underground. Many were constructed with concrete roofs and elaborate ventilation systems. In short, they were underground fortresses, not much bothered by shelling except for the rare direct hit. Of course, extensive use of these concrete fortifications allowed the Germans a certain economy of manpower.[34] While the noise of the bombardment was fearful, the actual death toll was often rather light. Since the defenders hurried underground as the attack began, most were unharmed.

Time after time, the defenders raced back to their posts as soon as the artillery fire stopped. Any still operable machine guns would have a target rich environment as the attackers charged what they hoped would be nearly undefended positions. Often what they found were still stoutly defended machine gun nests. Time after time, the attackers were slaughtered.

To escape this predictability factor in offensive operations, various stratagems were employed. Sometimes the attackers would pause the bombardment. But after just a few minutes, it would resume in full fury, hoping to catch the defenders in the open as they raced back to their front line defenses. Another strategy was a "rolling" or timed bombardment. Guns targeted a particular area, and then at a preset time, moved on to the next set of targets, allowing an assault force an opportunity to reach the enemy trenches before the defenders could recover.

One disadvantage of a bombardment was that the heavy guns could not reach both the front line trench and the second line of trenches at the same time. Trenches were constructed too far apart for simultaneous attack by one type of artillery. A pause, or perhaps more accurately, a delay, was necessary. After firing on the nearest enemy line, the artillery had to be moved, ever so laboriously, closer so that the enemy's rear trenches would be within range. The weight of the guns, the prevalence of mud, the possibility of enemy counter fire made moving the guns an exhausting and dangerous task. The heavier guns required teams of twelve horses on fair roads, and even more horsepower on the more common poor ones.

And that opens up still another dilemma. If the army planning an attack begins to dig gun emplacements closer to the enemy line, the enemy can see that activity and realize an attack is being planned. Then the enemy can make counterplans: reinforcing the threatened area, or even secretly withdrawing the bulk of the defenders to a rear and safer position. Recall that the British positions in the spring of 1916, as in most of the war, were on the lowlands, making the troops' activities easily visible to the Germans. In fact the Germans did continue to shell the British trenches as attack preparations were made. But the King's troops could not take time out. Instead, one man was assigned to "listen" for enemy shells, and if he felt one was about to hit his companions, he gave a warning and all ducked into whatever shelter was at hand. Needless to say, this was an imperfect system.[35]

A further disadvantage for the attacker employing heavy artillery was the surrender of all surprise. The very act of concentrating fire on one stretch of trench signaled to the defenders that an attack was imminent. This allowed the defenders to assemble reserve troops in the vicinity, but far enough behind the line that they were out of range of the attacking artillery. Then, when the shelling ceased, additional defenders would reinforce the line and repel the attackers.

Laborious preparations took place throughout the spring of 1916. Some men were briefly out of the line for unexpected reasons: for Noel Hoult, an outbreak of measles kept him and his fellow students confined to their machine gun school.[36] Some men were out of the line for more pleasant reasons:

> On the 30th [of June, 1916] we cleaned up and had a wash and shave, the first wash for ten days, my word it was a treat: "Sunlight" was "bon" soap, some of the boys had scented soap, but any old soap does out here [as] we do not have time to study our complexions.[37]

The deficiencies exposed in the shell shortage were now resolved. All these incoming supplies meant that the men had plenty to carry, as "...every man [was] loaded to the eyelashes with extra ammunition & bombs...."[38] Beyond munitions, many other supplies arrived in massive quantities. Even the horses were given new gas masks but the horses did not cooperate:

> We were now issued with different gas masks or respirators, a box-like affair [on the chest] and a mask to cover the horses' nostrils, attached to their nose bands. Instructions were given that, in a gas attack, the horses must be secured first, but when we tried this out, the horse reared up and plunged in all directions.[39]

Nor did the weather cooperate, and the men complained about the rain, rain, rain. Captain William Henry Bloor constantly recorded the wet. As early as 23 February, he wrote "I nearly got drowned leading the men into the lines—they were juicy." On 2 June he observed: "Wet. Working up a new [gun] position. Supply of timber is giving out and we are held up.... it is a practical truth to say the guns will be axle to axle." He continued on 6 June:

> Wet and miserable. Work held up. Food awful. All our covered space is filled with ammunition, which I have had to take in and we have no accommodation whatever. Piece of bread (wet) and cold tea for breakfast; bread and cheese for lunch!

Things were no better on 8 June when he noted "Wet and stormy. I am fed up to the back teeth with the beastly weather." But he was making progress, albeit slow, as he recorded on 10 June: "I have got 1,800 rounds of the 8,000 we are to start with, and am to get the rest at the rate of eight wagons daily. Don't know where the devil to put it!" One suspects Captain Bloor was an extraordinary officer after reading this take on his men:

> I cannot help every day admiring and liking the men. They are most excellent workers; will "go" from daybreak to night and often all night, too, without a murmur. They live a life a thousand times harder than an officer's, and have no relaxations or amusements—nothing whatever save work and danger and wet and rotten food. They have no blankets now, and sleep on the ground or on boards or on anything they can get.[40]

Some recent scholarship on the backgrounds of the common soldiers has concluded that many of them "...were intimately acquainted with hard labor—both at home and at work—long hours, in many cases for subsistence wages."[41] Such men were only enduring their "normal deprivation."[42] Captain Bloor further observed that his troops exchanged life stories. The former miners explained the ins and outs of mining to the former factory worker soldiers and *vice versa*. Lastly, he recorded that one of the most common conversations among his men concerned favorite beers.[43]

As the preparations continued all that spring, the regular unpleasantries continued as well. Harold Brooks noted that "There is usually an evening hymn of hate from the [German] guns; a '"let you know we're still here although its getting dark...."'[44] Sometime later, W. J. Grant observed a dangerous accident. One of the ammunition storage areas caught fire, blowing up thousands of hand grenades and other munitions, "...pieces flying for nearly a mile round."[45] This soldier may have been speaking for thousands like him: "Of course we had our grouses; but they were really only appetizers to keep us occupied when the trenches were unreasonably nasty."[46] One wonders what was meant by "unreasonably nasty."

Every once in a while, something new would occur. Captain Bloor observed that 28 January 1916 was:

> A day to remember! Gas attack on the whole front with lachrymatory[47] shells mixed. One could hear the civilians in Suzanne coughing and moaning—they had no gas helmets. Our eyes all watering and smarting terribly, had to wear goggles and helmets.[48]

Robert Graves also had an experience with gas masks:

> Gas had become a nightmare. Nobody believed in the efficacy of our respirators, though advertised proof against any gas the enemy could

send over. Pink army forms marked "urgent" constantly arrived from headquarters to explain how to use these contrivances: all contradictory. First, the respirator was to be kept soaking wet, then they were to be kept dry, then they were to be worn in a satchel, then, again, the satchel was not to be used.[49]

Anthony Eden, who ended the war as a captain, and later became Foreign Secretary and Prime Minister, also experienced gas masks on the Somme:

These masks, effective only against chlorine, were damp and impregnated with some unpleasant-smelling stuff which, as we were soon to learn, could bring out an ugly and itching rash on the forehead.[50]

Lieutenant Victor Hawkins experienced a gas attack:

The effect of the gas was to form a sort of foamy liquid in one's lungs, which would more or less drown you. A lot of the men died pretty quickly, and the others soon came down—they were in fact drowning from the beastly foam. Out of the 250 men we started with at 5 o'clock, we were very soon down to about forty or fifty men.[51]

There were also poignant moments that individual soldiers remembered long after the war, including this one:

There is one of our officers hanging on the German barbed wire and a lot of attempts have been made to get him and a lot of brave men have lost their lives in the attempt. The Germans know that we are sure to try and get him so all they have to do is put two or three rifles on to him and fire every few seconds.[52]

In an interview conducted in 1974, Gunner Leonard Ounsworth remembered:

Robbins pulled up some undergrowth and as we fished our way through there was the dead Jerry, his whole hip shot away and all his guts out and flies over it. Robbins just had to step back, and then this leg that was up in a tree became dislodged and fell on his head. He vomited on the spot. Good Lord, it was terrible.[53]

Yet in the midst of the death, destruction and misery, there were also the occasional morale-building intramural competitions. On 9 January, one soldier's battery played a football match against another, while on 18 February a number of soldiers witnessed a boxing competition.[54]

All that spring, the supply depots were enlarged. Men were withdrawn from the trenches and shown large scale models of the sections they were to attack. Kitchener army soldiers were assimilated into the trenches and acclimated to the prevailing conditions. Captain Bloor filled his diary with interesting observations. On 3 June he noted: "The roads behind the line are packed day and night with British and French transport bringing up ammunition and new material." He added on 9 June that "*Toujours il pleut*. [Always it rains]. Mud is knee deep. Our horses are being killed with work. Ten teams out every day pulling big loads of lumber, etc."

There are countless references to the mud in the soldiers' writings. In his post-war reminiscences, one soldier recalled:

...we were now issued with trench waders, a sort of boot and leather covering right to the top of the leg. [A soldier's] horse sank in mud and he jumped off, and was right up to his waist in this sticky mess.... I leaned over my horse's head, and undid the reins, tying it to my saddle. [My horse pulled him out, but] he had only one trench wader on, as the other had broken under the strain.[55]

On 12 June, a very busy Captain Bloor was visited by two generals who:

...came up and looked round. They asked the usual foolish questions and made the usual suggestions of the staff gentry, e.g., that one should have cover on the top of a dug-out, etc.! These people who live in chateaux miles behind the line have no conception of shell fire. They have the most amusing and grotesque ideas as to what shell shock can or cannot do, and their remarks are accordingly out of focus.

Ten days later, Captain Bloor was "strafed" by his Colonel Stanley who saw him coming by without having on his "iron hat." Captain Bloor wrote in his own defense: "The beastly tin helmets are awful things, and, anyhow, I always carry it in my hand."[56] One wonders how much good it would do for his head while in his hand. No doubt Colonel Stanley was right to correct him.

Some of the more senior officers were highly regarded. The Buxton memoir includes this: "I remember Brigadier Philip Howell... coming into my dug-out in the front line and sitting down and asking me about the situation there, and whether I needed anything. I asked for some barbed wire and had it by evening. He was killed a few days later on a similar tour."

As far as equipment, the British helmet had recently been substantially improved. Patented in the summer of 1915, the improved model designed by John Brodie was a one piece "soup bowl" of non-magnetic hardened manganese steel, virtually impervious to shrapnel from above. Within six months, a less glossy model was issued. At first, helmets were in short supply, and were treated as a "trench store", something to be used in the front trenches and left behind for the next group of soldiers to use. As helmets became more plentiful each man was issued his own.[57]

As all this preparation continued, the Germans watched and responded with their own preparations along the Somme river. They began shipping huge quantities of cement down the Rhine River, using it to construct underground troop shelters.[58] This would allow them to defend the area with fewer soldiers, releasing some to join the attack at Verdun.

Captain Bloor remained a keen observer as the month of June passed. On the 23rd, he saw "...perhaps 3,000 wagons all with six horse teams on the road." What a massive amount of supplies! The next day he recorded: "The best day yet!...There is to be a six day bombardment of the hostile trench system for the purpose of cutting wire, battering trenches and demoralizing the enemy generally." They were also to fire all night to prevent the repair of whatever damage they caused. But such constant fire caused great wear and tear on their equipment, and accidents, too:

> ...These prematures are the very devil but cannot be avoided. The barrel of the gun gets very hot with continuously firing, and this affects the charge of cordite or nitro-celulose, and the shell sometimes bursts too soon, but it is a thousand pities and an extraordinary mischance that we ourselves should shoot an officer of "ours."[59]

By late June, Bloor's battery had its assignment, to concentrate its five thousand shells a day on a target just 500 yards wide. And what would such a concentrated bombardment sound like? Captain Bloor described that on 26 June 1916:

> It is impossible to analyze the different sounds of the bombardment. The background is a constant rumble like thunder; this is penetrated all the time by the sharper "cracks" of guns which happen to be adjacent. This is also the sound which ten express trains might make, which is the shells whistling through the air. The air throbs and the ground shakes and the whole earth seems full of menace and danger.

While all this cannonade proceeded, Bloor still found time to note on 28 June "Pouring with rain and knee deep in mud everywhere" and then another accident when one of his men passed in front of a gun just as it fired—and blew the soldier's arm off. There was return fire from the Germans, of course. On the same day:

> ...Bombardier Greenwood got hit. It was a horrible wound right in the stomach, and all the bleeding was inward. In ten seconds this fine big fellow who was a strong as a lion and always had a beautiful ruddy colour, was writhing on the ground and his face was green in hue, and he was in awful agony. I knew there was no hope for him from the first, but told him the usual lies about it not being serious, etc.

The captain spent much of the next morning looking for a "Padre" to bury Greenwood, and "got that done."[60]

Captain Bloor's battery was not the only unit to prepare for this attack. By 1 July 1916, an astonishing total of nearly three million artillery rounds had been brought forward, 70,000 miles of phone cable had been laid and often well buried, and fifty-five miles of additional railroad track had been placed in service.[61] In the week before 1 July, General Rawlinson's heavy guns fired 188,500 shells at the German defenses, the heaviest bombardment thus far. But for the ground to be covered and the defenses to be overturned, even this unprecedented volume of destruction was insufficient.[62] As Whiteman noted in his diary, the Germans had retreated to their "fortress-like underground earthworks."[63]

Among the new supplies, each battalion of about one thousand men was receiving 1,600 flares to indicate its advance to friendly planes, sixty-four bundles of five foot wooden pickets for trench support, ten ten-foot-long bridges designed to cross shell craters or trenches, sixteen sledgehammers, 640 barbed wire cutters, and lots more as well.[64] Only a most profound optimism could justify hanging such an equipment burden on the assaulting troops.

The exact date of this massive attack was moved several times. General Haig aimed for mid-August, when his men and material would be at an all-time high. The French implored him to attack earlier, a request that grew more urgent as their losses at Verdun mounted. Finally, the "Chief" settled on 1 July.

To summarize, the situation by 1 July included all of these components. The British had plenty of troops on hand, and plenty of ammunition, too. An intense bombardment had been going on for a week or more, but no one could measure its effect on the enemy. The Germans already knew, from both the bombardment and observation, that a major attack was imminent. Another uncertainty involved the ubiquitous mud. A fierce bombardment had pummeled the German positions along the Somme for more than a week, but with what effect? How many shells had landed in the soft mud and failed to explode, or exploded causing only minimal damage? How many had actually harmed their targets? Was the enemy now in fact unable to resist the attacking infantry? The British generals believed that of course the Germans could not have survived such a merciless bombardment—no human could. At least one British soldier was convinced about the harm done to the German positions:

> By the time you get this letter the boys hope to be a lot nearer to Germany.... We are sure of a great victory.... I pity the German soldiers our artillery has been giving it to them day and night and there is not a bit of their first two lines of trenches left....[65]

And so well over one hundred thousand soldiers, carrying sandbags and shovels and rifles and ammunition and water bottles and emergency rations and altogether nearly sixty pounds of equipment per man as well as an enormous quantity of hope—each obeyed the officers' whistles to come out of the womb of their trenches and to cross no man's land in good parade order, some even kicking a football.[66] This was the "big push"; this was the first day of their victory over Jerry. Soldiers marched shoulder to shoulder into, through, and over no-man's land until funneled into particular lanes by unbroken barbed wire, presenting an irresistibly rich target that German machine gunners could not possibly miss. Brave men were slaughtered by the thousands. This was the way the terrible tale was told for many years. This is the way it came down in much of the literature. This was the tale of a valiant attack. This was the terrible tale of the bloodiest day in British history. This was the result of appalling generalship. Yet this is just not the way it happened.

Was there in fact actual kicking of a ball? In at least one situation:

> (Captain Neville came to me) and said that as he and his men were all equally ignorant of what their conduct would be when they got into action, he thought it might be helpful—as he had 400 yards to go and he knew it would be covered by machine-gun fire—if he could furnish each platoon with a football and allow them to kick it forward and follow it.[67]

The attacking troops were brave; they were well trained; they were patriotic; they were fighting for King and country; they were convinced that victory was finally at hand. But they were neither stupid nor suicidal. Without a doubt, this was a terrible day, the bloodiest in all of British history. However, more recent scholarship provides a very different picture of just how that day unfolded.

The specific details varied depending on just which section of that broad front is considered. For instance, one Irish unit did approach the battlefield in close to parade order—but while still behind its own lines, still moving up to do its part, it passed into range of German artillery. It was all but annihilated. In other places, troops crawled into the area just short of the German trenches so as to have a great head start when the order came to advance; these did not stand and march. Others awaited the results of another tactic, that of digging a tunnel under a section of the German trench and packing it full of explosives. Remembering how many Welshmen, in particular, had mining experience, it is not surprising that such skills were employed. More than a few tunnel charges were detonated close to or at zero hour—7:30 a.m.—in the hopes of blowing out a section of German trench and allowing the infantry to advance unimpeded by the deadly machine guns.

Imagine the soldiers' astonishment when the closer they got to the German trenches, the more machine guns opened fire on them. Men were mowed down as never before, to the right, to the left. This just was not supposed to be! How could those destroyed positions fight back? One soldier knew the answer, but could not get anyone to heed him in time:

> …we went to cut ways through our own wire & whilst there to take a first look at Jerry's to find, to our continued horror, that it was nothing like cut & in a few hours time our chaps would be just strung upon it like washing, a sitting target for the enemy machine gunners. We reported the matter back to headquarters but I don't know that anything was or could be done about it.[68]

Sweeney, the soldier who predicted a "great victory" on 29 June now had something else to record:

> You cannot realize what it is like to see poor lads lying about with terrible wounds and not being able to help them. We came out of action with four officers out of twenty-six and four hundred and thirty-five men out of one thousand one hundred and fifty.[69]

The BEF endured terrible casualties that day. "Casualty" is such a sanitized expression. To those who know battle, it is a hideous number representing the sum of those who died and those who were wounded, wounded badly enough to compel them to leave (or be removed from) the battlefield. It includes those who will never rise again, those who are no longer whole, those who just cannot be found. Nearly sixty thousand casualties on just the first day! Some of the men who survived that day and that week and that month left powerful eyewitness testimony, such as a soldier named Grant witnessing the German shell that burst inside a gun pit, wounding all four men and "…the pit caught fire, then fell in burning and burying the gun."[70] Grant also noted:

It was a terrible sight to see the wounded coming down in hundreds, the most serious in any conveyance that was handy... wagons, motor lorries, ambulances, or anything they could get. Those that could possibly crawl at all had to get from the trenches to the Dressing Station which was about three miles, as best they could. Each time we were coming back from the guns with empty ammunition wagons, we packed as many wounded on us as we could, as we passed the dressing station on our way back, but a lot of them were too badly wounded to stand the jolting of the wagon and preferred to go on their own.[71]

The records of particular units on that day are both heroic and staggering. What those men endured is almost inconceivable. Expecting to overrun a weakened enemy, they actually met a very strong opponent still operating numerous machine guns, still capable of a fierce and successful resistance. Despite the unexpected and staggering losses, the attack continued.

At what a frightful cost! The Leeds Pals, for example, sent 750 men forward; 539 casualties, 230 dead, not a yard gained.[72] The Newfoundlanders, fighting for the mother country, sent 790 men forward: 272 were killed, 438 wounded for a casualty rate of 90 percent. Follow-on attacks by reserve forces were planned, but could not be carried out because the support trenches were jammed with dead and wounded.[73] Like the narrow waist of an hourglass, the living just could not get by the dead. Bombardier J. W. Palmer recorded:

Our lads weren't moved for some days—the dead weren't moved, the wounded were—and for days after when I was laying the wire out I had to pass over those bodies, whose faces were turning more and more blue and green.[74]

Captain Peel observed:

The whole place was littered with debris of all sorts, Boche shrapnel helmets, charge boxes, and thousands of rounds of ammunition, also plenty of dead—and worse still, hands and legs....[75]

Despite the failure to destroy the barbed wire, the attack ground on, the dying continued. Whiteman was very clear in his opinion after the first day of this battle, writing in his diary that "Those still alive of our troops held on grimly using shell holes in no man's land as a defense until dark, so as to return and fight another day." He then added: "The German concrete deep dugouts won the day." He went on "...at the end of seven days struggle about 10,000 German prisoners were captured, but the death toll on both sides <u>was appalling</u>. I saw it." Realizing that there had been only a small gain, Whiteman lamented "But at what cost in life and limb! To say nothing of the British prisoners taken; wearily marching to the German cages [as they were called]."[76]

Another eyewitness saw "What began as ordered lines of men with rifles at the port & regularly spaced between each other became just like falling stalks of corn cut down by the cutting blades of the reaper."[77]

Captain Bloor remained in the thick of it:

Every inch of ground was strewn with equipment, rifles, hats, etc.; dead men, both British and German, lay about all over the place—some of them had been terribly knocked about, and the whole place was a succession of shell craters.[78]

On 6 July, a very tired Captain Bloor made another entry in his diary:

Bernafay Wood is in a horrible state, corpses lying everywhere, and there are wounded there who "got it" three or four days ago and cannot be attended to because of incessant shellfire.

Three days later, Bloor got a good look at the King's Liverpool regiment as it retreated:

…the King's passed us on the way out and looked absolutely finished, covered with mud, unshaven, and unwashed for three days, and very fatigued.[79]

On 10 July he added "The infantry who have been in the fight from the beginning are quite worn out and cannot carry on much longer without a good rest and a proper reorganization." One soldier tried to help a man with bandaged arms to fill and light his pipe until he saw "…he had nowhere to put it…" as his lower jaw had been blown away.[80]

The battle continued long past the first day. But neither the men nor the equipment could keep up. On 7 July Grant reported that "We had every one of our guns out of action, mostly through broken buffer springs."[81] Captain Bloor's battery had similar trouble:

We are having a great deal of trouble with the guns, which will not stand the excessive wear and strain. Springs of buffers are all weak and the gun has to be pushed by the men which is very hard work and prevents a rapid rate of fire.[82]

Captain Bloor may not have known why his guns were malfunctioning, but the cause had been diagnosed. Just as questions had arisen about the particular steel used in the hull of the ill-fated *Titanic*, it seems the guns, too, were ill made:

A gun had moving parts with tight tolerances; it could not be manufactured overnight, and hasty construction led to malfunctions and accidents. For instance, in 1915 British factories made recoil springs from inadequately tempered steel, and by mid-1916 up to 20 per cent of the 18-pounders were out of action due to broken recoil springs.[83]

Back on the battlefield, after nearly two weeks of attacking, a very tired Captain Bloor seemed to have lost his optimism:

We had the Bosche[84] beaten here on July 1, and could have gone right through, but we have stayed where we are, losing hundreds of lives through his shell fire and allowing him to bring up reserves and additional guns, both of which he has done in plenty. The sooner we get going again the better.[85]

While Bloor may have believed this with all his tired heart, on deeper reflection he would have realized that a local and isolated penetration of the German lines would probably be suicidal. As the attackers ran out of energy and ammunition, the defenders would close in from all sides. The salient would be treated like a painful splinter in a foot: the attackers would be removed.

In the midst of all this destruction, Captain Bloor also wrote a number of letters to his family. In one he told his father that "My diary has no claim to being a literary production or a war commentary, but will just help hereafter to keep my memory green as to scenes and faces, etc., which I encountered out here."[86] His diary continued with detailed observations such as this from the same day: "The one great pest is the perfectly appalling number of flies which simply swarm everywhere. There are a lot of mosquitoes, and the two combined are the very limit." His solution? "I shall send into Bethune (a nearby town) and get a quantity of flypapers."[87] Captain Peel also wrote to his family: "We get the continental *Daily Mail* here in the evening which is not too bad, but as a rule has not got much in it."[88]

Sometimes the soldiers tried to do the unexpected. For example, one evening Bloor's battery began firing randomly at a crossroads in a German-held town, "...in hope of catching hostile transport."[89] Meanwhile, their regular duties continued, including frequently moving the guns despite the amount of work involved. Each new gun pit required "2,000 sandbags, 8 reels wire netting, 200 yards green canvas, 10 barrels cement, 300 feet sawn timber, and 40 sheets corrugated iron—as a start."[90] The corrugated iron was often used as a roof over the pit to give some protection from enemy fire. An example of this roofing remains today in the preserved trenches on the grounds of the Hill 60 museum in Flanders.

The ill-advised but indefatigable attack along the Somme continued. In some places, the troops blew through to the fifth German line, way to the rear. But those soldiers were exposed on both flanks. Alone and unsupported, they had to withdraw, leaving behind many dead.[91] In fact, the senior commanders did not realize how badly the attack was going. Few reports came back: the assumption at headquarters remained that the objectives were being secured.

Nothing could be less true. Men were not reporting back because dead men do not talk. Yet it took some time for the reality to be comprehended. Few reports reached the officers in the rear of the battlefield. Few reports allowed those awaiting them to hope, to believe that the cause must be a grand success. It was just presumed that things were going so well that there was not time to report, there was not time to slow down to file dispatches. Even General Haig, the Commander-in-Chief—even his daily diary entries are quite confused. He notes reports of taking towns that were not taken, capturing landmarks that remained in enemy hands, and later corrects the misinformation. In many places ill-informed Generals, acting on misinformation, sent the reserves forward providing just so many more victims for the German guns.

Those German guns were in fact quite busy. Having seen the massive buildup on the opposite side of the field, they launched an artillery barrage of their own. So the massed British formations suffered from artillery attacks as they prepared for their assault, then machine guns decimated them as they advanced—or rather, tried to advance.

The British plan had been to blast paths through the barbed wire, and to blast gaps in the German trenches, but despite the unprecedented shellfire, shells exploding in mud just did not do enough damage. And since the Germans were not there in the trenches but were instead mostly in their shelters, what was calculated as an unsurvivable bombardment was in fact more sound than harm, more dash than destruction.

Units went forward; none came back; victory must be ensuing. No one foresaw the actual carnage. The high command believed in the plan. The officers believed in the artillery bombardment. The soldiers believed in their junior officers, who were, after all, right there with them. That all this effort was producing little more than huge casualty lists was incomprehensible to the leadership.

And so more and more soldiers were sent forward. Despite the nearly sixty thousand who were killed or wounded on that first day, more tried again the next day, and the next day, and the day after that. If just a bit more could not do it, then what had all the cost thus far achieved? It was not easy to admit that this spectacular effort was a disaster. All those casualties for just a few yards of muddy soil?

Gradually an awareness spread, an awareness that this great assault had failed to overwhelm the German Army, had failed to break the stalemate in this nightmarish war. The cost in human life was staggering. Morale was devastated. Headquarters were in stunned disbelief; individual homes, draped in black crepe, found the news appalling. From King to commoner, the news was just incomprehensible.

While this event is generally referred to as the Battle of the Somme, it was in fact a much longer conflict stretching over the next several months. As slight successes were achieved here and there, more troops were sent in attempts to exploit them, but nowhere was the promised breakthrough achieved.

At the small unit level, that was certainly not for lack of trying, or trying again, or trying still more. By 31 July, Captain Bloor's men were engaged over one simple point on a map called Maltzhorn farm: "There has been the most fierce hand-to-hand fighting in these ruins, and there are dead British, French and Germans by scores. It may be imagined what they are like in this heat. In my state I simply could not stand the stench and was violently ill three times...."[92] The next day he observed "It appears I have trench fever mostly with influenza and some effects of poison gas, of which I got a good doze [sic] a few days ago."[93] Another soldier lamented:

> I felt like crying with fury that men's lives could be sacrificed so easily. We all know [sic] that it was going to be costly, but this was just murder.[94]

Another soldier expressed it this way: "The horrible carnage was terrifying; parts of men's bodies, and parts of horses everywhere."[95]

The weather sometimes hurt the animals also: just as one group moved forward toward the line, a big storm scared the horses and they bolted off the road into a ditch where many suffered broken legs or broken necks; the soldiers had to destroy them.[96]

This battle and these casualties continued their protracted course. One observer noted:

> Of course our casualties are fearful tho. [sic]....But (the Germans) are stout hearted devils & no mistake & every yard of ground has to be fought for!! ...(the shelling) is the nearest approach to hell imaginable.[97]

It was this Battle of the Somme which brought the horrible reality of the war clearly and intensely to so many homes and hearths in the United Kingdom.

When units of men who had all joined as "pals" attacked together, the scythe of death paid a fearsome visit to their town or village. The ever longer lists of casualties published in the newspapers delivered the pain and sense of loss to the whole region. By the time the Battle of the Somme ended and the weather turned wintry in November and December of 1916, the casualty totals topped 430,000, more than 3,500 for each day.[98]

The outcome of this battle also led to withering criticism of the commanding General, Douglas Haig. He planned for, and as far as possible, directed this battle. The loss of 60,000 casualties on the first day, and all the rest of the casualties, occurring on his watch, were his responsibility.

But were those casualties Haig's fault? It's easy to blame him. He gave the orders, and men died. Early historians tore into him. Many who survived those days were caustic and public in their opinions. Liddell Hart, writing in 1923, charged: "Nearly two months of bitter fighting followed, during which the British made little progress at much cost, and the infantry of both sides served as compressed cannon-fodder for artillery consumption."[99] Churchill was equally blunt in his post-war account: "...if only the generals had not been content to fight machine gun bullets with the breasts of gallant men...."[100]

But as with so many things in this war, the reality is more complex, the truth more elusive. First, the whole matter had come a very great distance from a few shots fired by a teenager in the Balkans. Douglas Haig was coping with a situation that no one man could control. There was no British model for him to follow. He was inventing his position and his responses as he went along. No British general had ever commanded such a huge army, which at its maximum size numbered nearly four million men. Required adaptations to the challenges of trench warfare and poison gas attacks had not been foreseen. Strategic decisions had to take into account the emotional pleas and demands of hard pressed Allies. The science and technology of killing men and destroying equipment had moved forward smartly in the first decades of the new century. The science and technology of battlefield command had not. General Haig was in a unique and unenviable position.

Again recalling that General Haig knew he was writing for an audience, his diary gives firm evidence as to the number and variety of influences which shaped his views. He dealt with his sovereign, King George V; cabinet officials, such as David Lloyd George; more senior army generals such as Lord Kitchener, politicians, such as Ben Tillett of the Docker's union; he received the Prime Minister of Australia, the Prime Minister of New Zealand, and the Archbishop of Canterbury and many others at various times.

What was the subject of the interviews between the Commander-in-Chief and these individuals? That requires an astonishing broad answer. For example, he thanked Ben Tillett for keeping the Dockworkers union at work.

He told the Australian Prime Minister that the force from down under was too small to be designated the "Australian Army" as Mr William Morris Hughes wanted it to be called. He told the Archbishop of Canterbury that the Anglican chaplains in the Army must stop quarreling among themselves.[101] In addition to these examples, he received numerous individuals at the request of someone he respected. Amidst all these appointments, he sometimes found time to attend the War Cabinet in London, meetings in Paris, and even to take an occasional few days "holiday" at home. Beyond all this, he met with his senior officers, reviewed and critiqued their plans, appointed and removed subordinate commanders, inspected some front lines and some rear hospitals.

He was a whirlwind on a leash. It was not uncommon for him to summon a car and drive off on short notice to have lunch with a general, English or French, especially since he spoke excellent French. Yet he insisted that his day end with bedtime at 10 p.m. In fact, a physician on his personal staff was empowered to order him to bed if he seemed tired. On the days packed with even the worst news, he slept as usual—an interesting self-defense mechanism.

To maintain his control over so vast an enterprise, General Haig had his own system. First, the main army headquarters was at Montreuil where three hundred officers ran the Army. It was organized by departments. One was "military operations", including such responsibilities as appointments, promotions and honors. The Adjutant-General's department dealt with personnel and discipline. Other departments included Operations and Intelligence. One of the biggest was the Quartermaster General, dealing with transport and supply. But Haig was seldom at this headquarters.[102]

D. H., as he was often styled, maintained his personal headquarters in a French country home a few miles away at Beaurepaire. There his intensely loyal personal staff of about ten looked after his needs and maintained his daily schedule. Barring other business, General Haig followed a rather healthy regimen: first thing in the morning, he went for a walk or a run. He then spent some hours at his desk or meeting with senior staff, followed by lunch. In the afternoon, he was frequently "off" to somewhere. If his destination was close by, he would ride a horse. If further, he would take the "motor." Sometimes a horse would be waiting for him on the way home so he could get a ride in. After dinner, more office work preceded his early bedtime.[103]

Did his staff serve him well? Did this system keep him free to deal with only the most important issues? Were his gatekeepers effective in managing his time and attention? An examination of his diary shows that he seemed to have his attention torn among many subjects, some of which might have been kept away from him by better staff work. That said, his deputies, too, were inventing the system as they went along, once again recalling that never before had such a huge British army been put in the field. His deputies would have had to establish areas of responsibility, a daily awareness of what the "Chief" did and did not *want* to see, what the "Chief" did and did not *need* to see. They would need to be competent at their jobs—and then teach him to do his as well. Is not there a common tendency for the man who has risen through the ranks to micromanage?

As an example, General Haig's diary for 7 October 1916 concerns the reorganization of the supply services, including broad gauge and narrow gauge railways, inland water transport, roads and ports.[104] His diary from 27 October 1916 recounts a meeting he had with General Geddes, the Director General of transportation. Geddes wanted 16,000 more trucks, and more locomotives and more miles of railroads for moving the army's supplies. He also wanted to put experienced people into the concomitant skilled jobs. General Haig wrote:

> So, with the whole nation at war, our object should be to employ men on the same work in war as they are accustomed to do in peace...men of practical experience....To put soldiers into such positions, merely because they are generals and colonels, would be to insure failure!

If the purpose of this meeting and its details was to inform the general, that is one matter. If it was to invoke his intervention, it may be a symptom that he was being importuned. Were there too many such demands on his attention?

With his head full of alliance politics and strategy and concerns about his relations with the government in London and, to a lesser extent, the governments of the Dominions, it was difficult for him to concentrate on performing operational-level (or "grand tactical") functions appropriate to the commander of an Army Group.[105]

General Haig seems to have had an indomitable spirit. His diary indicates his unbounded faith in victory, but it also reflects that the price was heavy indeed. Haig had a realistic appreciation of what was going on around him. Others worried; he held fast to a grounded optimism. "...his maintenance of an air of great composure and confidence for most of his period as commander-in-chief was found by some contemporaries to be enormously reassuring, indeed inspiring."[106] In a revealing diary entry from 16 January 1916, nearly six months before the Battle of the Somme, Haig wrote that he cannot permit attacks which appear to the enemy, his own troops and neutrals "...as 'failures', thereby affecting our 'credit' in the world which is of vital importance as money in England is becoming scarcer."

General Haig was not, in Gilbert and Sullivan's famous expression, "the very model of a modern major general" and occasionally managed to offend his superiors. One of these moments occurred in May, 1916. Haig wanted to keep his cavalry divisions strong, always ready to break through behind the German lines. Maintaining the high numbers of mounted soldiers took a great deal of horse fodder, and that took up a great deal of shipping space. The War Cabinet in London wanted to reduce the size of the cavalry forces to reduce the "gigantic" demand for fodder. Since General Haig believed most of the fodder went for pack animals, that is, for the working horses, not the essentially idle cavalry, he essentially advised the War Cabinet to mind its own business.

That was not his wisest move. Such an attitude did not sit well with the Prime Minister, David Lloyd George, whose envoy to BEF headquarters reminded General Haig in no uncertain terms that the War Office was in fact his superior and that he would mind its directions. Haig, wanting to keep his appointment, acquiesced.[107]

Returning to the human cost of the battle of the Somme, there is a much-noticed line in his diary for 2 July 1916. He wrote that "The AG [108] reported today that the total casualties are estimated at over 40,000 to date." He then adds "This cannot be considered severe in view of the numbers engaged, and the length of front attacked…." The line stands there, the only mention of the cost in lives in this offensive. Is it callous? Indifferent? Cavalier? Fatalistic? Are these the words of a man who cares not, or who cares too much? Or is it giving the King a ready line of defense for the criticism that Haig believes is about to envelope all British leaders?

Despite the high cost of the offensive, Haig still had many other continuing factors on his mind. There was the fear that the unceasing German attacks on Verdun would force France out of the war. That was indeed the German plan. Another factor was that his Russian ally was practically on life support. Horrific casualties were rapidly undermining the Tsar's regime. Nor did Haig want to concede to the Germans the initiative of deciding where and when the next battle should be fought. Even just leaving the Germans alone, offering only minimal combat, had its price: it would allow the Germans unhampered time to further strengthen the fortress they were making out of their side of the battlefield. Haig felt compelled to shoulder Britain's share of the fighting, to make as strong an attack as possible, but to also realize that success here would not end the war, but would be an expensive building block of future victory.

Those who attack Haig most vigorously often assert that he ought to have waited for the new weapon just coming into service, the "land ship" or as it became more commonly known, the tank. Liddell Hart charged:

The first nine [tanks] rendered useful aid, especially in capturing Flers, but the greater prize—of a great surprise stroke—was a heavy forfeit to pay for redeeming in a limited degree the failure of the Somme offensive.[109]

Shortly after becoming Commander-in-Chief, General Haig ordered that 1,000 tanks be constructed. This was a mobile metal fortress weighing about thirty tons. It had a crew of six or so, and a top speed between two or three miles an hour. Its advantages were that it carried a modest field gun or multiple machine guns, could cross trenches on caterpillar-like treads, and had a thick metal skin so that it was close to being bullet proof. Thus its occupants did not fear German machine guns. Its disadvantages included its slow speed, a tendency to break down or to get stuck in mud, and a tendency to nearly asphyxiate its crew.

One early model tank is on display on the ground floor of the Imperial War Museum, London. It clearly could not have come through the front door, and there is no larger door into the building. Each of the large exhibits on display, including multi-stage multi-story guided missiles, Second World War vehicles and even a collection of aircraft suspended from the ceiling, all came into the museum the same way: experts took them apart and then reassembled them inside. As for the tank, a clear sheet has been installed over one side so that the cramped interior is open to view.

British tanks were first used in September 1916. The plan for their employment called for bombardment of a section of the enemy trench, but corridors one hundred yards wide were left open for the tanks to maneuver. The hope was that the tanks not be destroyed by friendly fire. When an individual tank failed to come forward due to mechanical breakdown, the Germans in the undisturbed portion of the line were able to take an extraordinary toll on the attacking troops. Because of small numbers, because of undeveloped tactics, because of undiscovered possibilities, the first employment of the tanks was not a grand success—and it did reveal this new weapon to the enemy before it was ready in adequate numbers to make a difference.

Haig personally decided on some tank tactics. For example, he planned an attack using fifty or sixty tanks but with no preliminary and telltale bombardment. This is an example of the complex character of this leader: planning new tank tactics to punch a hole in the German lines so his cavalry could pour through.[110] One historian summarized the criticism this way: "...technophobic cavalrymen failing to appreciate the potential of new war-winning weapons, notably the tank."[111]

Writing after the war, Churchill complained that the tank was "... improvidently exposed to the enemy on the Somme in 1916," but also gave some credit to General Haig who "... at least moved faster and farther along the new path [tanks], and in consequence, doubtingly and tardily, he realized in the end a generous reward."[112]

In a brilliantly written description, Gerald De Groote summarized the first bit of tank history:

The first successful tank produced in Britain was nicknamed "Little Willie." It was quickly replaced by a larger model called, predictably, "Big Willie." The later was then renamed "Mother" as it was the first of all tanks (even though it was actually the second). "Mother" came in two forms: male and female. The male "Mother" was bigger and had better guns, namely two 6-pounder naval guns and four Lewis machine guns, while the female had six Lewis guns. The female, rather inexplicably, had a tiny trap door, rendering it nearly impossible for the crew to escape if the tank caught fire. The crew's worst nightmare was to be trapped inside a burning female tank. For understandable reasons, they preferred a male "Mother." (Oh, what a surreal war.)[113]

While tanks may have had a promising future, their early debut was not so encouraging. They moved more slowly than troops on foot, so they actually slowed down the speed of an assault. They required a skillful driver to maneuver around impassible obstacles, trenches too deep, too wide, or too slippery. But when a tank got into range of an enemy machine gun, it could shoot its way through or just ride over the spot, crushing the defenses. While able to withstand most small arms and machine gun fire, a tank was vulnerable to artillery fire. As a small and moving target, it was hard to hit, but its early mechanical difficulties left it less-than-ideal weapon. Given time, it promised to be formidable, but at first, it was more a potential than an actual threat.[114] Perhaps it would be a game-changer—but not this month, not this year.

General Haig's strategy at the Battle of the Somme has been the subject of numerous modern studies. Why were those first day casualties so high? Because "...an inexperienced and partially trained force went 'over the top' with deficient artillery support and overambitious objectives."[115] One point of view is that "Haig's decision to attack such a formidable position has subsequently been questioned, but he had no choice."[116] Another historian concludes that the Somme campaign was "...not a blunder of mammoth proportion but rather a stage in the evolution of organization, tactics and weaponry," and points out the "depressing similarity" of battles in which "...gains are measured in hundreds of yards and tens of thousands of casualties."[117] There was a "...recognition now general that only a terrifying accumulation of killing devices could bestow success upon any offensive operation."[118] In fact, "...as long as most German machine gunmen and artillerymen survived the British bombardment, the slaughter of the attacking infantry would occur *whatever* infantry tactics were adopted."[119] Professor Gerald De Groote summarizes the argument in one typically well-written sentence: "It was technology, not idiotic commanders, which put the armies on the Western Front into trenches and kept them there for three years."[120]

While all this fighting continued, there was some effort at examining what was and was not working. Several memos survive containing senior commanders' reflections on these points. Among the most prominent was General Henry Rawlinson. In a document dated 13 October 1916, wondering "Why we fail", he listed five reasons. First, attacks were never a surprise, always beginning between noon and 3 p.m. Secondly, the poor weather always made observation difficult. Third was the problem of the enemy quickly recovering his power to resist. A fourth consideration was the lack of a clearly defined starting point which would allow a creeping barrage. The fifth and final point: the German machine guns remained operational.[121]

A close look at General Haig at this point of the war seems to find him with one foot firmly planted in each of the two centuries his career bridged. He was open to trying new inventions such as tanks and "aeroplanes", even active in discussions about how best to employ those. But he was unable to leave behind the horses he so dearly valued. From his diary of 15 July 1916:

> I visited General Horne (XV Corps) about 3 p.m. He told me that the report 7th Dragoon Guards (cavalry soldiers) charged last night and killed with lances 16 Enemy and took over 30 prisoners. All the cavalry are much heartened by this episode and think that their time is coming soon.

And what can one make of this remark?

> ...the object of the operations of the infantry aided by Tanks (was) to break through the Enemy's defenses *by surprise* and so permit the Calvary Corps to pass through and operate in open country.[122]

The Commander-in-Chief seems to have maintained a paternalistic attitude toward his troops. On 31 October 1916 his diary notes:

> ...I wanted definite information as to the state of the front trenches, and whether the winter leather waistcoats had yet been issued, also whether an extra blanket per man had been sent up.

In his attacks, Haig wanted to move with such speed that the enemy would not have time to bring forward reserves to plug the gaps he had created. On the other hand, and perhaps more realistically, General Rawlinson wanted to "... bite and hold" pieces of the enemy trenches, move his guns forward, and take another bite, then repeat this process until victory.[123] One of Haig's modern critics argues that "Haig ignored [many of his generals] and overreached, fatally dissipating his firepower."[124]

By remaining on the offensive, Haig was wearing down his own armies at a much faster rate than he was wearing down his opponents.[125] He was prepared to spend lives. His diary of 22 September 1915 contains this harsh yet realistic advice to one of his subordinate generals: make sure you keep two or three officers at headquarters "...ready to fill the places of Brigadiers who might become casualties...." Does that mean he believed that Brigadiers were interchangeable, just moves on a chessboard? That rather than carefully matching a man with a task, any old cookie cutter general would do? Or was he being extraordinarily practical, in having a trained man at hand to fill an urgent gap? No matter how much he felt compelled to support his allies, no matter how much more of the burden he deemed it necessary to carry, Haig's strategic choice to relentlessly attack rather than remain on the defensive was unsustainable. To keep this up would lose the war.

General Haig's political superiors knew this. Prime Minister Lloyd George was reluctant to replace all the casualties, believing the army would just chew them up, too. In the modern vernacular, where was the plan for victory? Where was the "endgame"? What was the "exit strategy"? How would the British know they had won? What exactly would they win? How long would the public tolerate this interminable war before turning on the politicians in office? There were some men available, yes, but that was not a bottomless well, and no end was in sight. This "more of the same" just wasn't going to do it.

Yet in Haig's professional judgment to ease up would be to lose.[126] If he reduced pressure on the Germans, they would use the opportunity to continue to strengthen their fortress-trenches, thus costing even more British casualties when they were attacked and taken next year or the year after that. There is no hint in his diary that he ever thought the war would be lost, although he certainly did have what might be termed some bad days. So the Commanding General extended the Somme offensive with its traditional attacks by artillery and infantry, well beyond July. His diary of 28 October 1916 indicates he had some awareness of what:

> [the men endure]... the long carry to this part of our front... Otherwise necessities such as water, food, ammunition, bombs of all kinds etc. cannot be kept up. The carry is roughly 5000 yards each way.... One man does one round journey carrying a load per 24 hours.

General Haig also noted that "The communications are still very bad. In fact we are fighting under the same conditions as in October, 1914, i.e., with rifle and machine gun only, because bombs and mortar ammunition cannot be carried forward as the roads are so bad."[127] The weather remained a frequent obstacle. Captain Bloor reported on 29 August that "During the afternoon had the worst thunderstorm and most torrential rain that I have ever, I think, experienced. The marsh we are in has become a lake! Raining all night."[128]

The Captain was not alone. One soldier quipped:

> We are having very wet weather—it came down in torrents this morning and
> if it had kept on we would have had to have a few battleships or submarines
> in the trenches.[129]

One odd feature of trench life has not yet been mentioned. At great risk
to themselves, the men often had to crawl out into no man's land to perform
a vital chore. At the risk of their very lives—they had to cut the grass, what
there was of it. Otherwise, they learned at no small cost, the enemy could use
it to conceal their approach.[130]

The soldier's letters home from these months are sometimes more sad, more
candid than earlier in the war. One soldier observed: "More shells over 2
Lancs (Lancaster Regiment) killed. Pitiful to see pieces of them blown up in
the air."[131] A soldier named Buxton wrote a letter to his aunt on 19 September
which included this unusually melancholy passage:

Dearest Aunt,

A hot bath and a clean set of clothes a white pair of spats[132] and a dry metal
roof would be heaven. The trenches are simply awful and we are all drenched
to the skies.... Do you remember when we left Doncastle that tall officer and
his fiancé on the platform as the train pulled away? He was wounded last
winter and married and came back here as my company commander and has
just been killed.[133]

The opportunity to bathe became a recurring topic in the diaries as in this
note from H. T. Williams which he titled "#11."

> Very seldom was there the chance of hot water for a wash, or bath, even
> when the Battalion was out of the line resting, so when orders were posted
> that we were going to the baths, a shout of pleasure went up, we had been in
> and out of the line without much rest for months, coming out of one sector,
> then into another almost at once.
>
> And the whole Battalion was in bad shape, a clean up would be good for
> our morale, so we were all looking forward to this treat, so rare in those
> days, we were in a filthy condition.
>
> Each platoon was to march to these baths, get it over as soon as possible,
> as the whole regiment had to go, then be followed by another regiment in
> our division and so on until every regiment in the Division had been done.
>
> When we arrived, we found that the [engineers] had fixed up some piping

in an old barn, these pipes had been placed about six feet from the ground, so as to form a makeshift shower, about every three feet, there was a few holes in the pipes.

Then started the rush to get undressed, and many jokes at this pleasure to come, after that the hot water started to come through, then the joy was unbounded, but alas very premature as the water flowed so slowly that at most of these holes just a trickle flowed, it was not enough, not like a shower should be, but there it was and nothing could be done about it, so there was really a fight to get the best spot, if there was one, it was funny to see men pushing together to get some drips of water on themselves, we had been given just a small piece of soap each. This soap was removing the dirt from our skins where the hot water was running down our bodies, but hardly touching the rest, so most of us looked like black men with white stripes, the result was really funny. It caused great fun, for in those days all mishaps were turned into some joke, although it was a tragedy to miss the chance to be clean, even for a few days.

The fresh issue of clean shirts and underwear which would free us from vermin at least for a few hours was small comfort to what we had lost. Another incident to remember.[134]

Buxton's letter of 24 September included three different themes. The first was thanks for the gifts which had arrived in the mail, the "...socks, cake, chocolate, post cards and sardines." He then mentioned the mud, the "...deep thick mud was awful—almost a practical impossibility to move your feet as you walked up to your knees." Lastly, he included this account:

Two or three days ago while on duty I saw 4 Bosche put a machine gun in their line—I marked the place exactly—got the artillery on & in the first 3 shells the gun was blown up and the men running down the trench. I was ready for them with snipers and machine guns and about ¼ hour later, 3 very bandaged Bosche received a rude reception to their renewed appearance.

Captain Peel kept up his steady flow of observations with this one from 30 September:

The row going on here is something awful. The guns never stop, day or night, and at night the flashes light up the whole sky for miles around. There is no doubt about there being a war on now....

I spent a happy (?) afternoon yesterday burying dead horses, killed by an aeroplane bomb. They had been dead for some days!! I saw the tanks for the first time yesterday.[135]

One soldier and his friends were quite angry over some publicity photos taken of them. As they left the trenches for a bit of a rest, they were ordered to "smile." Just then some photographers took their picture. A little while later, they came across the photo in the newspaper with the caption: "HAPPY EAST YORKSHIRES GOING INTO ACTION." They greatly resented this misrepresentation. They well realized nobody was happy to go into the trenches; to purport otherwise was, they felt, an unpardonable lie.[136]

That same soldier also recorded in his diary that a party of British soldiers were detected digging a tunnel under the German lines. The Germans pumped gas into the tunnel, and the British soldiers were removed "...frothing at the mouth."[137]

The usual nasty observations remained as the summer turned to fall. One soldier's first impression of the town of Hometz (?) was "...that caused by the smell of decaying corpses, not yet buried."[138] Captain Laidlaw wrote to his wife:

> We are in a kind of Camp now in a sea of mud, but I expect we won't be here long. You people at home can't realize what our fellows are going through out here, it is quite a common thing to be up to the armpits in mud, and there is such a lot of traffic that even on dry days the place does not get a chance to dry.[139]

Captain Peel was in almost a poetic mood that October when he observed:

> It was a glorious morning with bright sunshine and a touch of frost in the air, a real good autumn day, and it seemed impossible to realize that we were right in the centre of the great push; at least it seemed a shame to kill anything on a day like that.... It is indeed a promised land, but when will it be ours? ... It was perfectly ripping to look over at the Boche lines and see all the green fields and woods in the distance, as yet unspoilt [sic] by shell fire, instead of the dreary drab scene of the country over which we have advanced.[140]

The usually more optimistic Captain Peel must have been having a very bad moment when he recorded: "I don't think I have ever felt so miserable as I did then. I was cramped from lying in a hole where there wasn't room for me, hungry, tired, and bitterly cold."[141]

Captain Peel was not alone in his negative opinion:

> The area into which we had now come was one of desolation and mud and more mud much worse than when we left it in July, occasioned not only by the intensive artillery fire but by the incessant rainfall too.[142]

Some mundane events could be irritants as well. One unit of soldiers was billeted near a particular French village. At the end of their stay, "...the battalion was presented with a colossal damages bill by Mousuier le maire [*sic*] & as deductions were made from our pay we saw red & were glad to turn our backs on the place."[143]

On the other hand, sometimes the simplest things could cause a moment of joy or happiness or at least relief. There was modest joy when "...two men carry[ing] a thermos of soup on a pole between their shoulders...." arrived safely.[144] There was happiness when "...French farmers sold us eggs & chips...."[145] There was a warm feeling when an arriving deliveryman was greeted with "...a mug of tea, and [the men] looked upon me as a godsend for their mail and rations."[146] And there was sometimes a moment to brag to one's brother:

> Did I tell you I have a little dog who kills rats at the rate of 4 per night (some of them nearly as big as he is) and lays them out stiff and stark in a line by my bed for approval. He's a nice little fellow with one black ear and no tail. I call him Cannibal because I feed him his own flesh and bone namely bully beef.[147]

No doubt both brothers understood the subtle humor in the reference to the soldiers' rations as dog food.

When on leave in London, many of the soldiers found themselves met at the train station by senior citizens, men and women, who wore a form of a grey uniform. Their task was to keep the men away from prostitutes. To aid this endeavor, the seniors offered the soldiers a "good time", a bed for the night, a fish and chips meal, and all this value for just one pound, about five U.S. dollars.[148] Precisely how many soldiers availed themselves of this wholesome opportunity is not documented.

As September turned to October, despite the high cost, General Haig refused to stop the offensive. One recent study offers an explanation for his maintaining the pressure on the Germans. J. P. Harris asserts:

> When the weather [became worse] at the beginning of October, Haig then behaved as if he could, by sheer willpower, overcome the frequent blindness of the artillery, the collapse of his logistics, and the misery of his infantry."[149]

Harris continues that General Haig wanted to push on because of "The streak of almost maniacal stubbornness in [his] character...."[150]

Haig had his reasons for continuing. He had always believed in a simple formula for victory: the war could only be won if Germany were defeated, and that the Western Front was the only place where that could be accomplished. He may have kept the attack going partly because he wanted a "...notable success to strengthen his position at home before closing the campaign."[151] And finally, the Army had to keep up this "expensive attack" or spend the arriving winter at the bottom of a valley, wide open to German attacks.[152] The attack could not go on much longer, however, as:

> By October fresh troops were, in any case, in exceedingly short supply. All fifty-one divisions of the BEF had by now fought on the Somme and its infantry strength had fallen dramatically.[153]

It is easy to overlook what was just stated. To repeat: *all fifty-one divisions had by now fought on the Somme*. What an extraordinary intensity of effort! Some battalions which had a rated complement of 800 men were down to just 350, and reinforcements were not arriving in sufficient numbers. Just why success remained so elusive was not clearly understood. According to the Australian historians Prior and Wilson:

> ...the command failed to analyze why the achievements fell short of the original expectations. This proceeding might have provided [the Generals] with some comfort but it denied them the chance to learn from their mistakes. At this rate the learning curve would be very flat indeed.[154]

Perhaps the generals were not drawing the right conclusions, but they were reviewing tactics. General Rawlinson wrote some "Tactical Notes" in June 1916, which included this: "The ideal is for the artillery to keep their fire immediately in front of the infantry as the latter advances, battering down all opposition with a hurricane of projectiles."[155] General Haig's diary of 14 October 1916 lists reasons why a particular attack was not a success: the British attack went forward between noon and 3 p.m., the regular time for such things, so surprise was lost. Meanwhile, cloudy weather grounded the observation aircraft, the enemy had time to recover from the barrage, and they used machine guns in their defense at distant ranges.

As the fighting dragged on, Captain Peel was pleased to record:

> I have been at the School of Mortars for five days, learning drill which is never used and practically wasting my time. However there is quite a decent crowd here, and we manage to have a cheery time and do as little work as possible.[156]

Back with his unit, Captain Peel wrote about home leave: "Still perhaps around this time next year, or the year after that they might begin to think about it!!"[157] That same month, he wrote that he was grateful for gifts from home, including "…biscuits, cheese biscuits, gloves, crème de menthe, sweaters, books, tobacco, pipes, chocolate, socks." One cannot help wondering how the one fragile item, the liquor, survived the trip to the trench, and whether having it in the front lines was within regulations.

Despite being an artillery officer with his guns located well behind the lines, Peel did have occasion to visit the front lines, and on 24 October 1916 reported that "It was very unpleasant up there, cold and miserable and plenty of shells, and also a damned long way to walk." Six days later, he recorded: "The weather continues beastly, or gets beastlier every day." November did not improve his spirits much, as these two notes from the tenth indicate: "No one who hasn't seen it can imagine what serving the guns means, even with packhorses as we do; wagons have been out of the question for weeks." Why no wagons? He provides a clear answer in this second observation:

We have had the most glorious days, yesterday and today, real good ones, and they have done a lot of good, but as for drying up the mud—???!!! My horse was nearly swimming yesterday along a so-called road.

When possible, men continued to lavish care on their horses, although perhaps this is an exaggeration:

The horses, although a big lot and many of them big boned and long bodied, carrying the best of coats and are all in perfect condition. The drivers love their horses and take the greatest pride in them and in their harness also.[158]

Soldiers were constantly reminded of the fragility of their individual lives. Many became nonchalant, even fatalistic. If it was to happen, it was to happen. Thus this barebones description: "Gunner Bowles was all ready to go on leave when a shell burst right in the cooker house blowing it to pieces and killing Bowles."[159]

Leave was a great morale builder. By early 1916, the actual transport of the individual soldier had become well organized. For soldier Harold Brooks, leave began in his trench at 5:30 a.m. By 10:30 he was in Boulogne, in a "rest camp" by 11:45, embarked for home the next day at just after noon, arrived at Folkestone by 1:48, Victoria station by 4:45 and was actually in his home by 6:45 that evening.[160]

Soldiers returned from leave and new men arrived from training stations constantly. The new men were not as healthy as those who had already enlisted:

When they came to us they were weedy, sallow, skinny frightened children—

the refuse of our industrial system—and they were in very poor condition because of wartime food shortages. But after six months of good food, fresh air and physical exercise they changed so much their mothers wouldn't have recognized them.[161]

Along the same lines, there is this: the minimum height for a recruit in 1914 was five feet eight inches. Massive casualties forced changes. After the first battle of Ypres, the minimum height became five feet five inches. By the end of 1914, the standard became five feet three inches. By the last adjustment, the minimum height required was just five feet, and men already fifty years of age were welcome to enlist.[162]

Meanwhile, the mud remained a constant problem and source of complaint. Buxton sent his mother a postcard on 16 November just packed with news: "I am put in command. I am awfully pleased! Awfully busy. Mud awful. We have thigh boots issued." Ten days later he wrote to his father: "We were just out from a really shocking time snow rain mud over knees heavy shelling." He added:

> It is very nice having a company (240 men 5 officers if up to strength) & looking after them, arranging the work & deciding what to do in exciting moments also you have a horse which is always a joy to me.

A month later, Buxton sent a more cheerful letter which included "Just had a new gas helmet issued. They are simply splendid—far the best issued."

In addition to the letters and diaries of the soldiers, there are also the poems that they wrote. Some are famous and well known: others reflect a more private anguish. Siegfried Sassoon included these poignant words in "A Working Party":

> Three hours ago he stumbled up the trench;
> Now he will never walk that road again:
> He must be carried back, a jolting lump
> Beyond all need of tenderness and care.[163]

Another soldier poet, Charles Hamilton Sorley, died from a sniper's bullet on 13 October 1915. Some of his work was published in January 1916, including these lines:

> When you see millions of the mouthless dead
> Across your dreams in pale battalions go,
> Say not soft things as other men have said
> That you'll remember. For you need not so.[164]

Above: Two wounded Canadians being load onto an ambulance during Battle of Passchendale.

Below: Dump of 18 pounder shell casings near Fricourt, 1916.

Above: Water filling point near Theipal Wood, September, 1916.

Below: Royal Engineers construct canvas water trough for horses; Carnoy, September 1916.

Above: Troops bathing near Aveluy,
7 August 1916.

Right: Rescuing officer from dug-out
blown in by shell fire, Mouquet farm
September 1916.

Above: The ruins of Mouquet farm October, 1916.

Right: "Sammy", the mascot of the Northumberland Fusiliers. This dog went to France with the Regiment from Heysham, in April 1915, was wounded in the Second Battle of Ypres, and was gassed on Whit Monday, 1915. Has been with the Battalion in all trench tours and burned by shell fire on several occasions; this dog was also with the Regiment during the advance on the Somme Front.

Above: Sleds carrying wounded. LeSars, October 1916.

Below: Twelve horse team hauling a wagon over heavy ground, near Bernafay Wood, September 1916.

Left: A pack horse loaded with rubber trench boots (waders) is led through the mud near Beaumont Hamel on the Somme battlefield, November 1916.

Below: Unloading an ammunition limber in the Ancre Valley, November 1916.

Right: A regimental cook; Ancre Valley, 1916.

Below: Animal Welfare: British troops scraping mud from a mule near Bernafay Wood on the Western Front.

Above: Clearing mud from a trench: near Trones Wood, November 1916.

Below: Icicles hanging from the roof of a dug-out; Bernafay Wood, November 1916.

Right: Wounded British soldier holding his steel helmet, which has been pierced by a piece of shrapnel, during the advance on the Somme Front near Hamel.

Below: Pack horses taking up ammunition to the forward area: near Hamel, December, 1916.

Above: British Cavalry on the Cambrai Road, 26 May 1917.

Below: The Somme advance. British troops crossing newly captured territory by a road made of wooden planks. Miraumont, 26 May 1917.

Left: First Army Horse Show at the Château de la Haie, 25th June 1917. A horse jumping competition.

Below: A horse-drawn limber takes ammunition to the forward guns along the Lesboeufs Road, outside Flers, November 1916. The horses are up to their knees in mud.

Above: A British soldier directs a Mark IV tank as it crosses an old trench in Oosthoek Wood, near Elverdinghe.

Below: Ruins of the Cloth Hall (Lakenhalle) and St Martin's Cathedral in Ypres, 23 January 1916.

Above: Men and horses of the Army Service Corps (ASC) undergo an anti-gas drill, somewhere in England, probably Aldershot. Note that, as horses breathe through their nostrils, their mouths are not covered.

Below: British cavalry horses being watered from barrels, Aisne area, September 1914.

The Buttes New British Cemetery is located near the town of Zonnebeke, Belgium.

Rifleman Valentine Joe Strudwick, Service Number 5750, serving with 8th Battalion The Rifle Brigade, was aged 15 when he died on 14 January 1916.

An iron harvest at Varlet Farm, Poelkapelle, Belgium.

Shell casings at Varlet Farm.

A quiet summer scene 2010, at Mouquet Farm, 'Moo Cow Farm' Pozières, near Albert, France. There was heavy fighting here on 25 July 1916, two days after the opening of the Battle of Pozières, with the Australians suffering large losses.

The Menin Gate Memorial to the Missing is a war memorial in Ypres, Belgium dedicated to the British and Commonwealth soldiers who were killed in the Ypres Salient of the First World War and whose graves are unknown.

Edmund Blunden was just nineteen when he enlisted in the Army in 1915. He spent two tears at the front, enduring and surviving both the battle of the Somme and the Third battle of Ypres.[165] Among his surviving lines—many were lost, by his own account, in the mud of Flanders—are these:

> Why are they dead? Is Adam's seed so strong
> That these bold lives cut down mean nothing lost?
>   Indeed, they would have died: ourselves ere long
> Will take their turn.
>   That cheque is signed and crossed.
> But, though this dying business still concerns
>   The lot of us, there seems something amiss
> When twenty million funeral urns
>   Are called for. Have you no hypothesis?[166]

Not only in poetry, this long Battle of the Somme had far-reaching consequences. More than ever before, it became clear that both sides were so evenly matched that despite the cost and effort spent thus far, so much more would be needed. The French must be supported; the Russians must be supported. If either of them fell—both perilous possibilities in 1916—the task of Great Britain would be just that much greater. And while there were some who called for a negotiated peace, such a gospel did not resound among the people of the island: they wanted victory to reward their enormous sacrifice. They wanted Germany punished.

As the end of the year approached and as the cost of the war grew shockingly greater both in lives and national treasure, a few people began to think about ways of curtailing the price Britain would have to pay. The total casualties of the Somme campaign were a staggering 420,000 killed, taken prisoner or wounded.[167] That just could not be sustained.

The Prime Minister met with General Haig in London on 25 November and informed the General that:

> … [Lloyd George] considered the political situation serious. Lord Lansdowne had written a terrible letter urging that we should make peace now, if the Naval, Military, Financial and other Heads of Departments could not "be certain of victory by next autumn."[168]

The terrifying truth was that some had lost faith in ultimate victory, or rather, were no longer willing to pay the price it seemed to command. Just how long could the nation endure these human losses, this destruction of national wealth? Again, where was the certain path to victory? And if there were none, better end the suffering now rather than later.

There was very strong newspaper reaction to the Lansdowne letter. The *Pall Mall Gazette* summarized what the London papers declared this way: *The Times* called it "unpropitious", the *Morning Post* "mischief", the *Daily Telegraph* thundering "no compromise on sea rights" and the *Daily Mail*'s succinct: "He surrenders, We don't." The *Pall Mall Gazette* of 7 November 1917 spoke for many when its tongue in cheek editorial denounced any thought of negotiating with Germany:

> Belgium was protected by negotiations. Londoners are secure against bombs,[169] and merchant shipping against torpedoes, so far as negotiations have any effect upon the matter. The bombardment of hospitals, the shooting of stretcher-bearers, and the shelling of seamen in their open boats are all absolutely impossible, if the results of negotiations are of any account.

That the newspapers reacted so strongly to the Lansdowne letter while just about ignoring the high casualties so far in this war may seem surprising. Without a doubt, the popular press served Athena far more than Alatheia, served patriotism more than truth. In many subtle ways, the newspapers supported the war. For example, as the British made minuscule gains on the battlefields, the papers printed maps that changed scale over time, so that tiny gains appeared substantial. That conclusion can only be reached by looking at numerous maps over time; the change was incorporated quite gradually.

Meanwhile, the lengthy list of dead and wounded, columns headed "Roll of Honor" appeared in small print, minimizing their total numbers. When Lord Kitchener died, for example, the account of his bequests took up one and a half columns of standard size type—while on the same page five columns of much smaller type listed the casualties.[170] Sometimes what was printed as news reports was less the news and more a cheerleader's exhortation. Sometimes it was sheer nonsense. On 1 July, readers of the *Daily Telegraph* were made privy to this drama:

> A staff officer had whispered a secret to me at midnight in a little room, when the door was shut and the window closed. Even then they were words which could only be whispered and to men of trust. "The attack will be made this morning at 7:30".... The preliminary bombardment had done their work with the enemy's wire and earthwork.[171]

Even the more highbrow *Times* reported on 2 July 1916 that:

> ...under the dreadful hurricane whole reaches of the enemy's trenches have

been battered out of existence; his nearer communication trenches have been obliterated, ... and almost every discoverable shelter where an enemy might hide has been searched out and pounded by our guns. And still it goes on mercilessly.

On 3 July 1916, correspondent Philip Gibbs of the *Daily Telegraph* let his readers know this:

At first, it is certain, there was not much difficulty in taking the enemy's first line trenches along the greater part of the country attacked. Our bombardment had done great damage, and had smashed down the enemy's wire and flattened his parapets.... When our men left their assembly trenches and moved forward, cheering, they encountered no great resistance from the German soldiers who had been hiding in their dug-outs under our storm of shells.

While Gibbs might have believed it with his whole soul, it just was not true. But how would he know any better? He was not permitted anywhere near the front lines. Meanwhile his colleague W. Breach Thomas included these phrases in his account in the *Daily Mail* of 3 July 1916:

...we have beaten the Germans by greater dash in the infantry and vastly superior weight in munitions....plucky, merry groups of our more lightly wounded who were hurried back like parties of beanfeasters....[172]

The London papers kept pace with each other. The *Daily Telegraph* of 3 July 1916 reported bombarding the Germans for a week, then:

...full power of our artillery was let loose about 6 o'clock this morning. Nothing like it has ever been seen or heard upon our front before, and all the preliminary bombardment, great as it was, seemed insignificant to this.

The same paper included this line the next day: "The spirit of our men is so high that it is certain we shall gain further ground, however great the cost." On 4 July 1916, a photo caption of wounded men stated: "Wounded in France on Sunday, carefully treated in a London hospital on Monday....here they were home again, maimed, but enthusiastic, confident as to victory."

War or no war, the newspapers were going to conduct their business as usual. Next the casualty reports one could find an advertisement for "Good Books for Trench, Camp, and Hospital."[173] On the same day in the same paper one could find a by-now often-run advertisement by the Wilkinson Sword

Company for the "Bullet Proof Jacket, fitted by an expert."

This is not to disparage the press of Great Britain. They felt compelled to keep up the home front, and they felt a selective emphasis on what they reported was in the national interest.

Meanwhile, Prime Minister Lloyd George was calculating the national interest. Whatever his private reservations, he remained a public supporter of D.H. at least in part for an ominous reason: there did not appear to be a likely candidate to replace him.

That the achievements of the year fell so far short of promises was costly. Private Chaney was quite candid in his view: "From now on the veterans, myself included, decided to do no more than was really necessary, following orders, but if possible keeping out of harm's way."[174] That is only anecdotal evidence, of course, but it cannot be a surprise in light of the interminable bloodshed and suffering, once again without any near hope of success in the offing. Captain Hoult was most annoyed as the year ended. He had been sent a Christmas present of cigarettes which had not arrived:

> It must be beastly annoying for people when they send stuff over here to know eventually that it doesn't finish its proper journey: and that the pity of it is that a good deal seems to go astray, with regard to this base anyhow.[175]

As 1916 drew to a close, General Haig had much work in front of him. He would have to change the mood of the BEF. Captain Bloor's diary represents the common sentiment of the men that month:

> Was up all night wearing gas masks. The very worst experience I have ever had. I have never experienced any fire like it, and never wish to again. Feel the strain of this incessant fire a great deal more than I'd like, and as I am not in very good health and have toothache most of the time. I think I have never had or will ever have a less Merry Christmas than the present year of Grace (!)

Of all the diary entries for 1916, this by Captain Noel is among the most thoughtful:

> I often wonder what we men will be like at the end of the war. If England uses its finest manhood to serve its end in war 'tis a bad outlook for the future generations. 'Tis terrible to think that it is to be produced from the shirkers and physically unfit men at home, but speaking impersonally I think there is a lot of happiness ahead and most of those who come thro' will be given the work of helping England's women to build and raise a

greater England from a stricken nation.[176]

No one could doubt that when this horrendous war ended, there would be much to rebuild. Spirits. Lives. Treasure. If possible, that is. If possible.

CHAPTER IV

1917: Bite and Hold

*If the man can be found who wants war after this—he should be taken
to those rows upon rows of simple wooden crosses outside of Bailleul
and made to mark the ages thereon. He should be taken to this
horrible place and haunted day and night.*

—Harold Brooks *Diary*, 13 July 1917.

If 1916 began with much optimism, the soldiers who survived into 1917 were more callous. Witnesses to the expenditure of lives and material, they held a more somber view of the future. They would win in the end, of course, but the slogging part was not over yet. Such is the sense of their diaries. The British high command believed that more of the same—fine-tuned, perhaps, but essentially, more of the same—would lead to victory.

The army's political masters were not as certain. The War Cabinet as well as the broader Parliament was sensitive to the huge casualty lists. They had a genuine concern about national morale. Would it not be more economical, especially in terms of lives, to essentially remain on the defensive, to allow the naval blockade to strangle the German economy, to allow the German Army to batter itself to death on the British fortifications? General Haig and his senior commanders, although conscious of the cost, believed to the contrary. Allowing the Germans respite from attack only gave them more opportunity to strengthen their defenses so that the ultimate price of conquering them would be that much greater. Yet while there was some concern about General Haig's policies, about his leadership, there were also mixed signals coming from London, for on 1 January 1917, General Haig was promoted to Field Marshal, the highest rank any British Army officer could achieve.

By the beginning of 1917 the now massive BEF under the new Field Marshal's command consisted of fifty-six divisions of infantry with five divisions of cavalry and 1,157 pieces of heavy artillery.[1] Such a large Army was difficult to supply and the weather made sustaining offensive operations even more difficult. At last, the quantity of supplies was quite satisfactory. Getting them to where they were needed was the never-ending challenge. This was primarily a non-motorized army in which the bulk of transportation was horse-drawn.[2] Dennis Wheatley, who had a post-war career as a writer, remembered those challenging days:

> The roads were covered with ice on which at any moment a horse might slip, throw its rider and perhaps break a leg; so hour after hour one had to keep a firm hand on the reigns, never relaxing for a moment, which proved a heavy strain.[3]

Bringing supplies forward was dangerous: the Germans frequently shelled the visible movement. In his post-war memoir, Dennis Wheatley confessed his disobedience to orders:

> Our batteries were up near St Julian and to supply them we had to go round the dead end of the canal on the western edge of ruined Ypres. That was a really nasty spot, pounded by the Germans every few minutes. So when taking up a column I used to halt it a hundred yards short of the canal; then the moment a shell had exploded I gave the signal to gallop and carried the column hell for leather after me before the next shell came down. Of course it was a crime of the first order to gallop horses drawing ammunition limbers or wagons; but I did not give a fig for that.[4]

By this point in the war, the British were even operating veterinary hospitals. There was plenty of work for those treating the horses and mules. An artillery shell could fall among a corral of horses just as it might hit a group of men:

> There were dead [horses] lying all over the place and scores of others were floundering about screaming with broken legs, terrible neck wounds or their entrails hanging out. We went back for our pistols and spent the next hour putting the poor, seriously injured brutes out of their misery by shooting them through the head. To do it we had to wade ankle deep through blood and guts. That night we lost over 100 horses.[5]

The Imperial War Museum maintains a collection of photographs of horses undergoing surgery in the hospital at Abbeville in March, 1917.[6]

One officer summed up the difficulties in delivering supplies in this way:

> Troops had to go overland to all these shell-hole posts every day, the first

time to deliver rations and ammunition and the second time, at night, to bring the tins and hayboxes back, because there wasn't room to keep them in the little shell-holes. You couldn't chuck them over the top because they were needed again.

It was a terrible experience for the ration parties to make two journeys. The troops were from other battalions, because it was realized that the battalion on the line couldn't possibly do it. And they couldn't care less how they did it. The butter came in a round flat tin but bread was just bread and sometimes, when the fellow had fallen about a dozen times, there was a thick paste of dirt and mud all the way round it. Well, chaps started cutting this crust off and throwing it away, but then they found they had no bread left, so they had to eat it.

Oh, the conditions were terrible. You can imagine the agony of a fellow standing for twenty-four hours, sometimes up to his waist in mud, with just a couple of bully beef tins or his mess tin trying to get the water out of this shell-hole. And he had to stay there all day and all night for about six days, that was his existence. And when he got a hot drink, it was tainted with petrol, so he knew that for the next four or five hours he'd be filling a bully beef tin.[7]

That constant mud was perhaps the soldiers' greatest daily obstacle. "For days on end one was stuck in the trenches unable to move forward or backward. And it rained, and it rained, and one wanted to die."[8] "For most of the time it rained and the whole battlefield was one gigantic morass."[9] "I slipped into a shell-hole and got stuck in the mud. It was only up to me knees but it took three men to pull me out...."[10] The mud was so bad that "...half the fellows had their boots sucked off."[11] That wasn't the only obstacle. Pearson reported that "I saw a German pilot dropping bombs by hand", a new consideration.[12] Even those in the best of the available circumstances found the situation quite depressing. The Prince of Wales, the future King Edward VIII, wrote from his post at Army headquarters in Belgium: "Now isn't it about time this bloody war ended?"[13]

A further complication of the supply problem was that in the winter of 1916-1917 many canals in northern France were frozen and so unusable for shipping.[14] Worse, a freighter sank in the harbor at Boulogne in late December 1916 tying up operations there for a month.[15] Captain Peel's diary records the depressing news that "...leave is temporarily closed owing to congestion at [the port of Le] Havre."[16] Late in that year, Captain Peel had occasion to write about his leave: "As usual, we were told a fortnight, promised a month, and given 10 days, but still ten days at Xmas are better than nothing."[17] When a turn for leave did come around, it sometimes had unexpected aspects:

Home at last with my dirty body, lousy clothes and my rifle, which frightened my mother a great deal as she was afraid it might go off accidently...My father put my clothes into the oven and baked them [to kill the lice].[18]

And with regard to lice, no matter how hard the army tried to exterminate them, "...the ubiquitous louse was not banished for long & apparently returned to his nice, cleaned out residence bringing a host of others with him."[19]

The rain and snow and cold, all manner of unpleasant weather, continued unabated and exacerbated the supply situation. The men in the trenches constantly complained of the harsh weather, and meteorological tables bear them out. The winter of 1916-1917 was the most severe in the preceding twenty years. As a result, "Life became a constant struggle to don enough clothes, and to stamp about and flail oneself with sufficient vigour to prevent the blood seemingly freezing in one's veins."[20]

That winter's abundance of ice also formed an additional danger. In one soldier's experience, exploding artillery shells hurled deadly chunks of thick ice at the troops. The impenetrable ice also made it impossible to bury the dead. Water bottles froze and even picks could not open a hole on the frozen local rivers.[21]

In one letter home to "My Dearest Father", Buxton made the best of his situation:

[My new raincoat] has proved very successful in this bad weather. It is very short and so does not trail in the mud. The rest of your body is kept dry by long green thigh boots, a government issue.

We are in the line at the moment with snow & frost. How horrid you say—but this is heavenly compared to the dreaded thaw, when mud & trenches start moving. Clean cold with due precaution can be survived. Rain and mud to the waist as we had last week—is not an effective breeder of health and spirits.[22]

The following month, he thanked his parents for the gloves they had sent for his men since they would provide "invaluable warmth."[23]

Some soldiers experimented with what, given the low level of competition, might be termed cuisine. One fashioned an instrument which became known as a "trench cooker": candles wrapped round with pieces of sacking and placed in a suitable tin pierced with holes."[24] Another soldier became quite creative with the supplies at hand:

I took from our ration four hard army biscuits & moistened them with dilute [*sic*] condensed milk & from our fried bacon (occasional) at breakfast I took the fat & poured that into the biscuit & thus made dough which I then placed into two cigarette tins of the round variety, made a hole down the middle which I filled with jam, replaced the lids & then placed them in my mess tin of water by now boiling over a small fire of wood chips in the side of the trench. About 30 minutes careful boiling and presto, we had delicious steamed jam pudding and were they good.[25]

Another experimenter went into the nearby French town to buys loaves of bread and "Quaker Oats" which he mixed with jam to make a very popular treat which he called "burgo."[26]

There were not many ways to keep warm in the trench. One was to have a fire in a brazier, sort of a small charcoal grill, fueled by coke or dry chips—but the fumes from that in a low lying trench could kill, especially those sleeping in a hole dug into the side of the trench, a "funk" hole.[27] Another method was to use fur undercoats, and sometimes sleeveless leather jerkins: fashion was not a priority by this point in this war.

Life in the trenches remained an incredible daily challenge. Despite living in the open, the men developed few minor ailments such as colds, but trench foot and sheer exhaustion from lack of sleep were common.[28] The daily challenges remained fear, hunger, thirst, physical extremes, deafening noises, sudden flashes of light, cold, and sundry pains. "Intellect and reason had almost no place."[29] The simplest chore could bring disaster: "…one of our lads drove his spade into the ground just beyond us, there was a mighty bang & he lost his foot. He had struck an unexploded shell."[30]

With their minds free to wander, sometimes the soldiers believed preposterous things they would have dismissed out of hand in peacetime. Luther's diary mixes the truthful with the fantastic:

News leaked out that the Germans were starving owing to the naval blockade, and the dead German soldiers were being taken back to fry down for fat. We believed this, as German graves were not very numerous during our advance.[31]

Officers of course had extra burdens. Beside coordinating orders from above, beside maintaining good order and discipline, beside looking after the training and physical well-being of their men, they also had the burdens of supervising and inspecting and endless paperwork, keeping track of stores, equipment, casualty returns, and a thousand other details via reports to higher stations.[32] As the officers bustled about, performing their duties, they became attractive targets for sharpshooters. In fact, an officer stood a one in six chance of being killed and a one in three chance of being wounded.[33]

Pity the shy or very private person, the one who could not produce urine if there were another person in the same vicinity, the "bashful bladder" phenomenon. "If, for instance, you wanted to urinate and otherwise, there was an empty bully beef tin kept on the side of the hole, so you had to do it in front of all your men then chuck the contents, but not the tin, over the top."[34] Another soldier left this unique and uncorroborated testimony:

> (People) do not even know how we believe our bodies, how we urinate or empty our bowels. The answer is simple—it was easy to urinate even lying down, but men could or would not take down their trousers. What of excretion in a man's trousers—clean them out when opportunity arises.[35]

Of all the causes of wounds, those from bullets, as awful as they were, did the least harm to human flesh. Usually, the bullet inflicted a small entry point. On the other hand, shrapnel, which was sharp jagged pieces of metal, often did much greater harm to flesh, both because the shrapnel was bigger but also because it was irregularly-edged and whirling as it impacted, causing a much larger entry wound.

The puncture wound was visible and could be treated, but the less well understood complication was the infection caused by odd bits of cloth (from the uniform) and surface dirt that the foreign body dragged into the soldier's flesh, past the first line of the body's defenses, intact skin.

Visible infections, as earlier noted, were treated by "debridement", simply cutting away the infected tissue and irrigating the area with a mild solution, sometimes just plain salt water—which would often be effective. In fact, sources indicate that between 78 and 82 percent of the wounded returned to active duty.[36]

As the war went on, a new health complication arose. Modern medicine understands what happened much more clearly than did physicians and patients then, of course. There are particular bacteria which are present in the urine of horses and other farm animals. With all the churning of the earth caused by shelling, and with the large concentration of horses in the battle zones, these bacteria contaminated widespread areas. If a soldier was wounded and these particular bacteria got into the wound, a very serious infection was likely to occur. In its most extreme form, this infection is known as Weil's disease. Its symptoms imitate those of so many other diseases that it was hard to diagnose, or rather, without the support of a modern micro-bacterial laboratory, it was hard to be sure that the diagnosis was correct. Remembering that the soldiers lived in a "sewer of human and animal excrement," among the "decomposing carcasses of men and animals,"[37] it should not be surprising that infection entered the wounded bodies from their own filthy uniforms. Rats, too, just as in the plagues of earlier times, spread disease. Nor should one forget the lack of bathing opportunities, the infrequent change of uniforms and underwear, and the imperfections of the food supply, such as the bread dipped in mud mentioned earlier. One physician described the ground as being "...in a rather septic sort of condition."[38]

As the war dragged on and on, medical personnel increased their knowledge, honed their skills and did what they could. Often Colonel Helm's diary records that he was only able to provide painkillers to ease the dying, not postpone the death. But some of the techniques becoming available then seem quite modern: blood transfusions, anesthetic gas, even early model X ray machines. None of these eliminated long-standing enemies of good health including meningitis, an inflammation of the brain; scarlet fever, causing a rash and high fever; typhus, presenting a high fever and delirium: hepatitis, an inflammation of the liver causing extreme tiredness; pneumonia, a grievous breathing problem, and dysentery, whose primary symptom was severe diarrhea. Despite all the opportunities the Grim Reaper had during this war, of the battle casualties, thirty-one percent died; of those contracting sickness or disease, less than one percent died.[39]

This is not to say that all the ill were cured; quite the contrary. Some disorders may still not be fully understood, as recent U.S. military casualties attest. The whole concept of shell shock was controversial. At first, many thought it was cowardice. But then "...the mental and physical trauma of war caused mental instability ranging from headaches and shaking to complete mental breakdown."[40] Some soldiers reached the point of being unable to go on. Captain Robert Graves recorded one such tragic moment:

> [I] spoke to a man who did not respond.... I shook the sleeper by the arm and noticed suddenly the hole in the back of his head. He had taken off the boot and sock to pull the trigger of his rife with one toe. The muzzle was in his mouth.[41]

As time went on, physicians began commonly referring to mental phenomenon as "neurasthenia."[42] That was only one of many new concepts in this war. Another very useful term was NYD(N), which meant "Not Yet Diagnosed (Nervous).[43]

No description of the continuing life in the trenches is complete without repeated mention of the stench. Too many times to count, the two most common complaints in the soldiers' diaries are mud and stench, stench and mud. By this point in the war, the odor was a pungent combination from all of these particulars: chloride of lime, scattered to ease the risk of infection; creosol, to help control flies; latrines, with their natural effluent; smoke from braziers; sweat of thousands of unwashed men; double that number, nearly, of unwashed feet.[44] The picture is painted.

There was another as yet unmentioned health problem. Many soldiers had contracted venereal diseases. As early as the fall of 1914, one colonel had attempted to deal with this situation:

> Our colonel had issued a warning that anyone contracting VD if single he would personally inform the parents, if married inform the wife, also a forfeiture of pay.[45]

Nearly 800 men a month were admitted to the hospital.[46] The army believed the problem could be avoided, and in January 1917 declared that from then on, any man admitted to hospital for VD would be denied leave for the following year.[47] Two years earlier, the army had announced that the victim's wife, parents and family were all to be informed the patient had VD.[48] Those may not have been effective policies, as in 1917 twice as many men were hospitalized with VD as were for pneumonia, frostbite and trench foot combined.[49]

While their troops struggled with the elements, the senior staff of the British Army was deeply engaged in planning a joint campaign with their French allies. Disappointed in the course of the war so far, the French government had entrusted command to General Robert Neville. Exuding confidence while lacking common sense, General Neville promised a spectacular break-through followed by a romp to Berlin. In order to tie down potential reinforcements from intervening in the French attack, the British were asked to make a preliminary assault. Haig knew this would be costly. He knew this would be bloody. He knew this campaign would be ill received at home. However, he accepted that:

> We willingly play a second role to the French, that is, we are to make a holding attack to draw in the enemy's reserves so as to make the task of the French easier. We shall at any rate have heavy losses, with the possibility of no showy successes, whereas the French are to make the decisive attack with every prospect of gaining the fruits of victory. I think it is for the general good that we play this role in support of the French, but let the future critics realize that we have adopted it with our eyes open as to the probable consequences.[50]

The French explained their plans to the British War Cabinet in London in January 1917. One result was that the BEF was yet again to take over more of the French trenches, thus freeing those troops for the upcoming offensive. Meanwhile Haig was given just two additional divisions of troops although he had requested five. He was also ordered to start his next offensive on 1 April rather than his preferred date of 1 May.[51]

As the Commander-in-Chief continued his planning, the month of February brought significant developments. First, the German Army quietly pulled back from their existing trenches into a new fortified position known as the Hindenburg line. By carefully selecting exactly where to locate these new defenses, the Germans maximized the use of local geography, managed to reduce the holding forces by 12 divisions (which could then be employed elsewhere) and set up a new defensive strategy.[52] Captain Peel and his men hurried along behind the Germans, and he wrote:

> The Boche really is a swine. The absolutely wanton destruction all through the country where he has retired is wicked. All the big trees along the main road are sawn off within two feet of the ground, all the houses and churches wreaked and the fruit trees and gooseberry bushes cut down. Bridges and roads are of course of military importance but not trees and orchards.[53]

Another British soldier regarding the new enemy position for the first time was quite impressed with its formidability, since it had "...cruel large barbed wire in no man's land, concrete trenches, (and a) machine gun defense."[54]

The Germans had a number of good reasons for retreating to this new line. They had gotten wind of the Neville plan, the general outlines of which were quite widely known, even to the German High Command. As part of their reaction, the Germans would employ an elastic defense in depth. In front would be the thinly held outpost zone. Attackers against this would be canalized towards the battle zone of mutually supporting strong points. Behind those would be rearward defenses. The last piece of the new strategy was the inclusion of counterattack divisions to promptly expel successful attackers.[55] Such a plan demonstrated that the Germans had learned a great deal from their recent experiences.

February also brought news of a new policy at sea. Germany announced a resumption of unrestricted submarine warfare. That meant Germany was reviving the idea of a "war zone" around the British Isles, and a policy that any ship entering that zone was liable to be sunk. This was a logistical strategy,[56] intending to deprive the British army of the supplies needed to fight, and to deprive the British home front of the food needed to carry on. The German navy calculated that if they could sink 600,000 tons of British shipping a month, not only would the British be unable to feed themselves, but the British army, too would grind to a halt; out of gas, metaphorically speaking; out of ammunition, practically speaking; out of just about everything else, realistically speaking.

The British Admiralty reached similar conclusions. Senior naval officers firmly believed that *if* that much were sunk, the war was lost. "The Atlantic lifeline was Britain's centre of gravity: the thing which, if attacked successfully, would cause maximum damage to its war effort."[57] A great volume of munitions was arriving by ship from the United States and Canada. But as was so often the case in planning for this war, there is that grand subjunctive, the nebulous "if." In this case, much was riding on "if" that much were sunk.

At first, the submarine policy was a success: 259 ships sunk in February, another 325 in March—nearly twenty-five percent of all the Britain-bound ships that month failed to arrive. In April, 849,000 tons of shipping became new homes for fish.[58] Not only were those particular cargoes lost, but that same ship would never sail again. In modern economic terms, the "opportunity cost", the number of future loads that ship might have carried, were also lost. Sinking an individual ship has a multiplied effect far beyond just the current cargo.

It might surprise the modern reader to know that even with a war on, the British continued to publish sailing data every day. For example, *The Times*, confident of victory, published this data on 15 March 1917. These numbers represent all ships sailing or arriving at all United Kingdom (England, Scotland, Wales and Northern Ireland) ports for these three weeks:

	March 11	March 4	Feb. 23
Arriving:	1,985	2,587	2,280
Leaving:	1,959	2,477	2,261

They seem to have had a cocky confidence that even if Germany had this data, they could not do much about it. Meanwhile, projecting such confidence helped keep the insurance premiums for the ships from becoming prohibitive. The attitude seems to have been that yes, Germany will sink some of our ships, but not enough to matter—except that it will bring into play the immense power of the United States.

That new German unrestricted sinking policy did come with a grievous consequence. Earlier rounds of submarine activity had moved the United States of America much farther from the "neutral" column, much closer to the "at war" column. President Woodrow Wilson had made it abundantly clear that the American Congress would be asked to enter the war on the Allied side if Germany kept killing U.S. civilians, if Germany kept sinking neutral merchant ships. The Germans knew full well that the American population was double theirs, that America could become a great military power again.[59]

This offered a clear if terrible choice for the Germans. Their foremost experts asserted that a really effective submarine campaign would take the British out of the war before American power could come to bear. The Allies knew from their own recent experience how long it would take the U.S. to become an effective military power. That time would be measured in many months, if not years. Meanwhile, the American army as calculated in Berlin was both puny and very far away. In 1864, at the end of the civil war, the United States army had been perhaps the strongest in the world. In the intervening fifty years, it had lost both its combat-experienced officers and its grand size. There was little respect for its recent mission of chasing Mexicans in border skirmishes. By the time it could become a real power again, were all to go according to German hopes, the war would be over, Britain starved into submission, France defeated, Russia overwhelmed, Germany triumphant—and the U.S. left with no place to bring its army ashore. So, all things considered, Germany moved to end the near deadlock on the western front by unleashing more than one hundred submarines onto the British lifelines.

The Americans were already angry with Germany over the Zimmermann telegram. This was a secret proposal to the Mexican government that if war broke out between the US and Germany, if Mexico would ally with Germany, Mexico would regain the states of Texas and Arizona at the conclusion of the war. The British intercepted this message and made it public. The previous sinking of the *Lusitania*, the fresh insult of the Zimmermann telegram and the sinking of seven American ships was enough to have Congress declare that war existed between Germany and the US on April 6, 1918. While there was little immediate change on the battlefield, within 13 months there would be over one million American soldiers in Europe, and those would be backed by the enormous industrial might of the United States. The German gamble over submarine warfare would not end well for them.

Meanwhile, there was some more immediate bad news for the British. In March, 1917, just as feared, a revolution erupted against the Tsar and the suffering caused by the war, and a new government took power in Russia. While that government professed its desire to continue the war, its actual ability to do so, especially in light of Russia's already fearsome losses, was questionable. The consequence to the BEF was, of course, that if the Russians stopped fighting, more German troops could be brought from Russia to fight on the Western Front, to fight the already rather thin British lines. Even the common soldiers followed this news: "...the Russians were in a bad state & their collapse could release countless men for the Western front...."[60]

With all these matters and many more on his mind, the Commander in Chief moved forward with his plan to decoy the Germans away from the Neville attack. The BEF would attack at Arras. Again, the hope was not so much for a brilliant victory here as it was for a distraction to help the French in their much touted effort.

The target area was more than twenty miles wide centering on the Vimy ridge. Very detailed plans were constructed for this battle. It would use all four divisions of Canadians as well as British divisions. A large scale model of the German trenches was constructed using aerial photographs taken from planes and balloons. Each man was trained in his own task as well as what the man on his right and on his left was to do, so that even as casualties thinned the attackers, the attack could push forward. Specific tasks were assigned each man.[61] For example, some carried rifles while others specialized in carrying grenades and throwing them at machine guns, while still others carried light machine guns themselves. A preliminary bombardment of more than one and a half million shells was planned, a theoretically non-survivable hellfire.

Numerous mines were dug under the area and used as temporary shelters for the massing troops. Using them, soldiers were brought up close to their starting points but still under protection until the last possible moment. Hiding them from the Germans increased the chance of a surprise attack. Meanwhile, the Germans refined their defensive tactics. Now they would station their new counter-attack troops fifteen miles behind the lines—but that was too far back to be speedily deployed if needed in what had been up-to-now a "quiet sector."

Some of these mines were as much as thirty feet below the surface. Using as a rule of thumb that the modern office building is constructed with about ten feet per story of height, this means these soldiers descended the equivalent of three stores below ground before they began to move toward the enemy. At the same time, the Germans were also constructing trenches, and there were occasional subterranean conflicts to join those in the air, at sea, underwater, and now, underland. From time to time, one side would set off explosives near the other's underground efforts. Special devices called "geophones" and looking very much like a stethoscope were used to try to hear the enemy miners.[62]

The story of the mines in this war is another fascinating tale. Some truly brutal battles were fought entirely underground among soldiers brilliantly termed "military troglodytes."[63] For example, when the British detected German miners nearby, they tried to locate the enemy mine as precisely as possible. Men whose civilian occupation had been as miners had invaluable skills in such matters. Once located, a small shaft was drilled into the enemy mine, and then either poison gas or a small explosive called a "camouflet", a sort of underground hand grenade, was used to kill them. A second small shaft was sometimes drilled further back along the enemy tunnel in an effort to kill the rescue party sent to aid the original miners.[64] So now this chessboard war of move and countermove had an underground component.

Mines had multiple purposes. They were used as an undercover walkway, that is, a protected path to get from one point to another. They were also a storage facility, sheltering ammunition and water supplies, even sleeping areas and hospitals. A different type of mine was tunneled toward and beneath the enemy trench. Once packed with explosives, it became another weapon in the ever-increasing arsenal. The hope was that a large explosion, set off in conjunction with an infantry attack, would blow a huge hole in the enemy trenches, kill the enemy machine gunners, and allow a rapid advance through what had been the nearly impenetrable enemy line. The problem, of course, is that while it may have ripped a big hole in the defenses, it also left the ground so rough and debris-strewn that it was still a serious obstacle to the heavily laden troops trying to advance.

The farmland of modern Belgium still suffers from these days of mines. As the mines were dug, the dirt had to be hidden from German observation. It was in fact spread stealthily and at night on top of the farmland nearby. Yet this soil from so deep beneath the surface turned out to be remarkably infertile—and today some formerly productive farmland which was covered with this sterile waste still cannot grow crops.[65]

With the preparations as complete as time allowed, the battle of Arras was begun in less than ideal weather conditions. Sleet and snow blanketed the entire area, making both observation and movement extra difficult. Tanks were quite ineffective this time. There were only sixty available, and they suffered ditching, breakdowns or damage from shellfire.[66] One of the British generals reported to Haig that the snow and shell holes had made "the going... very bad indeed."[67] Yet at first, the 9 April attack moved forward rather well. The less-well defended forward trenches fell to the British. But all too soon the usual problems arose. Men who had raced across no-man's-land were soon exhausted. The German resistance became stronger, especially two days later when reserves began to arrive. After the first hours, not a great deal of progress was being made, but the Field Marshal was reluctant to call off the effort, as the French offensive, he knew, remained in deep trouble. He kept it going with varying degrees of intensity until 23 May and at the price of over 150,000 fresh casualties, the British had gained a few miles of strategically insignificant territory. It is important to recall, however, that Haig remained convinced these costly battles were the price that had to be paid to keep the Germans off balance and to wear down their army until it was unable to stop the Allies.

By early May, Haig was privy to the devastating details about the French attack. The Neville offensive was not just a failure, it was a catastrophe. Not only had the French army failed to win, but it had nearly destroyed itself in the effort. In three weeks of fighting, the army had suffered more than

200,000 casualties.[68] Worse still was the defeatist mood of the French troops who remained in the trenches. Promised victory, they felt betrayed. Having given their all, they felt let down by the Army's leadership. In fact, the French army was in a state of near mutiny. Having lost faith in itself, feeling that winning the war was beyond its capabilities, it cast off General Neville and waited to see how General Pétain would go about healing it. The new French commander visited Haig:

> General Petain showed me his latest reports. According to those there are today only 35,000 men in the depots to meet wastage.[69] This he said must mean that each month <u>one</u> French Division must disappear, unless the Americans can be induced to send over men to enlist in the French army! I think there is very little chance of their doing so![70]
>
> Meanwhile, the French army was unreliable: yes, it would defend its trenches—but it would not advance beyond them.[71]

There was more bad news. The German submarine campaign was utilizing several ports in Belgium as home bases for submarines. Haig was urged to consider attacking in that direction to deny these bases to the Germans. This concentrated his attention once again to the area around Ypres and he considered another major offensive there.

These developments along with the weakness of Russia, the failure of the Neville offensive and the submarine losses passed the burden back to the British. The Russians were in distress, the French near collapse: only Great Britain remained powerful and determined, if bloodied. In fact, 1917 saw the apex of British power: her military effort topped out at feeding 2,700,000 men as well as 400,000 horses and mules and providing fuel for 50,000 motor vehicles, a military presence unprecedented in British military history before or since.[72] For the supply officers, just having an adequate number of horses on hand for immediate needs was never enough, because by the very nature of war, many of them were destined to die in combat or related activities and need to be replaced.

All this movement of supplies had to be sustained by vast amounts of cross-channel shipping. Docks to send it were available: docks to receive it had to be enlarged. Big ships, little ships, tiny ships: the cross-channel traffic was terrific. Harbor masters, officers setting priorities for access to ship docks and anchorages, traffic controllers of seagoing cargos, were very busy indeed.

The British Grand Fleet was charged with protecting the dock areas. Stationed in the north of Scotland to be safe from submarines, it was in position to block any German raids on the shipping—or to cut off any would-be raiders as they tried to return to German bases. To be clear: German ships could probably raid the ports, but it would be a 'suicide mission, as the Royal Navy all but definitely would to be able to cut them off from home.

In the first few months of the renewed submarine offensive, the Germans enjoyed remarkable success. However, at the insistence of some junior officers in the Admiralty, a convoy system was instituted. Ships of all sizes and speeds were gathered into a group shepherded by small warships called "destroyers" which escorted the little flock from port to port. These small but seagoing vessels were ferocious defenders of their charges. Spotting a U-boat, they would shoot at it or attempt to ram and sink it. Failing those, they would drop a new weapon called a depth charge into the sea as close as possible to the submarine. Looking very much like oil drums these were filled with explosives. If they detonated close enough to the submarine to crack its waterproof hull, the ocean would finish the job. Before convoys were instituted, German submarines were terrifically successful; after the convoys began, much less so.

The early successes of the German submarine campaign truly frightened even some very senior British Admirals. The most prominent among them was Admiral Sir John Jellicoe, who had gone from Commander-in-Chief of the Home Fleet, the premier naval command, to First Lord of The Admiralty, the individual most responsible for all things naval. As such, he sat in the War Cabinet and rendered professional opinions. Field Marshal Haig's diary records a very strange session in exactly this way:

Secret

[A most serious and startling situation was disclosed today]. At today's conference Admiral Jellicoe as First Sea Lord stated that owing to [the great shortage of shipping due to German submarines] it would be impossible for Great Britain to continue the war in 1918. This was a bomb shell for the cabinet, [and all present] and a full inquiry is to be made as to the real facts on which this opinion [of the Naval Authorities] is based. No one present shared Jellicoe's view, and all seem satisfied that the food reserves in Great Britain are adequate. [Jellicoe's words were. 'There is no good discussing plans for next spring. We cannot go on.']73

Jellicoe must have been under a terrific strain. Earlier, while Jellicoe was in command of the most powerful British fleet, Churchill remarked that "Jellicoe was the only man who could lose the war in an afternoon."74 Whatever the Admiral's opinion, the facts of the matter were quite different. Of the 5,090 ships convoyed, only sixty-three were lost.75 In fact, not only did a busy flow of supplies continue but an astonishing total of 800,000 parcels—gifts from home—reached the BEF in each week of April 1917.76

The German calculations were grievously flawed. They miscalculated the available cargo space of Allied shipping, they overestimated the British dependence on grain imports and they underestimated the British ability to ration. "The British government indeed operated a siege economy so successfully that by the end of 1917 its grain reserves had actually doubled."[77]

The British managed to reduce the amount of shipping required in some rather interesting ways. For example on 5 May 1917, Haig ordered the Quartermaster General "...to make hay on all possible areas which have been recently taken from the enemy."[78] In fact, he also authorized a "Farm Directorate" "to grow crops and ease the strain on shipping by food production."[79] What previous British general had ever given orders to start farms, to plant crops?

Just how serious was the submarine menace? In his book published after the war, Winston Churchill argued that the Germans did not operate from Belgian bases to any great extent but rather from their home bases. He believed his successors at the Admiralty had "misled" Haig and his staff:

> It seemed to throw the Army into the struggle against the submarines. It confused the issue, it darkened counsel, it numbed misgivings, overpowered the dictates of prudence and cleared the way for a forlorn expenditure of valour and life without equal in futility.[80]

Did the German submarine campaign seriously hurt the British war effort? Sir Arthur Yapp, who was in charge of food production, told the *Pall Mall Gazette* in 1917 that Britain had to help Italy and France with food, because France that year produced less corn than it had in 1914. The British had it to spare. In fact, on 12 November 1917, the same official announced an increase in the home front food ration for everyone. All was not hunky-dory, there were some shortages but massive suffering, no.[81] To publicize the successful food conservation program, the *Pall Mall Gazette* of 15 November 1917 reported that the King himself visited the dockyards and viewed a giant granary apparatus that could discharge grain from a ship at the extraordinary rate of 300 tons an hour. To publicize this action was to twist the hungry German eagle's tail.

Field Marshal Haig often repeated his argument as to how the war must be fought. Each time there were heavy casualties, he had to explain or defend his policy. To halt now, to wait for the Americans, would discourage his army, allow the Germans to build even more formidable defenses, pass the initiative to them, and cost far more in the long run.[82] No, argued Haig, better to carry on with the "...wearing down character..." of these battles.[83] He was clear and emphatic in his view, as he wrote to General Robertson: "...it would be unwise, unsound and probably in the long run more costly in men and money to cease offensive operations at an early date."[84] His point of view was buttressed from time to time by modest success. Gone were the early months of the war when vast movements in short time were still possible. However, there were moments of sharp hope: Easter Monday, 9 April 1917 was the most successful day for the BEF since trench warfare had begun, in terms of land retaken.[85] Fully three and a half miles had been reclaimed on just that one day, and hopes were high for more. But the price paid for these modest triumphs was still so high:

In a typical offensive men would have to go over the top time and time again, attacking, fighting off counter-attack, being shelled, receiving neither water nor food, nor being able to take more than a few minutes sleep for days at a time.[86]

Not everyone agreed with the commanding General's strategy. David Lloyd George was troubled by those horrific casualty lists. The Prime Minister and some of his colleagues "...worried about British manpower, which they considered a precious, finite resource."[87] Churchill wrote after the war that by this point in 1917, "Mr. Lloyd George was now content to await in the main theatre the arrival of the American armies. He wished for Sir Douglas Haig to maintain an active defensive for the rest of the year and to nurse his strength."[88]

On the other hand, Field Marshal Haig had his supporters as well. In those days, before the idea of a press conference, ministers would accept speaking engagements before various audiences, such as a local meeting of their political party, and use the moment to review national issues and political questions. In 1917, Neville Chamberlain was the Director-General of National Service (and a future Prime Minister). He spoke before a crowd in Cardiff, Wales, and told his audience that:

...we shall be breaking the German line when we chose and where we chose... our ability to carry out that operation depends on one thing, and that is that we should be able to supply our gallant Field-Marshal Haig with the drafts of men that he will require when he has shaken the foe and when the time has come to throw fresh forces into the field to clinch the victory that has been begun.[89]

While the Field Marshal had his supporters, not all military authorities agreed with him. One of his own Generals, Sir William Robertson, worried that Haig would "...get carried away and exhaust the one reliable army left to the Allies...."[90]

General Robertson had a point. Conditions for the men in the trenches were no better. While leaders reflected and debated, men in the trenches lost fingers and toes to frostbite, lost their lives to German shells and sharpshooters. One soldier wrote thanking his mother for the "...six dozen pairs of gloves and the 2 dozen pairs of socks" she had sent for his men.[91] In early February he reported that "...the thermometer has certainly never been as high as freezing for 3 weeks..."[92] Captain Peel had this observation: "This place looks very funny in snow, all the humps made by shells, and the stark remnants of woods on the top of the hills."[93] Yet by now experience had taught him what was to come as the snow melted: "This will be a lovely spot in a few days, right up to the eyes."[94] The harsh weather made the care of the horses more difficult: a fresh four inches of snow meant "We had a busy time roughing the horses to get them along."[95]

Another soldier remembered his residence from this time very well: "At times our living shacks were self-constructed from ammunition boxes & biscuit tins filled with earth & used as bricks for wall building ...(with) salvaged lumber for the roof...."[96] He also remembered seeking divine intervention, a rare comment in these diaries: "Oh! God, look after me now & bring me safely through this & I'll be a different and better chap when I get out...."[97]

There were some disturbing situations as well. As the Germans retreated to the Hindenburg line and the British followed, they found unburied bodies of their countrymen from the battle on 1 July 1916, bodies that had undergone six months of decomposition.[98]

That March was cold. In fact, there was "...wind enough to cut you in two; in fact the horses would hardly face it."[99] And yet there was also joy, sometimes from the most mundane events, such as when a new pet arrived; "Peter", a collie who was "charming with all."[100] Not all animals were as fortunate as Peter: Trooper Stanley Dawn recalled that "...often one could hear the howling of a starving and homeless dog somewhere in the ruins."[101] Of course the food complaints remained:

> About 12:30 all men were finished (digging new trenches) and then tea was served—what a mockery! About two tablespoonful's for two of us.[102]

Field Marshal Haig was pleased with the rate at which supplies were coming forward, but perhaps not many of his men would have agreed with the first part of an observation he made on 13 April:

> It is fairly easy work moving these great heavy guns nowadays by means of tractors. The real difficulty is getting the large amount of shells forward. Luckily our railways are following our advance well.

Haig did recognize the difficulties many faced in supplying the army:

The motor lorry drivers have been doing very well. Regularly night after
night they have gone through Ypres in spite of heavy shell fire, and [suffering]
a considerable number of casualties. These men have shown that they have
the same spirit as the fighting soldiers![103]

No matter how hard the supply personnel worked, there was always an
unexpected occurrence to reduce availability and complicate their task. For
example, one soldier recorded that the "...Germans shelled the wagon line
and it was a hard job to stop the horses stampeding about 40 of B Battery did
get away."[104] Late in the year he noted that German shelling killed 5 horses
and wounded 14.[105] All of these had to be replaced.

Personal supplies were arriving in great quantity as well, and some soldiers
presented "wish lists" to their families:

My dear ones,
I can do with parcels in the shape of hams, fruit, in fact any dainty which
is not issued by a munificent Government.... I have just remembered the
brandy balls and plain chocolate are boons, and speaking of same I want a
small bottle of Martello.[106]

By 1 May, there was a break in the weather, which was just fine with
Captain Peel: "The horses are looking very happy in the sun; warmpth [sic]
and light will have done wonders for them." Having moved closer to the new
German trenches, his own accommodations had improved: "We no longer live
in deep damp and dark doughouts [sic]....." He was infected with this grand
note of optimism: "Well, we're winning anyhow, and we shall all be home
for Christmas if not before." On 7 May he added: "The papers are coming
very well now. I got yesterday's times [sic] like I always used to." By the time
August came, he was almost jolly:

This really is quite a bon spot, we have got the gramophone up at the guns,
and all sleep in pyjamas, so it is not too bad. Also one had a lovely view from
the [observation post] and can see towns and trains and all sorts of exciting
things.[107]

By mid-May, 1917, the battle of Arras was over. Little progress had been
made, but Haig had higher hopes for his next planned effort, to take the
ridge almost due south of Ypres. Capturing the Messines ridge would, he
believed, open the door for a renewed attack close to Ypres, and victory

there would open the long road to Berlin.

General Herbert Plumer was tasked with capturing the Messines ridge. He skillfully planned to use every weapon in the arsenal. There was a concentrated and intense artillery bombardment. Tanks and poison gas were on hand. A "creeping barrage" was designed: just as the infantry moved forward, the artillery would slowly change their targets from the front to further back, thus offering the foot soldiers the most protection possible. There was also another tactic: twenty-one mines had been laboriously dug under the German trenches. The hope was to simultaneously detonate all of them. In the midst of the resultant death, damage and confusion, according to the plan, British troops would pour into and over the German positions.

Not all went according to plan, however. The barrage by more than 2,500 guns terrorized the enemy for more than two weeks. When it suddenly stopped at 2:50 on the morning of 7 June, the German troops hurried from their shelters back into the trenches and the machine gun emplacements. Forty minutes later, the order was given to detonate the mines, and nineteen of them went off. The resulting explosions may have been the loudest man-made sound ever generated until then. Some sources say it was heard as far away as Dublin.

The actual damage was spectacular. The huge holes in the German lines were soon the route of advance for nine British divisions. They quickly occupied their targets and prepared to hold on to them. German counter-attacks were beaten back, and the British had a victory at a cost of nearly 25,000 casualties. Haig recorded:

The operations today are probably the most successful I have yet undertaken.... Our losses are reported to be very small. *Under* 11,000 for nine divisions which attacked. Our front of attack was 9 miles in length.[108]

Does Haig's phrase, "*Under* 11,000 casualties", indicate how realistically he viewed casualties, or does it indicate a stoic acceptance of them?

There are several important things to note about this battle. First, as a result of the mines, the defensive power of the trenches was seriously compromised before the first attacker went over the top. So, obviously, the key to victory henceforth would be extensive mining, would it not? Unfortunately, in a word, no. The picturesque windmills of Flanders are not there just as public art; they perform a real and necessary service in pumping rainwater out of the below-sea-level fields. With the skills and technology available at the time, a mine might be dug, yes, but it could not be kept dry.

Within the last ten years, a remaining section of British trench in Belgium passed into private hands. The new owner attempted to preserve the site, and spent a great deal of time and effort to pump out the water, especially in the bunker part that was in places twenty or thirty feet underground. Today there is a locked steel gate over the entrance, because the trench has re-flooded, in some places, back to thirty feet deep. It simply cannot be kept dry at an economical cost. It also would not be safe to open it to tourists without a great number of expensive safety upgrades, such as making sure there are no live munitions where tourists could hurt themselves. In sum, then, mines, so prone to flooding both now and then, would not end this war.

One more point about Messines concerns the mines themselves. Twenty-one were constructed: only nineteen were detonated. On 17 July 1955, almost forty years later, the twentieth mine did detonate—set off by a lightning strike on the electrical tower that had been unwittingly constructed above it. The only casualty was a dead cow. The last mine may have been found nearby, but it seems that no efforts are underway to deal with it.[109]

A very serious point about Messines is that it gave the impression that all the tricks were now learned, the rest of the war would be less difficult. It was so easy to overlook the effort that had gone into this, the intense preparation, the stockpiling of artillery shells, for example. This could be used as a template for future efforts, perhaps, but that did not mean the next "big push" would be any easier. Most bluntly stated, at this rate, needing this many lives and this amount of supplies to advance this distance, did the nation have the means to win? That is a valid question, and schools of thought, serious and deadly schools of thought, supported each side. Haig made his position clear:

> For two weeks in June, he had to defend his plans in Whitehall (with the army high command) and Westminster (with the Prime Minister and politicians). At stake was the fundamental issue of whether the government would permit the British army to mount the major offensive in Flanders that Haig planned. Constitutionally, His Majesty's Government had every right to forbid it.[110]

But they did not, and Haig proceeded with his plans to move out from the Ypres salient, to fight a third battle of Ypres, this time named for the village just north east of Ypres, the soon to be famous Passchendaele. Once that crossroads was secure, Haig hoped to turn north and reach the seacoast, further securing his supply lines and turning the German flank. A powerful additional benefit would be pushing the submarines out of their Belgian bases.

Training for the next battle incorporated all the hard-won lessons of the war thus far. Individual soldiers had specific tasks, whether grenade throwers, machine gunners, pill box destroyers and the like. Sharpshooters held places in artificial trees, and camouflage was used more and more.[111]

Additional artillery was brought forward and ammunition was stockpiled.

On 18 July 1917, an intense artillery barrage was launched and kept up for ten days until more than four million shells were fired. By now such a barrage was *de rigueur*, Lord Kitchener's earlier advice to "practice economy" long gone.

There also was a unique feature to this battle. The plan had called for British troops to land along the North Sea behind the German lines, in an amphibious attack similar to those at Normandy during the Second World War. But a heavy German bombardment on the assembly area for this amphibious attack blew it, as it were, out of the water. In addition, the Germans also used a new poison, mustard gas, which:

.... may have been the most heinous of all the gases used in the war. Unlike the earlier lung gases such as phosgene, mustard gas attacked the entire body, inside and out. The results were horrifying: it seeped through clothing and caused grotesque blistering and lesions, actually peeling off layers of skin. Infection invariably set in. Victims went blind and began to cough up blood as their lungs were eaten away. Worse, unlike phosgene, it lingered, so that doctors and nurses themselves were quickly infected when they tried to remove the victim's clothes – or just from the fumes of contaminated clothes. Then they, too, began to turn yellow; even their hair turned yellow.[112]

Captain J. C. Hill had this experience with mustard gas:

The men were blinded and couldn't see at all, and they were choking— thousands had to leave the line. Fortunately, one or two of these shells hadn't exploded, so I got one of them and nursed it on my knees all the way back to the research station. But it took our best chemist weeks to find out what this new substance was. It was a dreadful oily liquid called dichlorodiethylsulphide that evaporated very slowly. Because it had such a faint smell the troops tended to take no notice of it, then when they did feel their eyes smarting, it was too late. If they got it on the soles of their boots it would go through and burn their feet. And if they got some on their boots then went into a hut or a dugout and slept there, they would gas everyone else in it too.[113]

Perhaps worst of all, mustard gas would linger on clothing affecting rescue personnel, even days later.[114]

While gas may have been a pretty terrifying weapon, it was not all that effective. It was in fact surprisingly non-lethal. While one third of the soldiers hit by shell fragments or bullets were killed, less than one in twenty of the gas casualties died. In fact, ninety-three percent returned to duty within a few weeks.[115] Gas attacks did consume precious resources, however. By the end of the war, the British manufactured thirteen million gas masks.[116]

The Germans also tried a few new tricks about this time. One soldier recalled that:

> Suddenly, a mounted man came galloping... shouting to us as he passed: "Get Out! Get Out! The Germans are coming!" Afterwards we were told that the enemy had sent a number of their men ahead dressed in captured British uniforms, whose job it was to spread panic in our retreating army.[117]

Meanwhile, British and German aircraft contested for control of the skies over Flanders. Airplanes were quite new, of course, and airplanes used as weapons newer still. But each side wanted to observe the other's gun positions and troop movements. Each side wanted to bomb the other. Together, the British and French planes outnumbered the German aircraft over Ypres by two to one.

The total attacking force, British and French combined, was nearly 500,000 men, 3,000 guns, and 136 tanks. In light of the qualified success at Messines, it appeared that all was in order for another victory. Careful planning, adequate stockpiles of munitions, clearly chosen targets, well trained troops: the factors that could contribute to victory were as much in line as they could be. The one crucial factor beyond either side's control was the weather. For much of the next several months, the weather did not aid the attack.

The British path at Passchendaele was essentially uphill. They underestimated one effect this would have on the attack. The more they shelled the German positions, the more they interfered with rainwater drainage. A pre-war series of canals, ditches and trenches had carried off excess rainwater. But now, that system was essentially destroyed, and each shell explosion, of which there were millions, made it just that much worse. Men do not move well in mud, horses do not move well in mud, mules do not move well in mud and tanks do not move in mud at all. What an irony: the more the German trenches were shelled, the worse the ground conditions became for the attacking British. "No doubt thousands and thousands of our shells just plodded into the earth, making more water filled shell holes, making it impossible to advance."[118]

Over the next few weeks the troops fought the weather almost as much as the Germans. From 30 July to 31 August, to hear the soldiers tell it, it never stopped raining.[119] One artilleryman, W. T. Grant, observed: "Saturday morning it was still raining it not having ceased since the day of the advance; it was a pitable [sic] sight to see this state of the men, especially the infantry who were up to their waist in mud and water."[120] He also wrote on 31 July:

"At night the rain came down in torrents making the ground like one vast sea of mud nearly up to the men's knees." He added on 16 August 1917: "...the infantry went over but it was terrible for them being nearly up to their waist in mud and water made it very hard and difficult to advance...."

Grant was certainly not alone in recognizing the difficulties the mud presented. Bombardier J. W. Palmer saw it also:

> It was mud, mud everywhere: mud in the trenches, mud in front of the trenches, mud behind the trenches. Every shell-hole was a sea of filthy oozing mud. I suppose there is a limit to everything, but the mud of Paschendale— to see men sinking into the slime, dying in the slime—I think it absolutely finished me off.[121]

The Commander-in-Chief was aware of the difficulties, writing in his diary on 1 August: "A terrible day of rain. The ground is like a bog in this low lying country!" He added: "I judged we are fortunate not to have advanced to [today's assigned target] because it would not have been possible to supply our guns with ammunition. Our troops would thus have been at the mercy of a hostile counter-attack and a check might have resulted." He was pleased with the action of one of his subordinate generals, Lord Cavan:

> Owing to the mud, he made special arrangements for passing up freshly cleaned rifles to replace those clogged with mud and grit. 'Armourer shops' were sent forward for that purpose.[122]

The mud was so bad that in places the newly laid railway lines were actually sinking halfway up the boilers of the engines.[123] One soldier wrote to his parents: "...the ground we had to go over was awful, full of shell holes and nearly all of them full of water. If you got in one of them you would have a poor chance of getting out for they are 6 or 7 feet deep and full of mud and water."[124]

The soldier just quoted, Percy Smith, marks a new presence in this study. He was not a volunteer. He was a conscript. Beginning in 1916, as the pool of volunteers ran dry, the government resorted to the draft. While the other major powers had long used conscription, even in peacetime, this was new to the British. Reading Smith's diary and comparing it to all the others read up to this point, there is a profound difference. This is only anecdotal evidence, of course, but there is a quite noticeable change in tone: Smith complains, complains, complains. To tag him with a classic phrase, Shakespeare's *Henry V* would have accused him of "remembering with advantages." He wrote this on 17 September 1917 about mail censorship:

The reason is that if the relations and wifes [*sic*] of us boys know the real state of affairs and how they would worry more and most likely there would be an unrest on the country and so to carry on this terrible work which after three years of plunder and sacrifice is still likely to go on for a long time yet, you are not allowed to know what the boys have to go through out here.[125]

On 18 September 1917, his letter to his parents recalls a "...pontoon bridge about 2 miles long for all the ground was flooded by the Belgians" and adds that the Germans began firing at him: "He [the Germans] opened out with artillery and threw Krupps Factory at us." Krupps factory, of course, was the world famous and enormously large armaments factory in Germany. Needless to say, he exaggerated the intensity of the attack he endured.

Smith also breaks another unwritten rule of the brotherhood of the trench dwellers. He is too candid. Again writing to his parents, Smith laments: "[This] is not a war of fighting for rifles are not used like they used to be in other wars, it is a war of machines, terrible machines."[126]

Other individuals in the King's army also suffered, but also managed to see a brighter side, sometimes in the simple things, such as the new pet dog mentioned earlier, or in the box of gloves, a gift of love from home. On a rare day in that muddy July, Barclay Buxton wrote a moving letter to his parents:

I think of you today—a lovely sunny evening, as I sit in the tent with the band outside playing. Your wedding day. God bless you both in all your love for each other, for us your sons & for the greatest of all His work.[127]

What makes this letter all the more poignant is knowing that just five days later his brother George was killed, and he wrote another letter to his parents regretting that he could not be at home to help them deal with that.[128]

There is more bad than good remembered in the soldiers' diaries. An artilleryman named Grant recorded an attack on 14 July 1917 that left "60 [men] going stone blind." On 20 August he reported that a German plane dropped a bomb that killed one man and 110 horses and mules. A month later he observed:

...the whole way from Achonvilles being a mass of ruin and desolation, not a tree or building of any sort standing, there were small cemeteries both British and German all along the roadside with hundreds of small white crosses and black iron crosses dotted over the recent battlefields with an occasional tricolor rosette to mark the grave of a French civilian.[129]

In the Imperial War Museum are the papers of Sir Jonathan Peel. He is not a famous war poet, but in March, 1918 he wrote this poem which his family preserved in this form:

Ypres—July, 1917

Nothing but filth and sandbags, rotted and torn to bits,
Debris, and scraps of iron, the guns in their shallow pits,
The ammunition beside them, handy, with fuses set,
And not even enough protection to keep out the soaking wet;
   The men in their cheerless dugouts—just holes in the side of a trench,
With a sheet of tin on the top—and the loathsome sickly stench
Of mud and nothing but mud—of men, and guns, and shells—
This is the way we fight the war, and this is the tale it tells—
   Gone is the glory of battle—the old-time glamour & shout
The charge, and the flash of sabers, the foemen in headlong rout.
No galloping into position, no cry "Halt! Action right!"
Those are the days that are passed afore, and it isn't the way We fight
But crawling along in the darkness we pass up shell-torn tanks—
Mud to the gun wheel axles—the ammunition in packs,
(For it's easier thus to manage, when the thick clay clogs like glue)
It isn't the way men used to fight, but now it's the way we do.
   We traverse what once were roadways, broken by shell and mine:
The shrapnel stabs the darkness, the bullets hiss and whine;
Ahead the trench flares flicker, the great guns boom around;
And over all is the reek of gas, and the smell of the rotten ground.
   "This way up to the gun-pit"—"Unlimber—be off—good night!"
"Manhandle the gun back quickly! Steady! "Trail left—that's right"[130]
"Rig up the camouflage over her—darkness will soon be gone !"
It isn't the way things used to be—but now it's the way they're done.
   Nothing but filth and sandbags, rotted and torn to bits,
Debris and scraps of iron—the guns in their shallow pits.
That and an aching weariness, the slumber of tired men,
Who have scarce closed their eyes for seven days, and may not again for ten.
   This isn't the sort of war it was in the days of old,
It isn't the same, and yet the selfsame tale is being told
By the iron voice of the guns, in their never-ceasing roar,
"We mean to finish today, as we've always finished before!"

                   St Quentin, March, 1918

Peel was not alone in writing poetry, of course. It was during the

Passchendaele campaign that Wilfred Owen's *Dulce et Decorum Est* was composed, including the lines:

> ...Men marched asleep. Many had lost their boots
> But limped on, blood-shod. All went lame; all blind;
> Drunk with fatigue; deaf even to the hoots
> Of gas shells dripping softly behind.[131]

Despite the harsh conditions, despite the record amount of rainfall, despite the increasing casualties, Haig felt compelled to maintain this campaign. There were occasional pauses because the guns could not be moved in the mud; there were occasional pauses while the guns were laboriously moved through the mud; there were occasional pauses while the British prayed the mud would dry.

What is usually termed the battle of Passchendaele is actually more accurately described as a number of smaller "bite and hold" actions, each one costly in lives and each one gaining just a little ground. Individual villages and crossroads such as Pilkem Ridge, Langemarck, Polygon Wood: such places each saw fighting, such places each saw dying, such places each saw the creation of a well-kept cemetery, a permanent reminder of the price paid by hundreds from each side, the price of "bite and hold."

By early October, a significant amount of the high ground the Field Marshal had intended to conquer was still controlled by the Germans. If that did not change, the enemy artillery would be able to harass the British all winter, with the British ill positioned to respond. So, despite the ratio of high cost and modest benefit, Haig continued the attack into November.[132]

The mud is just an inescapable theme of this campaign. An eyewitness recalled: "The trench ran like a river and gradually our dougout began to flood until it reached the top bunk."[133] The same soldier recalled it was "...the most unfortunate for the destruction of men, animals and armaments."[134] A contemporary historian has written that "Much of the battle area became a shallow lake with sucking mud beneath.... Even for a fit man who had suffered no wounds, falling off the boards could mean death by drowning."[135] Captain Peel called the mud "simply atrocious."[136] He also took note of a modest advance: "Here we are out of the salient and at rest at last.... We have only come twelve miles from our old wagon line, but still we are clear of that hateful spot."[137]

It rained nearly every day in August. There was plenty more in September. In October heavier rains resumed. Indeed, the ground became so waterlogged that at least some artillery shells would not explode on contact: they simply became buried in the mud, unexploded.

These shells remained after the war, numbering in the millions. In fact, modern Belgian farmers uncover unexploded munitions every spring as they plow their fields, and other times more serendipitously. On the Varlet farm near Poelkapelle, for example, just a short bike ride from Ypres, the proprietors have established a modest but interesting museum of items discovered on and under their land. They have become experienced at determining whether a newly discovered shell is highly dangerous (such as still having gas within; such shells often make a "sloshing" sound when gently rocked), or questionable, or harmless (just a hollow casing). The Belgian army maintains bomb disposal units throughout the nation, and assists the farmers with the "iron harvest." Today it is not unusual to hear explosions in the early evening outside the village of Poelkapelle as the Belgian military bomb disposal squads detonate nearly one-hundred year old munitions.

Other contemporary remnants of the Great War are not hard to find. The author walked into a farmfield in June 2010 and within three minutes picked up just on the surface of the field three palm-sized shrapnel fragments. There are also millions of "silent pickets" everywhere there once was a trench. These are iron bars about six or seven feet tall. They have a corkscrew on the bottom, similiar to a dog's outdoor tie-up. Soldiers would leave their trench at night, screw this silently into the ground, and then string barbed wire from pole to pole. The wire has rusted away—these fields are now rich in iron—but the "silent picket" has remained, a mute witness to a bloody time.

German barbed wire posed a particularly nasty threat. One common variety employed sixteen barbs to the foot, and was often strung in beds four feet high and thirty to forty feet deep. Iron spikes helped pin it to the ground.[138] Corporal Jack Dillon remembered: "I'd never seen such a depth of barbed wire. It was ten yards deep, four feet high, and so dense you could barely poke a broom handle through it."[139]

Even when not directly engaged in fighing that bloody autumn, the soldiers' suffering continued. All the usual difficulties of keeping the troops supplied with basic necessities during battle remained. Corporal Clifford Lane recalled a particularly unpleasant moment:

> We were so thirsty that we actually drank out of shell-holes, and God knows what a shell hole contains. It could hold anything—very often parts of a human body. But we were so thirsty we drank it cold and without boiling it, because you couldn't get a fire very often.[140]

By the end of this campaign, there were 350,000 more British casualties.[141] Churchill's post-war observation was "By sublime devotion and frightful losses small indentations were made upon the German front."[142] In fact, the

British had advanced about five miles in a few places. But the loss of so many men had startled Prime Minister Lloyd George. The setbacks on the Italian front[143] gave him an opportunity to urge the transfer of troops from the Western front to Italy. The Prime Minister wanted to send twelve divisions. Haig opposed this, of course, just as he had opposed weakening his forces in favor of the Dardanelles campaign two years earlier. The Prime Minister wanted to so reduce Haig's strength that he would have to go over to the defensive and await the arrival of the Americans. The Commander-in-Chief was more concerned with the imminent threat from the Eastern Front. More than a million German troops would soon be free to re-enforce their western front. He was going to need every man. Haig managed to limit the transfer to General Plumber, one of his best, and just five divisions.[144]

Just as Haig was criticized for the terrific number of casualties at the Battle of the Somme in 1916, he has been held responsible for the nightmare his troops endured around Passchendaele in 1917. Writing in 1930, Liddell Hart was an early critic:

> Perhaps the most damning comment on the plan which plunged the British Army in this path of mud and blood is contained in an incidental revelation of the remorse of one who was largely responsible for it. This highly placed officer from general headquarters was on his first visit to the battlefront—at the end of the four months' battle. Growing increasingly uneasy as the car approached the swamp-like edges of the battle area, he eventually burst into tears crying "Good God, did we really send men to fight in that?" To which his companion replied that the ground was far worse ahead. If the exclamation was a credit to his heart it revealed on what a foundation of delusion and inexcusable ignorance (Haig's) indomitable " offensiveness" [*sic*] had been based.[145]

No reference or source was indicated in Liddell Hart's book. Dennis Wheatley reports what may have been the same moment in his 1974 memoir, but also with no source indicated:

> [When the car could go no further forward due to the mud] Sir Archbald Murray (chief of staff to the Field Marshal) stared appalled at the endless sea of mud. Then he exclaimed "Can we really have been sending men to attack across this!" And he burst into tears.[146]

A much more recent book, published in 2002, identifies the officer as General Launcelot Kiggell.[147] Again, however, no source is listed. Perhaps very similar events occurred; perhaps no such event occurred; perhaps this is an example of how an apocryphal tale may become taken as fact.

A review of the whole "chateau general" idea fits here in this study. There is ample evidence of friction between front line soldiers and the generals who had certainly more cozy accommodations well behind the lines. "Trench soldiers hated the staff and the staff knew it. The principal disagreement seems to be about the extent to which trench conditions should modify discipline."[148] In reality, the speed of communication between the headquarters and the front line was so slow and so tedious that the generals could not exercise battlefield control. Put another way, one hundred years earlier, Napoleon could see well enough despite smoke and rain and other obstacles to have a good idea that his enemy was *there* and his forces were *here*. A galloping messenger could deliver his orders to his subordinates.

But in the Great War, a general at the front lines could only effectively command perhaps fifty men. For that reason, he had no place there. Rather, he ensured his local commanders knew the attack plan and then relied on local leadership, that provided by captains and lieutenants, sergeants and corporals to carry out his orders. Indeed, many trench personnel did not welcome generals in their little world; who wants the boss looking over their shoulder? Captain Bloor made this observation: "Inspected by Corps Commander.... Generals are more nuisance than hostile fire!"[149] In sum, "Generals had inadaquate knowledge of events & were unable to communicate quickly enough to control the fight."[150]

The question of casualty rates and war wounds among generals is a point of disageement. Troops in the trenches were convinced that generals were so seldom in the line of fire that they died of old age, not warfare. In point of fact, to take just the 1915 Battle of Loos as an example: three major generals were killed, three more wounded and one was captured. In the entire war, 232 generals were casualties, and seventy-eight were killed.[151] Was the death rate among generals proportional to those of the men in the trenches? Probably not. But neither was their presence in the war zone a guarantee of good health. Perhaps the best summary of this matter is by an officer who saw it all:

> The feeling between the regimental officers and the staff officers is as old as the history of fighting. I have been a regimental officer in two minor wars and realized what a poor hand the staff made of things and what a safe luxurious life they led; I was a staff officer in the First World War and realized that the staff were worked to the bone to try and keep the regimental officers on the rails; I have been a Higher Commander in one minor and one major war and have sympathized with the views of both staff and regimental officers.[152]

Returning now to the high cost of Passchendaele, while many blamed Field

Marshal Haig, some thought he did the right thing. In an interview almost sixty years after the war, one veteran concluded "If it hadn't been for Douggy, we shouldn't have won the war [Because of the French collapse]. He <u>had</u> to carry on with Passchendaele or we should have been slaves of Germany."[153] Lending credence to Haine's opinion is the fact that he was awarded the Victoria Cross "for valor against the enemy" which is the highest medal in the British system.

With the Passchendaele campaign less than a great success, Haig was open to an alternative plan. He thought there was time for one more short campaign before winter would prevent advances. The new target would be at Cambrai, a French city about forty-five miles south south-east of Ypres. This battle would employ different tactics. There would be no great days-long bombardment in advance, always a dead giveaway of an impending attack. Instead a combination of infantry and a planned 500 tanks would make the surprise assault. On 20 November 1917 a sudden bombardment from a thousand guns, some of them firing smoke shells, disguised the rapid advance of 476 tanks.[154] Both the attackers and the defenders were shocked and surprised, the British at their ease of penetration of up to four miles, the Germans at yeilding up to four miles. However, with few reserves present to carry on the attack, the Germans were able to quickly pinch off the British advance.

One eyewitness remembered a retreat during this campaign very clearly:

> We reached the gun pits from which we had set out, and here found hundreds of men on stretchers, lying in the road, waiting to be picked up for the rear. Suddenly, out of the sky, enemy planes appeared, and poured their machine gun bullets all over us. Those of us who could move, dived into any shelter for cover; but the poor wounded, face up, had to meet their fate. We shook our fists at the murderous airmen now flying away, after completing their dirty work. But this was war.[155]

When word of this minor success reached England, many believed it grander than it was. Church bells rang all over the country for the first time since the war began. When a few days later the news arrived that the Germans had successfully sealed the breach and taken back much of the modest gains, Haig's reputation suffered.[156] The actual cost of the attack was 44,000 total British casualties as well as 179 tanks in just the first assault.[157]

A few techniques which would be useful in the future were pioneered at Cambrai. For example, many of the tanks attacked in "unicorn" posture, three tanks forming an equilateral triangle with the two rear ones followed by platoons of dismounted infantry.[158] One soldier suggested that tanks, not soldiers, be used to cut the barbed wire.[159] The combination of a sudden, brief, intense artillery barrage, followed quickly by a mass assault of tanks and infantry together was a tactic that would henceforth be used quite often.

As the fighting continued, so did the suffering of the soldiers. Some irritants were mundane but, nevertheless, real. Soldiers discovered, for example, flaws with their boots, each of which weighed about five pounds. These mass produced leather goods had little or no ability to stretch. Worse, the heels would fall off and the nails would come through.[160] Hardly a critical matter, one might think, unless the nail were in one's own heel.

Much more seriously, Private Harry Patch told this tale on himself:

> All over the battlefield the wounded were lying down, English and Germans all asking for help. We weren't like the good Samaritan in the Bible, we were the robbers who passed by and left them. You couldn't help them.[161]

Captain Peel continued his diary entries with this one on 10 November 1917: "Anyhow, there is no doubt who is winning the war, but I no longer believe in peace by Christmas as I did 'til quite a short time ago." He added on 21 November: "The battery position is in the midst of a regular sea of mud, and one can't move off the trench-board tracks."

Captain Peel's diary is generally upbeat. He seems to have found sunbeams poking through the darkest clouds. He reported to his family about a morale building competition, in which first the horses and tackle were judged—his "dazzled"—and then "<u>All</u> the officers and sergeants sang in turn, so you can imagine what it was like when it got to <u>my</u> performing."[162] He even turned an injury into a minor event:

> I had a most glorious spill this morning. I woke up at 9.0 a.m. in my bed, with boots, breeches and a shirt on, plentifully sprinkled with mud and blood, a very sore face, and stiff neck, and no earthly idea of what had happened even now, though I am told my horse put his foot in a hole and stood on his head, and that I rode home. I have not the slightest recollection of it. However there is no serious damage done.[163]

A month later he added: "Life is still very boring, though bearable, as one can always sleep and eat, which are about the only diversions available."[164] This excellent officer reported to his family in December: "We are busy preparing for Christmas now, buying pipes and things for the men."[165] At just about the same time, another soldier tried to reassure his family:

> ...the papers said last year was the coldest for 22 years—the coldest in my life. I lived through it out of doors without suffering ever from the cold

& wearing precisely what I am now. So you need not worry about my warmpth.[166]

Not everyone could maintain their spirits. By November 1917, the officers who censored the soldiers' letters home reported an increase of war weariness.[167] One physician reported that the men are "... medically unfit to carry on, owing to so many going sick principally caused through lice and vermin...."[168]

Even in the midst of these great battles, an astonishing variety of topics required Haig's personal attention. For example, on 15 August 1917, he received the Quartermaster General, Sir John Cowans:

He has come out with orders to reduce some of our motor lorries because 'spare parts' cannot be manufactured in sufficient quantities now, and petrol is very scarce indeed.... The War Cabinet and the members of the Army Council keep pressing me to make a few cheese-paring reductions (six Divisional cavalry regiments = 2500 horses out of 450,000 in the Army, some motor lorries, work on railways for instance) but they fail to see the huge beams in their own eyes. Such as 2 Army Staffs (northern and southern) at home, which swallow up many useful subordinates and cost much money.

I felt it a waste of time speaking to Cowans: he knows so little of the essentials which make for success in war. All the same he is most anxious to be friendly: he is feeble because he listens to too much gossip—e.g. he has an idea that 'Tanks' will never be of any use, when as a matter of fact they have already accomplished so much as to show that they have come to stay!

Field Marshal Haig's endorsement of tanks is all the more remarkable in light of this entry in his diary from 13 November 1917:

... the object of the operations of the infantry aided by Tanks [was] to break through the Enemy's defenses *by surprise* and so permit the Cavalry Corps to pass through and operate in open country.

Horses were often on Haig's mind. Also on 13 November 1917, he wrote:

Position of hay reserves is serious. I wired to War Office on 11th that only six days reserves are in hand and ships advised as probably arriving in next seven days, only carry about 5½ days hay for the Force in France. Situation seems likely to become worse.

Beyond his battlefield concerns, Haig had two additional matters on his mind. Winston Churchill referred to the first as "an acute crisis in Man-Power."[169] British casualties from January to November 1917 totaled more than 790,000. Haig wanted those men to be replaced. But there was continuing concern about this in London. There simply were not enough men to perform all the tasks at hand. The director of National Service, Auckland Geddes, had argued back in October that the whole economy simply could not spare any more men. Rather, he argued the Army should use more technology—such as tanks—and less manpower. The War Cabinet manpower committee established priorities in its report of 28 November 1917. The Navy, shipbuilding, Air Force, agriculture, timber felling, food stores: all of these had higher prorities on manpower. In fact, the Army was at the bottom of the list, dead last.[170] The BEF wanted 600,000 category "A" men, the strongest and fittest. The Committee decided the Army may have 100,000 men. Haig had fought this domestic battle before. He recognized the strains the war was placing on the economy. But he was also profoundly concerned about December's news from Russia. With the German success there, he recognized it would "... allow the Germans to employee some 30 more divisions on this front. They can be brought here at the rate of 8 to 10 per month if the enemy so will it."[171]

There was another matter that reduced the number of available men. Some individuals went to great lengths to avoid service, and a whole new catagory of criminals came forward to help them do that. An individual could avoid service for medical reasons. A particularly clever group of crooks found the name of a deceased physican who had kept no records. They began to sell "exemption certificates" and fake medical records supposedly from this doctor's office. The draft doger would obtain paperwork proclaiming him to have, for example, "V.D.H." which stood for "valvular disease of the heart." The twenty-two year-old Bernard Black presented himself to a physican for examination and offered the doctor's note. The examining physican smelt a rat and called the police. Pretty soon the whole gang was in jail: father of the draftee, the draftee, and the false papers salesman.[172]

So another very long year came to a close. Another high cost in lives and treasure, another disappointing result. But there were hints in the most recent battles that perhaps victory would arrive in the New Year. Victory would come in one of two ways, went the common wisdom. Either Germany would collapse under British pressure, or the arrival of American soldiers would finish the job. Either way, victory was assured. The only question remaining was still very important, however... at what further cost?

CHAPTER V

1918: Tenacity Rewarded

There has been wrong done since the world began,
That young men should go out and die in war;
And lie face down in the dust for a brief span,
And be not good to look at any more.

—*Nina Murdoch*[1]

Knowing who won certainly influences one's mental image of 1918, the last year of this horrific war. The reader of course knows. For the participants, it was a much bleaker picture. In fact, how very close the Germans came to winning is often overlooked. There is much truth to that old adage about the winner writing the history books.

It was quite difficult to see any particular cause for optimism as 1918 began. Fog and snow and ice and rain— and, of course, mud—were uppermost in the discomfort causes of the moment. Miserable weather had become quite the norm. Many battles, many dead, many wounded, high costs paid. Progress? Hard to measure. National mood? Downcast. Source? Soldiers' diaries. If the end were anywhere near, it was pretty well hidden. Most of the discomforts of trench warfare remained, and winter weather intensified others. Sergeant Laidlaw was quite honest about how much he missed being home, writing to his wife: "We are both lost when we are separated."[2] More mundanely, F. S. Cooke made this observation:

> ...terribly cold, mud froze around my legs, have to chip mud with bayonet to get free. 10 p.m. the boys have just come up with the soup. Hot too and it's great.[3]

Captain Peel had both good and bad news to report to his family:

We were just starting off when another train ran into us & knocked eight trucks clean off the line.... Not a man nor horse was hurt; so though we had to wait all day while they cleared the line.[4]

Captain Peel was surely furious on 18 March 1918 when he discovered: "Some swine stole four of my best horses the night before last. We are scouring the country but haven't found them yet. Heaven help the sods when we do." Another soldier reported his health news: "...cooty as you like, big uns and little uns, beaucoup itchy koo."[5] He was also happy about "Getting all the letters from home all right now."[6] That cold January and colder February led to the March thaw, and so the never gone long mud returned. One soldier reported "I'm carrying a soup canister on my back.... Got stuck in the mud and could not move."[7] A. S. Carter's "Account of Service" recalled: "In places the front line was six to eighteen inches deep in muddy water."[8] The ever observant Captain Peel found some happy moments in February:

> ...my dug-out is tophole. Two of us sleep there; there are two little separate bunks, about the size of a decent cabinet & a place in the middle where we wash, all lined with wood & painted blue outside, also a mine shaft going down from the center for use as a funk-hole so we are pretty well off....[9]

The Army was going to need a great many more officers like Captain Peel. So many officers had been lost in the Passchendaele campaign that just about every remaining veteran of 1914 found himself urged to apply for an officer's commission. For various reasons, such as high mortality rates, many men declined the position.[10] The Army was going to need more soldiers, too. In the aftermath of this most costly war, the pool of manpower was quite shallow:

> Lads of eighteen and nineteen, elderly men up to forty-five, the last surviving brother, the only son of his mother (and she a widow), the father the sole support of the family, the weak, the consumptive, the thrice wounded—all must now prepare themselves for the scythe.[11]

It was in March, 1918 that one soldier overheard an argument between two others. They seemingly had agreed to shoot each other in the ankle, but the plan had miscarried: "B had done it to A, but now A refused to fulfill his part of the agreement. They had used a tin of bully beef to shoot through & protect the ankle from powder stains." The ear witness to this bargain decided to walk away, unseen, but it remains one small piece of evidence about the mood of at least a few soldiers in the appalling conditions.[12]

As March arrived, the Field Marshal had a full plate. His Yule's cup had begun the year with a bitter brew. In the political arena, he was quite aware of upcoming changes, telling Churchill that:

> At the present moment, England is in a stronger position than she has ever been and by continuing the war she will get weaker [financially and in manpower]. On the other hand, America will get stronger, and finally will dictate *her* peace which may not suit Great Britain....[13]

His Army was weak, understrength, overstretched and in some places, especially the South, poorly fortified.[14] On the other hand, he now had plenty of supplies on hand, ammunition and food in abundance, yes. But he was also fully aware of a major problem expected to arrive just after the spring thaw, a powerful German offensive. His intelligence service reported the enemy was massing forces. The Germans were rapidly increasing their troop strength in the trenches opposite his. There, many divisions recalled from defeated Russia were preparing for the spring campaigning.[15] His senior commanders advised him that since the Germans were about to have a temporary superiority in numbers, they could be expected to try again for the endgame.

Yet as the German troops grew in numbers, as the unknown date of their attack grew near, the British were actually weakening. At least some of his own soldiers expected an attack and were surprised that leave was still being granted.[16] One Captain, Cyril Dennys, recalled an officer who requested leave in Paris. His reason for requesting leave was listed as "sexual starvation."[17] And another humorous moment in an otherwise most serious world: Pearson's unit was hurried over to France—and when they arrived, "...the army of all things ordered a payday & of course nowhere to spend it."[18] Not only were 88,000 men home on leave,[19] but the British were once again taking over more of the trenches from the French.[20] This while at that very moment their ordinary replacements were being withheld at home.[21] In mid-January, the British held 95 miles of front; by 4 February that had grown to 123 miles, with all the additional strain not so much on the quantity of supplies as on the transporting of those supplies to where needed.[22]

Anticipating an attack, Field Marshal Haig conducted an extensive analysis of his field position. Where could he lose ground without jeopardizing his mission? Where, if forced, could he trade land for time? Certainly not in the north, close to the sea. His supply lifeline ran right through Belgium to the coast. There were a number of critical bases in the North. Ypres was only about twenty miles from the seacoast. Just a dozen miles South of Ypres was the railhead of Armentières. Less than fifteen miles west of there was Hazebrouck and this triangle of supply depots was the very heart of the British supply system. An enemy disruption of the daily tasks of these supply centers would grievously impair the British ability to fight. If they were fully lost, the British might even have to surrender. That area was crucial; that area must be held at all costs. No, if the Field Marshal had to yield territory, he would miss it least in the southern part of the battle area. Here he calculated he could lose a great deal of territory with minimal risk to the long term outcome.[23]

The Chief looked for ways to strengthen his hand in a very tense time. By thinning his southern forces, he added to what limited strength he had to the North. Against his sense of proper timing, the War Office had decided to reorganize all infantry divisions. Formerly each had twelve battalions; now each would have nine. In addition, the five cavalry divisions would be cut to three.[24]

The Commander-in-Chief enacted his own significant changes at this moment. First, the whole philosophy was shifted to emphasize defense: let the Germans batter themselves against strong British trenches. To this end a new scheme was unveiled. The plan was to have a "forward" zone which would be only lightly manned, but with carefully sited machine guns. Then came the "battle zone" where the enemy would be stopped, using reserves if necessary. Last there would be a "rear" zone, four to eight miles back.[25] Yet this plan, incorporating the lessons painfully learned over the previous few years, was only applied here and there. It would not be uniformly in place when the Germans attacked. Quite to the contrary, many British officers were still adhering to the older policy of defending the front line trenches to the last man. By early March, 1918, in some areas as many as eighty-four percent of the British battalions were within 3,000 yards of the front line and thus exposed to surprise enemy bombardment.[26]

Haig was making other preparations as well. For example, he decided to transform three under-used Household Cavalry units into machine gun battalions, thus trading horses for firepower.[27]

The Germans fulfilled the expectations of an attack that spring. Having brought nearly 1,000,000 soldiers from the Eastern to the Western front, the Germans launched a very strong attack centered on the point where the British and French trenches met. The Germans believed that if they could destroy the British Army, the French would have to sue for peace. So, in a major gamble, the Germans planned four separate attacks.

The first was code-named "Operation Michael." It began at 4:40 on the morning of 21 March 1918 when nearly 8,000 guns opened fire on the British and French positions. The battlefield was familiar to both sides: it was the Somme River Valley—again. More than a million and a half shells blasted the Allied positions. High explosive shells and phosgene gas dominated. More than thirty divisions formed the first wave with an equal number ready to follow on. The British were outnumbered eight to one.[28] The British were expecting an attack, yes, but not with such strength, not an attack that captured almost 100 square miles on the first day.[29]

The Germans had utilized some new stealth tactics. Wagon wheels were wrapped in burlap, for example, to muffle the sound of the arriving German forces.[30] Very rapidly, the defenders were pushed back. Shockingly, the defenders were pushed back as much as four miles in some places. Concentrated German artillery, well trained attacking troops, vigorous leadership and a belief among the Germans that this attack would end the interminable war with, finally, a German victory gave the Germans a momentary edge over the stunned and outnumbered defenders.

A mix of high explosive shells, phosgene gas shells, and lachrymatory shells overwhelmed the targets. Cascading lachrymatory shells were designed to make the victims' eyes water, thus compelling them to remove their masks— which would then allow the poisonous gases to kill them. One soldier heeded the warning:

> ...Fritz would use a new kind of gas which made it essential that everyone should wear gloves and leave no part of their flesh uncovered or the gas would burn up right into them.[31]

There was not a great deal the Field Marshal could do in the short run to influence the unfolding battle. Were he an ancient Greek, he might have believed that the gods were against him when numerous little adverse things began to pile up. Soldiers returning from leave, for example, could not get back to their units: the leave boats could not cross the channel due to heavy fog.[32] In some places, fog also protected the German attackers from being clearly seen. An outbreak of Spanish flu hit his troops and his doctors advised the soldiers to "just sweat it out."[33] The Germans pushed his troops back so far, so fast, that both sides were cut off from their own supplies, from their own reinforcements: F. S. Cooke complained of no rations and no water on 27 March, and of no artillery support on 28 March.

There was no artillery support in this sector at this instant because the guns were in full retreat to keep them from falling into the hands of the rapidly advancing Germans. In six days, the Germans penetrated nearly forty miles,[34] gains not seen since the earliest days of the war. The retreating British were surprised at the continuing strength of the attack against them: "Jerry with great numbers attacks vigorously. Heavy fighting all morning, but we hold on like grim death."[35] Cut off from their supplies, the British soldiers returned to living off the countryside, such as taking "... as many rabbits and chickens as we could carry from the abandoned farm to keep it from the Germans."[36] Sometimes a mini feast ensued:

> ...We found a litter of young pigs so with the help of one lad whom was a
> butcher & another a cook we had, for two days, roast pork garnished with
> new potatoes and peas.[37]

The civilians who had been trying to farm behind the lines soon found
themselves fleeing again:

> ...it was a very pitiful sight to see the French civilians trying to get their few
> household things along the roads away from the Germans, they were taking
> them on wagons, barrows, perambulators, or anything they could get hold
> of little babies and poor old men and women were being almost dragged
> along and when it rained it was a thousand times worse.[38]

Weary soldiers returned with great reluctance to quite familiar places:

> On March the 26 we dropped into a trench. It was a trench we knew of old.
> We had started to retreat on the 21st of March, 1918, and here we were back
> in the trench wc had started to attack from on November the 13, 1916.[39]

What accounted for the German penetration of the British line? Aside from the
sheer number of troops, it was also due to new tactics. They declined to attack
British strong points. Rather, they employed an intense but short barrage, and
then they flooded the field with infantry trained to avoid strong points, to let
those be taken later by follow-on troops with heavier weapons. They were
emphatically ordered to concentrate on a continuous infiltration, to keep the
defenders off balance.[40]

There were several other important facts making this March different than
that of a year earlier, and Haig made sure that his King knew them all. In a
conversation with George V on 29 March at the General's headquarters, the
Chief told his sovereign:

> 1. British infantry in France at the beginning of the battle were 100,000 less
> than a year ago!
> 2. We now had three times as many Germans on our front as we had last
> year.
> 3. We had also extended our line (by order of the British government) fully
> one-fifth more than it was last autumn. This may have been necessary,
> because the French had inadequate numbers and the Americans had not
> arrived, but it rendered our front precarious.[41]

Despite the new tactics, despite the deep penetrations, the British line bent but it did not break. When units realized that they were being out flanked, they conducted orderly if hasty retreats. The Commander-in-Chief's policy of retreat in selected areas gave him just enough flexibility that he could send forward limited reinforcements—sometimes cooks and mail clerks and other rear area personnel and dismounted cavalry—just in the nick of time. Even as the British line benefited from these limited reinforcements, the Germans quite literally ran out of everything else but desire.

They had crossed the fields carrying two days' rations. Those were now gone, their energy was far gone, and their own supplies found it just impossible to keep up with them.[42] Knowing how the mud and shell craters formed such obstacles to the British system, one can only imagine how hard it must have been for the German supply effort. They did not have the light rail network to bring supplies forward into the newly taken areas; they did not have pre-planned supply depots. The primary direction of their attack, for example, shifted from North to West, so they just could not maintain a supply line. No one could have supplied that much that fast. It was simply beyond the infrastructure of the day. From day to day as the battle unfolded, the forward elements, the point of the German spear, did not even know where they would be that night. Their objectives kept shifting based on British resistance. How could supplies possibly keep up?

Winston Churchill tried to explain the situation to Prime Minister David Lloyd George using this analogy:

> ...Every offensive lost some of its force as it proceeded. It was like throwing a bucket of water over the floor. It first rushed forward, then soaked forward, and finally stopped altogether until another could be brought.[43]

With the Germans losing about 240,000 irreplaceable men and the Allies about the same, the Germans ceased their attack on 5 February. The losses may have been near equal in numbers, but not in significance. There simply were no more men for Germany to call. On the other hand, troop ships from the United States were landing thousands of troops in France every day. The promise of the submarine campaign advocates was proving hollow. American might was becoming an important factor in the military equation.

The costly German attack was called off because it had stopped advancing, and now the Germans were in vulnerable salients sticking into the British positions. They had captured much territory but of limited strategic worth. Germany had expended a great number of irreplaceable lives and a great amount of irreplaceable supplies to conquer badly damaged farmland, of value only to its former occupants. Many of those Belgians and French were dead and many others could no longer recognize what might have been their home for generations.

The Germans had used their limited resources in a massive effort to separate the British and French armies. That had failed. This was a crucial point, although it was not yet clear to either side. Perhaps a more valuable achievement would have been the serious disruption of the British supply system. That had not occurred. In hindsight, it is easy to see just how close to the end Germany was. If this last big effort was not a success, there would be nothing left. Despite four years of exhausting effort, despite victory over Russia, Germany would lose the war.

Believing it imperative to continue attacking, using what resources they had remaining, the Germans unleashed the second of the four planned attacks. Having decoyed the British into sending reinforcements further south, they now moved the fresh thrust further north, this time along the Lys River— again, for this was in the shadow of the Passchendaele battlefield of the previous year. The Germans termed this second stage "Georgette."

Vast fields made near impassable by deep shell craters and deep water pools were no easier for the Germans to cross and to conquer than they had been for the British. For three weeks, the Germans threw 500,000 men toward the major British supply base at Hazebrouck. More than 100 Allied supply trains routinely unloaded there every day. Should the Germans get that far, their supply problems would be eased, at least for a while.[44]

The same old names returned to the news reports: battles were fought, lives were lost, men were maimed over such familiar places as Messines, Ploegsteert, Ypres. The Germans came so close that Field Marshal Haig ordered the opening of the dykes protecting the ports of Calais, Dunkirk and Boulogne precisely so the Germans would not get those Allied supplies and thus refresh their power to fight.[45]

The Germans made gains. Still more familiar names returned to the news reports. St Eloi, Kemmel, the whole ring of Belgian towns around Ypres changed hands again. The towns, smaller villages, basic hamlets saw more deaths. By 12 April, the Germans were once again at the gates of Ypres. It appeared that the seacoast ports were in grave danger of falling to the Germans.

This was again a near run thing. For the first time since those earliest days of the war in 1914, the pendulum could swing either way. In the entire conflict, this may have been the only time Field Marshal Haig came close to losing his composure. Recognizing how vital it was that his Army hold what it had, he issued what became a famous "order of the day", a message addressed to:

ALL RANKS OF THE BRITISH ARMY IN FRANCE AND FLANDERS

Three weeks ago today the enemy began his terrific attacks against us on a 50 mile front. His objects are to separate us from the French, to take the channel ports and to destroy the British Army.

In spite of throwing already 106 Divisions into the battle and enduring the most reckless sacrifice of human life, he has as yet made little progress towards his goals.

We owe this to the determined fighting and self-sacrifice of our troops. Words fail me to express the admiration which I feel for the splendid resistance offered by all ranks of our Army under the most trying circumstances.

Many amongst us are now tired. To those I would say that Victory will belong to the side that holds out the longest. The French Army is moving rapidly and in great force to our support.

There is no other course open to us but to fight it out. Every position must be held to the last man: there must be no retirement. With our backs to the wall and believing in the justice of our cause each one of us must fight on to the end. This safety of our homes and the Freedom of mankind alike depend upon the conduct of each one of us at this critical moment.

(signed) D. Haig, FM, Commander-in-Chief, British Armies in France.[46]

What an extraordinary message! D. H. did not often issue such messages to his troops, and this one certainly raises the "threat level" to the highest notch. In issuing this order to the entire Army, including those involved in heavy fighting and those in quiet places along the front, he risked spreading alarm and even panic. Obviously he took the gravest view of the situation. Which was what? The Germans had crashed through some Portuguese soldiers who were holding the line in a supposedly quiet sector. Haig did not hold his Portuguese allies in high regard:

We don't want to quarrel with ally, Portugal, because they have many suitable submarine bases for the Enemy! On the other hand, the Portuguese troops with their Portuguese officers are useless for this kind of fighting.[47]

As the Portuguese fell back they exposed the British troops on either flank to attacks. They too had to retreat. But they did retreat, they did not run. Yes they were falling back, and yes the Germans were advancing, but the same old problems remained: the supply service just was not adequate. Soldiers can only shoot if they have bullets. These exhausted Germans ran out of bullets and bread and water and time and energy and had to stop, again. Once again, they had only punched an indefensible salient into the British line.

By 12 April, parts of the BEF were in retreat again. But as it had done multiple times before, the British Army was not running away, but rather was conducting an orderly if reluctant movement back to more defensible lines. As both sides had learned earlier, a shorter line gave the defenders more flexibility. It released some men from the reduced length of trench to be reinforcements where they were most needed. Perhaps not so much by design but by happenstance, the Germans were creating numerous new salients in the British lines, new places where when the moment came, the British could counter-attack with advantage.

This is not to say that the BEF was conducting a careful and deliberate policy. Retreat was not so much a choice as it was a necessity. German strength was pushing against British weak spots and the British were yielding under pressure. There was a real sense, indeed, a real danger that the Germans just might win this ghastly war after all.

Two key factors determined the outcome although they were far from clear at the time. First, the British did not panic. True, the situation was grave and pronouncements from headquarters only underlined the seriousness of the situation. But there was a sense in the trenches as if the soldiers believed that we did not go through all this to be licked now: setbacks, yes, but no sense of permanent defeat in the soldiers' diaries.

The second factor is war material. The mini museum on the Varlet farm in Belgium was mentioned earlier in this study. Even nowadays, when new German shells are unearthed, the proprietors can often date them based on the fuses. The older fuses are from 1914 and are made of high quality brass. Later fuses used inferior metals and the late war fuses are made entirely of zinc, a barely adequate substitute. This is just one example of how the British blockade cut Germany off from so many needed war materials. So many items were in short supply that Germany just could not make do with the available resources.

When these final offensives began, Germany threw into the cauldron all she had left. It was truly a last chance gamble. Either defeat the British and French now, or wait until ever-increasing American strength guaranteed defeat.

How close Germany was to exhaustion was not at all clear to the British. They could be told over and over again by their intelligence services that the Germans were close to the end, but that did not make the artillery shells any less fatal to those caught beneath them. Meanwhile, the British caught their breath and hurried men over from England. Churchill was urging that men be sent to replace those lost, but that no new offensives be undertaken. Even he was shaken by the terrific losses at Passchendaele the previous autumn.[48]

The BEF welcomed the brief respite between the German attacks. One soldier rejoiced:

How lovely it was to be able to have a shave once more followed by a bath however primitive the conditions; even the fresh shirt & socks felt wonderful & it is surprising how such simple things could help restore one's morale & attitudes; there was no thought of having suffered a reverse & the line was holding.[49]

But not every soldier felt his efforts appreciated:

We at last get relieved after ten of the heaviest days of fighting any regiment has had in this war and we are not even thanked or mentioned in dispatches and nobody knows anything about us.[50]

Some of the men worried about their suffering horses as well:

…The horses being completely done up they not having had their harnesses off since the retreat started, and only what food the drivers could pick up for them, the men are pretty well done as well, not having hardly a wink of sleep since [the retreat] started….[51]

Many of the horses required a visit from the saddlers who had to tighten the saddle cinches as the horses lost weight and girth.

As these German campaigns continued, as they spent the last of all they had, even when they ran out of everything except hope, they were aware they ironically had pushed the British closer to their supplies. In the beginning of April victory for either side was possible: by May only a German optimist could hold such a view; by June most in the German leadership had become realists. The war was lost. The only remaining issue was on what terms would Germany be forced to concede.

Men in field commands had no such clear view. Men in the trenches had no such clear view. Moms and dads and wives and children at home had no such clear view. To the contrary, the view from the trenches remained as gruesome as ever. On 8 April 1918, F. S. Cooke recorded: "We have to make the best of things lying in shell holes filled with dead and dying and we cannot help them."[52] He added two days later: "We still struggle through bravely never thinking of the great odds against us. Just buried a chap named Kendall, just been back a week from being married, both legs gone."

There is a great sense of depression, of demoralization, sometimes of despair in the diaries of these months: not that the war would be lost—that sense never comes through—but victory is taking so long, is so costly. Towns and trenches, villages and vineyards that had changed hands in 1914 were doing it again. Places long ago passed over were occupied again. Where was the forward momentum? When would victory be achieved? Who would still be alive at the end of this horror?

As the war continued, so too did the devastation. The carnage was terrific, the numbers incredible. In March and April 1918 the BEF lost 301,340 men to all causes.[53] That is more than the entire force first landed on the Continent in 1914. To make up those losses, 372,330 "category A" men were sent over—the most fit men.[54]

By 12 April, the Germans were once again at the gates of Ypres, closer than they had been in 1914. Even so very late in the war, there was a real danger that the Germans would again get a pincer's movement to work for them as it had earlier in Russia. Just as in the German campaign leading to their victory over the Russians at Tannenberg, the Germans moved some strength north and some south of that beleaguered Belgian town of Ypres. Again, they came just so close—and no closer. By 29 April, the advance toward Lys was halted, once again short of any crucial objective. The German effort failed for the same reason, inability to keep the attacking troops supplied. As so often in this war, the troops were willing but the wherewithal was short.

The misery of trench life continued unabated. One soldier observed his trench mate's injury:

> I proceeded to examine his wound finding that a bullet had passed through both cheeks and smashed his teeth fortunately missing his tongue....I plugged the holes in his cheeks with cotton and ...set off for an aid station.[55]

He also emulated the Good Samaritan:

> I saw a lad of the East Lancs [Lancashires] with a shattered hip & a look of intense longing on his face. I put him in a wheelbarrow for a mile to an aid station....[56]

Perhaps it was at this time that Henry T. Williams wrote his undated poem, all in capital letters:

> SO REST IN YOUR MUDDY GRAVES CONTENT,
> THAT MANY OF US HAVE EVERY INTENT
> TO REMEMBER YOU ALWAYS AND NEVER FORGET.
> BUT YOUR WASTED LIVES, WE WILL ALWAYS REGRET
> BUT SLEEP ON MY COMRADES, AS I SAY.
> THERE SURELY WILL, AND MUST COME A DAY
> WHEN ALL MEN WILL REALIZE ONCE MORE
> THE WASTE AND EMPTINESS OF WAR.[57]

There are so many tragedies recorded in the soldiers' papers that the occasional piece of good news really stands out. The Army realized early on that many of its new recruits had experienced less than ideal medical care. Many had never been to a dentist. On 14 April 1918, one soldier made a simple entry in his diary: "Got new teeth"[58]. At the same time, another soldier realized a new concern:

> ...the Germans started shelling with a new kind of 11 inch shell which was absolutely terrible, it killing and wounding men before you heard a sound and when it did burst it had a double report, which was most nerve shattering.[59]

The war ground on. As the Germans pressed their attacks around Ypres, Haig was in touch with his French counterparts. They promised him aid, and did move their troops to support him. The French Prime Minister wrote directly to D.H. with his concern about the town of Bruay. This was just fifteen miles or so from Hazebrouk and so in the path of the probable German advance. Bruay was important because of its coal mines which were providing seventy percent of the French needs. There was only a five day supply on hand. The output of those mines was crucial to the war effort. This is one more example of the demands on the Commander-in-Chief's time even in the midst of a major battle.[60]

The German High Command was absolutely desperate. Repeated offensives had cost many lives and purchased only more mud: soggy, militarily worthless mud. In fact, the math of the attacks was frightening. The numerous German soldiers taking part were being chewed up by the British defenses. The hoarded supplies for the attack were being consumed with great speed. There was very little more that could be brought forward. There seemed to be no light at the end of the tunnel. Quite to the contrary, the tunnel only grew darker and more hopeless for the Kaiser's Army. There was only strength enough for one or two more attacks. After that, the military course of events would be irreversible. The well-equipped, un-bloodied and immense American Expeditionary Force would dominate the exhausted combatants and donate its unearned victory to the British and French. The exhausted old world powers would be subordinate to the will of the idealistic American President. German leadership could not accept the consequences of defeat, so they refused to accept defeat, and slaughtered on.

"Georgette", the attack that so stressed Field Marshal Haig, was called off on 29 April. The causes were the same. The attackers were out of supplies and were offering flanks to the British. The Germans decided to shift their attention to a new area in an effort termed "Blücher-Yorck." Recalling how small this entire battle area is, it is not surprising that this new battle was over previous battle sites. The British termed this "Third Aisne", another of those French Rivers giving its name to a place where men died by the thousands—again. This time the surprise bombardment of the French and British trenches caused very high casualties among the French. They were still in what was by now the old style of defense: plenty of troops in the first trench. These were literally blown away in the German barrage of 27 May. The modern visitor to the great Cathedral at Rheims will find pock marks in the stone sides of this grand edifice, memories of this bombardment. The German troops actually reached the Marne River again—as they had done in 1914—but once again, ran out of all they needed to even stay there, let alone advance. No more men, no supplies, no hope—and exposed flanks. While the Germans tried one or two additional attacks against the French, their offensive strength was now spent.

The German campaign of 1918 failed for the same reasons as the campaign of 1914. No matter how willing and motivated the men, there is an incontestable line that cannot be crossed. Soldiers simply must have food, ammunition and rest to carry out their mission. But just as French *élan* could not conquer German machine guns in 1914, neither could German desperation defeat British machine guns in 1918. The best intentions could not put more ammunition where it was needed, could not manufacture munitions without the embargoed supplies, could not lift exhausted soldiers across that damned muddy shell-holed field. Men can only run so far, carry so much, endure so much, before they just cease to function due to exhaustion.

The Germans had reached the end of their line. They knew that as they stretched their supply lines beyond the breaking point, they had pushed the British ever closer to their own well-stocked supply depots. Just as in a classical Greek play, Victory was removing her mask to reveal the ugly face of Defeat. At the beginning of April, victory was in the balance; in May, it was on a see-saw; by June, Germany could no longer win.

But the war was not over. Much pain and suffering remained. Honor had to be satisfied, but the supreme issue no longer was in doubt. What had changed was the momentum. For years, Haig had argued that the path to victory required that the British keep pressure on the Germans. Now, the Germans had exhausted their offensive power, but they still maintained very strong defensive positions. The Hindenburg line, constructed at such expense, remained a very strong position for the British to take. If the Germans remained on the defensive rather than surrender, there was still much hard fighting to endure. The Germans were not going to just go home quietly. They, too, had suffered beyond the point of just withdrawing. Sadly, with the ultimate conclusion of the war no longer in doubt, hundreds of thousands of men still were to become casualties.

The Grim Reaper continued his harvest. One soldier noted "It is like heaven right now to be away from the line and we have a roll call the larger amount of 160 out of 800."[61] That is an eighty percent casualty rate. On 10 April, 1918 Haig recorded in his diary that:

> The French losses in this battle are about 20,000 to 25,000, ours are about 160,000 and will be more. This shows their share in the fight so far!

How this war changed perspectives. That offhandedly mentioned 160,000 would have been half of the original strength the BEF brought to France in 1914. By this point, it is just a number on a campaign's tallies. This is not to insult the Field Marshal's sensitivity. It is to point out the need for the human mind to desensitize itself to the horrors of this ongoing conflict.

The horrors continued that spring into summer. In July there was a great explosion at the Chillwell munitions factory in Nottingham, England. How ironic that this close to the end of the war, nearly eight tons of TNT exploded, killing 134 and wounding another 250. Many of the victims were young "canary girls", women who contributed to the war effort by hazardous service in that plant. Little publicized at the time, it was the worst single explosion in British history.[62]

Meanwhile, as the Army continued its progress, in F. S. Cooke found much to record during those months:

> We follow a railway track to Underdam as ordered instead of a track across the fields which was safer. Get shelled and lose 150 men out of 196.[63]

Six days later he added: "Jerry pushes us back. There seemed to be millions of them." And four days later: "Dare not move, snipers everywhere. Good job I'm like a matchbook." No reader of this study can be surprised by this observation from 28 June 1918: "Mud and mud again everywhere even hot sun cannot bake it up." July wasn't much better: "Don't know the name of our sector but it lines up well with the rest of Ypres: mud, rats, rain, sunshine, smells, etc." Cooke may also have been one of the lucky ones:

> Found two holes in my mess tin, bullet holes and looks as though one hit some scissors I had in it and perhaps deflected it outwards. Anyway I'm still here.[64]

How utterly incongruous that is compared to Laidlaw's experience while behind the lines in reserve, as he wrote to his wife, "Sweetest":

...last night we had fresh fish, lamb and chips, peaches and cream and a baked fruit pudding, and they put up a bottle of fizz, so your old man is all right just now.[65]

Meanwhile, Haig had some fresh problems to solve. One concerned his personnel. Some of the less physically fit units were now taking their place in the line where their stamina raised concerns: "They can shoot and will hold a position, but cannot march very far, say, five miles slowly as is the normal."[66] It was also at this point that the Chief began to express his concern for disabled officers who had served the nation but been unable to return to duty. He recognized all too well that: "Now the officer in many cases has risen from the ranks, and in most cases is quite without means outside his pay."[67] Even after he withdrew from active duty (a Field Marshal in the British system is never considered "retired"), he remained engaged in veterans' affairs for the rest of his life.

As the German offensives wound down, the British made some changes in their tactics. Rather than attack the strongest parts of the enemy defenses, they went for a "bite and hold" philosophy.[68] Attack the weak spots, not the most well defended. Artillery would continue its massive role. In fact, in the last eight months of the war, the British fired between one and three million rounds a week.[69] What a change over the shortages of 1914 and 1915. Haig also paid more attention to his new tank corps:

> Remarkable progress... has been made with Tanks. Tanks may now go first, covered by shrapnel barrage, and break down all opposition. Enemy in strong points and machine gun nests are then flattened out by the Tanks. The latter then signal the infantry to 'come on', and these then advance in open order and mop up the remaining defenders, and collect the prisoners.[70]

Ultimately, the Germans tried in five separate campaigns to end this war by victory in 1918. In March they attacked along the Somme, in April, along the Lys, in May along the Aisne, in June toward Compiègne and in July in Champagne. Neither the British nor the French collapsed, and Germany had no offensive power left. After a short pause to rest and refit his Army, the Field Marshal was ready to begin what became known as the "Hundred Days." At long last, Haig's years old policy of keeping constant pressure on the Germans was about to yield results. Germany was not defeated. Much more human suffering would occur. But as the maps in the British daily newspapers made clear, the Germans were returning—at a controlled pace—to Germany.

Following the exhaustion of the German effort, the British and French moved forward. Their advance was not so much one grand battle as it was the "bite and hold" expanded to "bite and hold and move on." More specifically, the new style was to attack in "waves." A few soldiers would move forward and concentrate on "points of resistance." The next group bearing the "main weight of attack" would reduce these strong points. Next came reinforcements for the first two types, and finally some troops to remain in the newly taken territory.[71]

One of these attacks near Amiens began on 8 August. A large number of tanks were employed. By the end of the day, the German line had been penetrated to a depth of about seven miles on a front nearly fifteen miles wide. Numerous German soldiers, thoroughly demoralized by this point, took the opportunity to surrender. General Ludendorff is supposed to have called this day "the black day of the German army."[72]

Just about every place mentioned in earlier dispatches for the valour of its defenders as it was lost to the Germans was now triumphantly listed in the newspapers as retaken. The names of these, the details of these, exceed the scope of this study, but that in no way diminishes the sacrifice of those on both sides who fought and suffered on those fields of mud and blood. Even as he began the final campaign, Haig remained a modest man. His profound faith led him to believe that "...I am only the instrument of that Divine Power who watches over each one of us, so all the Honor must be His."[73] His religious convictions may have helped him through some of the darkest hours of his command. He used the month of August to make sure some of his ideas were carried out. For example, while he wanted constant pressure kept on the Germans, he did not want any more of those large scale attacks which had led to those horrendous casualty lists. Rather, the new method was to "Reinforce where we are winning, not where we are held up!"[74] Similar to the recent German strategy, the British were to keep moving, to attack the weak points, to bypass the strong points, and to use a future term for this method, allow those bypassed points to "wither on the vine."[75] He put it this way:

> Now is the time to act with boldness, and in full confidence that, if we only hit the enemy hard enough, and continue to press him, that he will give way and acknowledge he is beaten.[76]

Talking with one of his subordinate Generals, the Chief put it this way:

> I told him that owing to shortage of men I was opposed to doing more attacking than was absolutely necessary. Our object is to keep the battle going as long as possible, until the Americans can attack in force....[77]

Haig was keeping the casualties very much in his mind. In a letter to Sir Henry Wilson in London he acknowledged that if those numbers became too high, it might cost the Field Marshal his command.[78] At the same time, he kept his eye on one of his new favorite things, tanks, noting that on 23 August the tanks had done well—until they ran out of petrol and had to withdraw. Aware of the critical nature of his supply situation, especially if the Army began to move fast into the German-held lands, he conferred with his railway expert, recording:

> He has laid over 200 miles of track since last battle [8 August] began. He asks for 120 miles of rails [standard gauge] every month from now on to enable him to follow up the Armies through Belgium. The railways have kept up with the advance of the troops in a most praiseworthy way.[79]

At the opposite end of the technological spectrum, he also monitored cavalry matters, such as this directive:

> I directed [the staff to] augment Cavalry Corps by the addition of good infantry brigade in buses, and extra machine gun batteries in motors, with the object of exploiting situations which I hope will arise....[80]

Just a few weeks later, he added: "On Tuesday I am holding an exercise for the Cavalry Corps against a marked enemy, in order to practice all ranks in the pursuit."[81] The Duke of Wellington might have written the same order one hundred years earlier.

As September unfolded, the Field Marshal must have realized that the Germans were pushed out of Flanders, this time for good. His Armies took and retook what had become familiar names: Menin Road, Passchendaele, Messines. September saw the end of the fourth battle of Ypres with a British victory. Highly encouraged, Haig wanted all the men who were still in England to be shipped over at once in order to keep his pressure upon the Germans—even Royal Navy sailors, who he felt were underemployed:

> Within the last four weeks we had captured 77,000 prisoners and nearly 800 guns! There has never been such a victory in the annals of Britain, and its effects are not yet apparent.... Reserves in England should be regarded as reserves for the French front and all yeomanry, cyclists, etc., now kept for civil defense should be sent to France *at once*.[82]

There was never a shortage of fresh problems for D.H., seemingly never a day without something new. Sometimes the most interesting details got his attention. His diary notes that on 25 September 1918 he worried that a railway strike in Britain might affect his supply of ammunition. The next day, when one army unit was to cross a canal, for example, they borrowed life jackets from the cross-Channel steamers. Haig admired that kind of care being taken of his men.

While the Commander in Chief worried about the grand themes, his men continued to endure life while at war. In September, the mood in the trenches took a decided and realistic upswing:

> We continue to advance, but there was no panic in the German forces. Theirs was an orderly retreat. Their engineers had blown up all bridges. At cross-roads there were craters at least twenty yards deep, which slowed us up immensely…. The end was definitely in sight.[83]

A retreating army traditionally put obstacles into the path of the pursuers. This was a recognized strategy to slow down the chase, to allow the retreating soldiers to retire in good order. But some of the British thought that some of the German effort was just plain malicious. On 5 September 1918, the *Daily Mail* thundered its opinion that "…wanton destruction in France will be punished inevitably one day by stern reprisal in the form of destruction of German properties in like manner." This newspaper was fairly typical in its prose on war topics:

> There never was and there never will be finer troops than those of ours who have shattered the Kaiser's idea of world domination. Yet they are the soldiers of a citizen army, to whom war is not their business but their detestation, and their antagonists had been making ready for the struggle for more than a generation.[84]

Needless to say, a heavy diet of this jingoism was going to complicate the work of those politicians who would shortly be called upon to fashion a political end to this conflict. Moderation was certainly not going to be in style. The idea is not quite there yet, but undertones of "Germany must pay dearly" were certainly crystalizing. The *Daily Mail* did become a leader in another matter, one dear to the King. There were already and there would be many more disabled officers and men. There was only a rudimentary system for assisting them. Having met many such men on his trips to the battle zones and the hospitals, the King took the lead in establishing "The King's Fund for Disabled Officers and Men." It set a first goal of three million pounds. One of the first donors was the King himself, with his gift of £78,000.[85]

Every horror that had occurred earlier in this war recurred during the Hundred Days. The Germans used gas shells again, and "…the horses would not face Neuve Eglise village which was full of gas."[86] Destroyed countryside remained commonplace: "The banks of the Somme are all ragged with neglect and trenches and the river is full of bridge debris."[87] The personal discomfort remained severe: "I think it is not necessary to mention that I am everlastingly cooty, although I manage a clean change every now and again."[88] The tragic accidents remained as when a "...premature shell blows a crewman's arm off...."[89] And this:

> ...Where we are now it is awful, mud mud and more mud and a downpour of rain but we are smashing old "johnny" [sic] so we are all full of good spirits.[90]

In addition to leading the British Army, Haig also tried to share his hard-earned knowledge with the newly arriving Americans. But just as the colonials offered minimal respect to General Burgoyne one hundred fifty years earlier, the Americans did not seem to want much coaching. The Field Marshal seemed to have a rather detailed knowledge of his new American ally:

> The Americans are very ignorant of war requirements and insist on each man carrying 5 bombs! I said ½ bomb per man was now our average in the attack.[91]

The BEF formed "demonstration platoons" to instruct Americans. One British officer gave a speech to some U.S. troops but felt he was ignored, as some of the audience chatted with their neighbors or even slept. When he asked the American officers about his reception, they excused the conduct by telling him that those particular men were from New York, and that sixty percent of them did not speak English.[92]

The British soldier did have plenty to teach the Americans. After all, the British troops now wore a steel helmet, carried a magazine rife, and carried hand grenades, none of which were standard issue for the BEF of 1914.[93] Nor could there have been in those early days a battle like that for Amiens in 1918. In just that one battle, the British hurled 350,000 shells from 700 guns at the Germans, more shells than were fired by the Royal Artillery in all of 1914. Fully 504 of the Germans' 530 batteries were identified before the attack and very quickly put out of action.[94] The British also launched more than 550 tanks at the German lines. Taking advantage of the dry ground and a creeping barrage, the British pushed the Germans back up to eight miles. This was the first strong gain of the Hundred Days Campaign.[95]

This was a very different force than the BEF of 1914. The junior partner of 1914 went on to capture more ground, guns and men in the last 100 days of 1918 than the French and Americans combined.[96] Even medical care had greatly improved. After reporting to his family that "This is wrote [sic] left handed as I have been shot in my right arm", this soldier announced: "Had X-rays. Found bullet had gone right through."[97] Another wounded soldier had to be rescued in an odd manner: "I opened my legs and had him half on top of me, I crawled back."[98]

The British advance was quite rapid. In September, they drove the Germans out of Flanders for good. They retook so many blood-stained places: the Menin road, Passchendaele, Messines—and hundreds more too small to list but precious to their residents. By 1 October, Field Marshal Haig had a novel complaint:

> Reports from the Americans [west of the Meuse] and from Belgian HQ state that their roads and communications are so blocked that the offensive has had to stop and cannot be recommenced for 4 or 5 days. What very valuable days are being lost! All this is the result of inexperience and ignorance of the needs of a modern attacking force.[99]

By 4 October, the British were eighteen miles out of Ypres, well on their way toward the German homeland.[100] The next day saw them past the last German defenses, now moving over unfortified ground.[101] Haig was close behind his troops when a German rear guard suddenly turned on the pursuing British unit:

> Such a check as has taken place here today is due to Enemy suddenly strengthening his rear guard and taking the offensive. This must always be expected in operations of this nature, when advanced guards are pushing on to keep touch and press the Enemy…. as soon as we organize an attack with adequate artillery support the enemy will fall back.[102]

The British were now following the German retreat. But it was an orderly retreat, and from time to time and from place to place, the Germans would resist, sometimes strongly. Then, the British would bring up heavier guns, bombard the German positions and move on again. On 18 October, D.H. wrote in his diary:

> It was only yesterday that the Enemy was driven from this great fortress [Bel Aise farm], and yet I was able to walk about today, 24 hours later, almost out of the hearing of the guns. The dead men were still lying about and one was able to see where the struggle had been fiercest.

How profoundly sad that this close to the end of hostilities, men were still dying in such great numbers. As October ground on, the soldiers kept up their steady stream of letters home. One wrote his "Darling Wifie" that "... we are getting our food pretty good food but how would you like your tea made with water out of shell holes, what a colour."[103] Three days later he continued:

> ...we are taking our food in a shell hole and it's wet and muddy, food plates etc. of course get dirty and it's not easy to get water, still we are all quite cheery, as long as we keep pushing him back we will stick anything.

As the Army continued its now relentless pursuit of the retreating Germans, there was a storm of diplomatic activity going on behind closed doors. The German leadership realized they were defeated, and were looking for the best terms they could obtain from the Allies. Germany was in a sea of trouble: her principal ally, Austria, was defeated; German contacts with a supposedly more moderate President Wilson had gone nowhere; at home, political instability threatened the ability to govern at all. The need to end the war was urgent.

D. H. was called to London to express his views. Meeting with Prime Minister Lloyd George on 19 October 1918, Haig advised the politicians that the French army was not fighting much, as no one wants to die with peace at hand. He also reported that the American Army was disorganized, ill equipped and ill trained. Furthermore, it was short on good officers. His own Army, on the other hand, had fought hard but was lacking in reinforcements. He favored a prompt peace.

Even during these last days of war, the soldiers continued to record their experiences. One soldier recorded a happy moment:

> ...on this day there were any amount of civilians released from captured villages, they almost cried for joy as they came back through the lines, shaking hands and kissing every soldier they met [*sic*].[104]

Sometimes the British advance was delayed by damaged infrastructure, such as "We had to wait on the banks of the river Leys while the Engineers put a pontoon bridge across the river."[105] There was also the occasional bittersweet moment: "Met Pete Hardy from Ponders End [i.e., an old neighbor]. Had his leg off, progressing all right."[106]

Colonel E. K. Cordeaux was very clear about the imminent end to the war in this letter to "My own Darling":

> [Germany will accept terms because] they are completely outfought and are incapable of further effort—outgeneraled & outfought; they trusted to force and force they have had. And without boasting, it is mainly due to our dear

land & the men it breeds that right and justice have won and that we can
hold the heritage our forebears [*sic*] died to acquire.[107]

The high cost of this war made such expressions of patriotism less
common at the end than at the beginning. One man who had certainly
suffered personally—his first-born son died in the Battle of the Somme in
1916—was the Prime Minister who had led the nation into war in 1914.
No longer Prime Minister, but still a public figure, Herbert Asquith gave
a speech in Glasgow on 1 November 1918 concerning his Governments'
initial decision to go to war:

> A great decision, perhaps in some ways the greatest in history, had then to be
> taken.... Nearly four and a half years have passed, and is there anyone in the
> Kingdom, in the Empire who after long and sustained experience of sacrifice,
> of suffering, of personal and material loss—is there anyone who doubts that
> we decided rightly? And I suppose it is impossible for anyone to realize the
> weight of the burden of the responsibility which lay upon the shoulders of
> those who had to decide.[108]

And then, the end. With minimal fanfare, the Great War was over. Not so
much a sense of joy as a sense of relief that at last this madness is at an end;
that is the sense of the soldiers' diaries. One soldier remembered:

> On armistice day [*sic*], we went down into a little wood and found the
> skeletons of some of the Manchesters still there. Lying there with their boots
> on, very still, no helmets, no rusty rifles or equipment, just their boots.[109]

The Armistice went into effect at 11 minutes past the 11th hour on the
11th day of the 11th month: 11 November 1918. The British Government
suspended all recruiting, all call-ups were cancelled, all military tribunal cases
were dropped.[110]

And in Flanders on that day, at that time: it was raining, and there was
mud.

And in England on that day, as the bells were ringing to celebrate, the news
arrived for Mrs Owen that her son Wilfred had been killed on 4 November
1918.

And on 14 November 1918, there was a little-noticed story in the *Daily
Mail*: the previous week there had been twice as many deaths as births.

And on 15 November 1918, a Mrs Simpson received a letter announcing
that her son Joseph had died on 12 November 1918.[111]

And one year later, at eleven minutes after eleven o'clock on the eleventh day of the eleventh month, a new tradition was inaugurated. It became known as "The Silence." At that moment, Britain paused. Trains stopped. Pedestrians halted. Workers laid down tools. Veterans, in or out of uniform, stood to attention. For two minutes, silence was observed. Today that custom has morphed into "Remembrance Sunday", the second Sunday in November, when all over the nation, led by the Royal Family and by local dignitaries, war monuments are decorated, locals heroes are recalled, wreaths are laid on tombs and monuments.

Returning to 11 November 1918, the war might be over, but not the suffering. Not the suffering. Much remained.

CHAPTER VI

Aftermath

Sit on the bed. I'm blind and three parts shell.
Be careful; can't shake hands now; never shall.
Both arms have mutinied against me, —brutes.
My fingers fidget like ten idle brats.

—Wilfred Owen, *A Terre*[1]

The war was over, but so much remained to be done. In fact, the two greatest challenges were nearly contradictory: maintain a military presence in and over Germany while at the same time getting nearly four million soldiers home. Beyond that would be providing lifelong care for those who would never heal.

Within the BEF, now fifteen times the size it was in 1914, the overwhelming sentiment of the soldiers was the same: let's go home. Volunteers totaling 2.4 million held one idea in common with the 2.5 million conscripts.[2] It was time to go home. *Cincinnatus* had served his country and wanted only to return to his family and neighborhood. One soldier wrote his wife: "I would walk home if I could."[3] Colonel Cordeaux wrote to his wife "...the only thing the bulk of the men want is to be demobilized as soon as possible."[4] The volunteers had enlisted "for the duration", and they believed the duration had now been endured. Nearly everyone in uniform wanted to go home. The few remaining professional soldiers wanted to go, at least for a bit of leave before returning to occupation or overseas duty. With the exception of a few men making the army their career, and a few others who realized an army presence must be maintained lest Germany attempt some sort of "do over", everybody wanted to go home.

This sentiment was no surprise to the Government. The Ministry of Reconstruction had been organized in 1917, charged with planning the conversion to peacetime. Unfortunately, some of its plans were perfectly silly. "In fact the Ministry scheme, the product of clever Whitehall minds, theoretically sensible and administratively convenient, was completely out of touch with reality."[5]

In the Government view, the most important component was to control demobilization in such a way as to minimize unemployment. There was a real fear among some upper class persons that a danger of socialism, a danger of social unrest such as was taking place in the former empires of the Czar and the Kaiser might spread to Britain. The *Evening News* of 2 April 1919 wondered "Does the Army have to stay longer in Germany to prevent Bolshevists?" The Czar was murdered and the Kaiser in exile, and pandemonium now reigned in their formerly tightly controlled capitals. Such political infections must be prevented from spreading to the British Isles. Consequently, only as many soldiers were to be demobilized at a time as the economy could absorb.

Demobilization rules were promulgated. In the belief that the most recently conscripted would have the strongest connections to their former employers, they were to be the first released. The policy: last in, first out. Men in particular categories, men whose release would expedite the return of others—supervisors in a coal mine, for example—would be released first to pave the way for the others. These lucky fellows were known as "slip men" since they generally had a written promise of employment.

Some thought such a plan sensible if insensitive. London's *Daily Mail* of 13 November 1918 reviewed the plans. Those who worked in employment offices, for example, would get out early as would husbands long at the front. The details were rather fuzzy, however. On 28 November 1918, *The Times* observed that it was "...hard to see the reasonableness" of the rules. The New Year's day edition of the *Daily Mail* announced "It rests with demobilization to say when production and labour shall shake hands and get busy."[6]

Not surprisingly, this concept of "last in, first out" enraged millions. Those who had fought for years, borne what scripture would have called "the heat of the day", were to be indefinitely retained? That simply was not going to fly, and was foolish. What made perfectly sound economic sense grievously offended the national sense of fair play. In fact, there were demonstrations by discontented citizen soldiers, not over deep political questions or proposed forms of government, but over simple things like the speed of demobilization. One soldier witnessed troops "...defying authority and rioting" in the French port of Calais.[7]

There was more of that to come. Soldiers wanted out, plain and simple. When discharge did not come fast enough, there were "disturbances" begun by "...malcontents and disturbers of the peace" who were often in cushy jobs in base camps, not front-line fighting troops:[8]

I must confess that some of us did not behave very well.... Nor did the troops. For instance they refused to sing the national anthem after morning service at the Garrison Church. Three times the organist played the opening bars. The men, so far from singing, remained seated and silent. The Colonel, ice-cold externally but internally fuming, walked slowly to the lectern and addressed his mutinous command; either they would sing or remain in the church until hunger had overcome their objections to His Majesty. They sang, without enthusiasm.[9]

This was not an isolated incident. On another occasion a more serious disruption transpired. A few soldiers actually seized their officers and began a negotiation with a General concerning their grievances. Lieutenant Worthington witnessed this:

...[at Calais]... several thousand leave men had imprisoned the officers and locked the Guard in their own Guard room. We had to sort them out, one depleted but armed Brigade versus 6,000 mutineers, unarmed thank goodness. A nasty situation indeed. The prospect of having to fire on our own troops was not alluring. Meantime all three Battalions marched into the compound in single file and occupied two sides, facing the sulking crowd. Ostentatiously we loaded.

Guarded by military police, the Brigadier invited the ringleaders to submit their grievance... they did not notice the Redcaps [military policemen's] cautious approach. By the time their pals had yelled out a warning it was too late & they were in handcuffs. The riot was over. The troops dispersed. The officers and the Guard were released. We unloaded. Would we have used our weapons? I don't know.[10]

So there was some slight evidence to justify concern over the political leanings of the returning veterans. But while some feared a unified veterans' movement might demand more than the government was willing to provide, this did not happen. Various veterans' associations formed, ultimately amalgamating into the "British Legion" whose policies were so benign that Field Marshal Haig himself was active within it. By the 1930's, their main goal was to have veterans compensated for "...intangible results of war service."[11]

But the political leadership was not about to lose control now. *The Times* noted on 18 January 1919 that "The phase of unrest among sections of the troops concerning the process of demobilization appears to be passing away." *The Times* endorsed the Prime Minister's "timely warning" that any "...irregular assemblies or marches... will not quicken the release of men."

The BEF thus had a new problem, great military strength, but no enemy to serve as its target. Standard military training seemed pointless to the many who were unwillingly there in the first place and only marking time until discharged. The countryside of Belgium and France was filled with numerous under-employed, well fed, youthful men wearing uniforms but with little apparent immediate purpose. The Army Command had to keep these men busy.

As early as Armistice Day, Haig had reminded his officers that one of their duties was to keep the men "amused."[12] Many officers worked diligently along these lines. As individuals were called from their units and sent to discharge camps, the remaining men were kept occupied. Lieutenant Worthington recalled: "All the time we were losing men, and morale. Hopefully we organized concerts, gymnastics, darts competitions."[13]

Soldiers who did go home on leave and then return brought back news, simple little things that marked a return to what the American President Harding would famously call "normalcy." For example, Harrods's department store ran ads in the *Observer* on 19 January 1919 which announced we were "Looking Our Best Again":

The old world is casting off its shadows and social joys return to cheer our days. Now of all times is the time to trust to Harrods and so make sure of what is newest, loveliest & best.

Moreover, newspaper readers would find that almond candy with chocolate was available once more, and Calvert's Tooth Powder had returned in its tin package, now that the metal shortage was resolved. Complaints about a shortage of buses on the streets, however, were justified. An inquiry by the *Daily Mail* published on 3 May 1919 found that in 1914, 3,000 buses a day were on the streets of London, but that number had fallen to only 1,840 on the day of the Armistice. Readers could take comfort in knowing that new buses were on order. Such were the social news headlines the soldiers could bring back to their duty stations in France and Belgium where they helped not a bit with homesickness.

In this immediate post-war period, Winston Churchill was once again tasked to solve a major problem. This time he was put in charge of demobilization. What a multi-talented office-holder he turned out to be. While his record while holding major positions is well known, he also provided a great deal of less heralded service. He began the war as First Lord of the Admiralty, of course, but lost that position as a result of his support for the failed Dardanelles campaign. He then served as an officer in the trenches in France until returning to Parliament. He followed David Lloyd George as Minister of Munitions in 1917. In that position, and benefiting from the work that David Lloyd

George had set in place, munitions production increased so much that the British could finally fight "a rich man's war" with nearly unlimited supplies of material.[14] Having such quantities of supplies set up "Extravagance with transport and *materiel* (that) bought economy in lives."[15] Then he became Secretary of State for War in 1919. In that last position, he scrapped the existing demobilization polices and enacted new ones, beginning with "First In, First Out." Immediately, anyone who had served in 1914 or 1915 moved to the front of the line for discharge. Army strength, reported for the month of November, quickly declined as this table indicates:[16]

1918	3,779,825
1919	888,952
1920	431,916
1922	217,986

As Churchill told Parliament, by April of 1919, the Army was releasing men at the "enormous" rate of 13,000 or 14,000 a day.[17]

There were excellent reasons why it could not be done any faster. One involved simple logistics. The French railway system had not kept up with demand, and demand had only increased since the armistice. That stressed system had to carry food for the newly freed prisoners coming home from Germany, transport the demobilizing French soldiers, supply the soldiers now going into Germany, and, by the way, bring home British troops. It was doing just about all it could in the opinion of *The Times* of 15 January 1919.

Even the best plans were not always fulfilled. One soldier recorded his experience:

Being a miner, I was given priority, and was drafted back to England, and was posted around Bexley Heath, London, to await my demobilization. It came in March, and I was given my train pass and two pounds, and told to expect a fortnight's field ration money and pay at my home address.

However, when he arrived at the coal pit, they were "full up" and he could not find a job there as his muscles were "too soft for mining", so he took a job as a laborer.[18]

Many officers, too, now had to find work outside the BEF. Many of them had come up through the ranks and ended the war with aspirations far beyond what they might have sought before the war killed off so many of their social "betters" and enhanced their aspirations. These new-made non-traditional officers simply could not afford to remain in the Army. Officers just could not live on their pay. They had to provide for their own uniforms, servant's outfits, a contribution to the mess and an annual mess expense, to name some of their costs. The mess was a sort of compulsory officer's club; one simply had to be a member. If they were in the cavalry, they had the additional expense of maintaining as many as six horses: a charger, two hunters, and three polo ponies. Being an officer was an expensive proposition.[19]

A letter to *The Times* made the problem of employing the now former officers very clear. The author was a placement specialist for officers. His clients were all looking for jobs as private secretaries and estate agents. Such positions were in short supply. On the other hand, he had multiple openings for jobs such as training to be an "articled clerk", a form of apprenticeship for positions in accounting, law offices, and other businesses—but these were seen as "beneath" the former officers by the former officers—who just would not take the lower paying jobs, but would rather remain unemployed and continue looking.[20]

Then there was the sensitive matter of military pensions. Their task was to provide financial security, health care, and re-education or training.[21] The problem? People entitled to them just were not receiving them. A Parliamentary Inquiry looked into the whole matter in May, 1919. Testimony taken before the House Committee on War Pensions from Sir Albert Flynn, the acting Secretary of the Ministry of Pensions revealed spectacular deficiencies. While the department received 40,000 letters weekly, mostly inquiries, each had to go through forty different departments to be sure all aspects were reviewed. He testified that the system he inherited was "utterly bad", reporting that every incoming letter was "put away in a laundry basket system." He also pointed out that the department was located in forty different buildings in London.[22] Needless to say, prompt improvements were enacted. And just in time, perhaps, because the workload kept increasing. By 10 June 1919, *The Times* reported that 200,000 applications for "Form Z-16" were on hand.

To keep up its peacetime strength, the Army retained only those men who were under age thirty-seven and who had fewer than three wound stripes. It also kept officers, many involuntarily as in this case: "I am being retained in the Army & shall be out here until the end of summer and may be out for a year."[23] Parliament recognized the need for a continuing military establishment in "The Naval, Military, and Air Force Service Act" of 1919 which kept the most recently conscripted men until April 1920, which Churchill told Parliament was justified on "practical and patriotic" grounds.[24]

The Army needed to maintain an occupation force. Germany needed to be monitored. *The Times* was quite candid in its advice to the Government:

[The Prime Minister] must make sure that the fruits of the victory which have been won by the sacrifice of so many lives, and by so many brave deeds, are not jeopardized by any apparent weakness on the part of Britain during the critical months of the peace negotiations.

The German army have not yet been demobilized, and are still very powerful.... Impatience now might lose in a few weeks all it has taken years of heroism and sacrifice to gain.[25]

The troops actually sent across the Rhine were those with the most spit and polish. Left behind were those with "...leaky boots, tatty puttees, stained and torn uniforms."[26] *The Times* of 28 November 1918 carried advertisements for new uniforms which could be purchased by the "Army of Occupation." Some of the soldiers sent to occupy the edge of Germany took advantage of the opportunity to study German and Germany. Many did not. "Yes, I am ashamed that I did not take the trouble to learn any German other than 'Danke, Bitte, Prosit, and Zum Wohl.'"[27] Since conscription had ended abruptly on Armistice Day, and for political reasons the Prime Minister was not about to reintroduce it, the Army needed a fresh recruiting strategy to keep up its strength.[28]

The Army was also becoming more modern. It had moved a long way from its culture of 1914. No longer could an illiterate be as sure of a successful army career. Now there was a need for technical personnel. "...wireless operators, motor cyclists, telegraphists, cablemen and drivers" were among the earliest of the modern military technicians.[29] To obtain these skilled personnel, the Army had to compete both with the Royal Air Force and civilian occupations. To entice men to join or remain in the Army, several incentives were offered. Wages were doubled, and a re-enlistment bounty was paid to as many as 75,000 men by the end of 1919. The age of entry was also lowered to just seventeen.[30]

The Army updated itself in other ways as well. The Army had begun the war with not a single dentist. But due to need, that changed:

We didn't have dentists in any great number until 1916. Then when the dentists came over and the men got their teeth put right, and the dead ones pulled out and so on, it certainly got them into another era of health, because their food could be properly digested.... I believe it began a tremendous change in the attitude of the working class after the war—quite new to what had happened before it. [31]

By 1918, the Army had 800 dentists, some of whom were retained. For many soldiers, the Army dentist was the first health professional who had ever looked in their mouth, let alone treated them. On the other hand, all the Army's eye care service built up during the war was completely dismantled.[32]

Other reforms were accomplished just after the war. In May, 1919, for example, the Army set up the "Directorates of Hygiene and Pathology", bringing together what had been a number of "isolated army research workers."[33]

Why would an individual join the Army at this time? One might think that military life would be out of favor after such a long struggle. For some men, remaining in the service was a temporary expedient until their civilian opportunities became more clear. A few others actually looked forward to service in what they still called Russia. Still others were attracted by the extra pay available for the gruesome but important work awaiting them in France and Belgium, that of finding a "missing."[34]

That work involved finding graves, disinterring the remains and reinterring what was found, all with profound reverence. Many men had not come home. Many men had no identified grave. In many cases, no grave would ever be found. In many others, the bodies had just vanished. It was often hard for the families at home to accept that there was no definite grave. Sometimes they hired individuals to attempt to locate where their loved ones' remains might be. Sometimes they paid to have a body exhumed and returned to British soil for final burial. Sometimes they paid to have an individual monument erected near where their loved one was believed to have perished. Sometimes a chapel was erected on such a revered spot. On average, remains of thirty-five British and Commonwealth soldiers are still found in France and Belgium each year. Discoveries are likely to continue, for perhaps as many as 165,000 Commonwealth soldiers remain missing.[35]

An expertise developed around finding unmarked graves. Soldiers walked the fields, looking for clues. Sometimes they would find the remains of a wooden cross, and knew to dig. Sometimes they would find an unusually rich growth of grass, and realize they had found a body fertilizing its surroundings. Other clues included a localized discoloration of the soil or groups of holes made by vermin. Often while conducting these searches they would find live ammunition, at the incredible rate of five unexploded shells per square meter.[36]

The exhumation teams worked diligently. Between 1921 and 1928, they found 28,000 bodies, or parts of bodies, and were able to identify nearly twenty-five percent of them.[37]

Beside the decomposing corpses, the recovery troops and the returning farmers would also find timber, which could be used for construction or fuel; sheets of metal, which might form roofs of farm buildings; water pumps, useful to drain the fields; tools by the thousands and brass shell casings galore.[38] The fields were a vast wasteland of "vulgar debris", both human and material.[39] In Belgium the government used some of the reparations money paid by Germany to subsidize farmers who wanted to reclaim their land.

Trenches were filled in, drainage restored, debris removed. It was a great deal of work, often difficult and dangerous work. Even today, the land itself remains wounded by years of war:

> Contrary to popular belief, the extent of devastation in the Salient was restricted to a narrow ribbon of severe destruction barely six kilometers wide, outside of which by comparison, damage was limited. Within this band, however, the contamination of static trench warfare and years of relentless shelling was so intense that today the physical remnants have actually been laid down as a distinct geological feature. Just under the surface between the clay subsoil and the surface loams lies a stratum of metalliferous debris, a ruddy and rusting callous made up of shells and shell fragments, cables, rifles, shrapnel, sheeting, rails, expanded metal, wire, all kinds of weaponry, pickets, timber—and men.[40]

In numerous well-tended cemeteries in Belgium today, there are markers with the names of persons and an inscription such as "believed to be buried in this cemetery." In at least one cemetery, there is a notation of the names of some soldiers who were buried there, but a subsequent bombardment tore up the grounds and so the specific location is no longer known. There is also the frequent nameless monument bearing the inscription: "Known only to God."

The landscaping care devoted to these cemeteries nearly one hundred years after the war is remarkable. It is as though a contest were held among the caretakers with a huge prize for the best. Today a variety of flowers, seasonal and perennials, occupy the spaces beside many of the grave markers, which are themselves in nearly perfect condition and in perfect rows. Neglected, damaged headstones? None. Modest signs of weathering? Of course.

In 1920, *The Times* published an early report on the war cemeteries, finding there were 1,600 British cemeteries in France and Belgium, and another 1,200 cemeteries in Belgium and France containing some British soldiers. The actual land for the cemeteries had been deeded to the British in perpetuity, and a tour of these little islands of Britain surrounded by France and Belgium left an impression of "noble dignity, quiet grandeur and solemn peacefulness."[41] The contemporary visitor gains a similar impression.

In 1984, British cemetery head gardener Robert Jack was interviewed about his work. He reported there were 100 British cemeteries in Flanders alone. New bodies are often discovered when farmers plow. When they do, the farmers report the discovery to the police who report to the military exhumation teams, who then attempt to identify the remains. If they can trace the family, they are notified. Then the remains are respectfully reinterred in a nearby Commonwealth cemetery.[42]

On some of the major monuments, such as the memorial of the Menin Gate just at the edge of the modern town of Leper, there are names, thousands and thousands of names, carved on the monument: names of individuals with no known graves. At the dedication of the Menin Gate in 1927, General Plumer's remarks included the exhortation: "They are not missing! They are here!"[43]

A rather special ceremony has evolved at the Menin Gate. Each evening just before 8 o'clock, members of the Leper Fire Brigade in uniform stop the vehicular traffic through the archway of the Menin Gate Memorial and march into the center of the street. Exactly on the hour, they play "The Last Post." This mournful tune is similar in emotional content to the American "Taps." Often a military detachment will place a wreath of remembrance near the name of fallen members of that unit. Sometimes it is just an act of reverence in general. While it is played, tourists and local residents stand by in respectful silence. After the music concludes, the musicians retire and the crowd moves on. It is considered appropriate for an individual to thank the musicians in a soft voice, but never to applaud. It is not a performance; it is a memorial. The focus is not on the musicians but on the meaning. It is the sacrifice of the fallen that is recalled, not the skill of the players. With the exception of when the Germans occupied this town in the Second World War, this humble but moving ceremony has continued every night since the dedication of the Memorial in 1927.

Despite the large size of this Menin Gate memorial, it was soon realized that it did not have nearly enough room for all the names of those with no graves. Not far away is "Tyne Cot" cemetery and memorial with another 35,000 names carved on the walls.[44] This huge cemetery and memorial has one rather odd feature. A German pillbox remained here after the war. Seeing it on his pilgrimage there in 1922, King George V suggested it be incorporated in the architecture, and so today it is enclosed by a cross of remembrance. An opening in the covering masonry allows just a glimpse at the pillbox beneath.

Today no matter where one is in the Leper area, one is never beyond walking distance of a British cemetery. On the other hand, while the Germans also suffered great casualties in this area, their cemetery is very different. Most German graves were consolidated into one large one close to the town of Langemarck. A huge ossuary just inside the main entrance contains the remains of many unidentified soldiers. Altogether this is the final resting place for nearly 45,000 German soldiers.

The numerous British cemeteries are well marked with clear road signs. The German cemeteries? Not so much. There is an unfriendly attitude toward Germans among at least some Belgians even today.

Returning to the discharge of soldiers, the Army did not simply dump men on the street corners. Recognizing that many would be remaining in the service for months to come, and recognizing an opportunity to improve their skills and thus their employability, the Army rapidly set up an education aspect to its daily exercises. By the end of this program, perhaps one-third of the discharged were skilled in some useful way; a second third benefited from Army schools, while the last third remained ill-educated, poorly equipped to seek civilian employment.[45] One officer remembered providing paper, pencils and literature for his men, but many of their efforts were "illegible."[46] His men were not too keen on school just then:

> The men's thoughts were on demobilization. To hell with arms drill. The few originals, and Kitchener's few survivors especially, had had their fill of soldiering. Last in first out: they could not understand why conscript miners should have a preference over volunteer cotton-workers for instance.[47]

The procedure for demobilization was not terribly complex. Orders would arrive for an individual to report to a particular camp that specialized in discharging men. Here the individual would complete paperwork and surrender crown property, received some traveling money and papers showing an honorable exit from the King's forces. The individual was then free to travel home, where some more papers would arrive by mail. Sometimes the individual would be particularly valuable to the unit he was leaving—perhaps the only skilled "typist"—and so the unit might not be as prompt as possible in releasing that person. In fact, there were many cases where an individual was held up until he completed the training of the man designated to take his place. This made many men angry: the better they were at their duties, the harder it was to get out? Often true.

While the ordinary soldiers and the junior officers looked for work, the senior officers were able to add to the vast literature about this war. Generals wrote memoirs, sometimes criticizing other generals. The criticized then wrote rebuttals. Letters to newspaper editors followed with this or that position, and the key decisions of the war were rehashed in endless detail. Repeating an earlier point, Haig was blasted in Churchill's 1923 book with well written lines such as:

> ...if only the Generals had not been content to fight machine-gun bullets with the breasts of gallant men, and think that this was waging war.[48]

Churchill also hurled these words at the military leadership:

> It is a tale of the torture, mutilation or extinction of millions of men, and of the sacrifice of all that was best and noblest in an entire generation.[49]

Liddell Hart's 1930 work was no more gentle and is peppered throughout with criticisms of such things as sending soldiers forward into muddy morasses. This school of writers may be summarized as perpetuating "...doomed youth led blindly to slaughter by cruel age."[50] A more modern historian reached this conclusion:

John Terraine argued that there was no shortcut to victory on the Western Front, that the way was always going to be hard and bloody, but that under Douglas Haig the BEF wore down the German army in a series of attritional battles before delivering the coup de grace in 1918.[51]

The British leadership is certainly more disparaged than exulted in the literature. Recall the already reported remark about "Did we really send men to fight in that?" Then there is the stereotypical character created by John Cleese and his then-wife Connie Booth for the British TV comedy *Fawlty Towers*, Major Gowen. That former officer bumbles about the hotel, oblivious to everything except sport scores and whether the bar is open.[52]

A more nuanced opinion is offered by experts on Field Marshal Haig, the editors of his diary. They offer this observation:

When the war began, no one could have predicted that Great Britain would become a major military power or that a British general, commanding more than one million men, would be required by the Government to launch them against the main forces of a first-class enemy. This was not the 'British way in warfare'.[53]

One of the most singularly difficult calculations about this war is its actual cost. One can review casualty statistics, one can study expenditure charts. There were five million Britons in uniform, just over twenty-two percent of the male population,[54] and the war cost seven and a half million pounds a day.[55] The *Daily Mail* boldly proclaimed on 20 November 1918 that the cost of the war was "Forty Thousand Million Pounds." The author actually began what would have been a difficult calculation to convert that figure into a contemporary value, but stopped. That is not the point. That is not close to the point. What follows next is not a matter of expended funds.

Every war has an incalculable cost. This may be defined as that which might have been accomplished had the time, talent and treasure consumed in this endeavor been channeled elsewhere. Consider just these few famous persons and some of their accomplishments, remembering that all of them participated in but survived the Great War: A.A. Milne, forever associated with *Winnie the Pooh* and Christopher Robin; John Reith, one of the founders of the British

Broadcasting Corporation; Dennis Wheatley, the author of over seventy books, with over fifty million copies sold; C. S. Lewis, and his *Chronicles of Narnia*; J. R. Tolkien and *The Lord of the Rings*; Basil Rathbone and his fourteen Sherlock Holmes films, along with Nigel Bruce, his Doctor Watson; Alexander Fleming whose discovery of penicillin is estimated to have saved over 200 million lives; Bernard Montgomery, who would defend his nation in the next war; Peter Davies of the Peter Pan stories; Harold Macmillan, a future Prime Minister; Winston Churchill, likewise; J. B. Priestly, a novelist and broadcaster.[56]

Beyond this list of the well-known there are the numerous lesser known persons whose descendants have written to the author expressing their gratitude that their loved one was spared and enabled to raise the family of which they are a part. If these few people accomplished so much in the time they had, what might they have achieved had the call to arms not interrupted their civilian pursuits? Even more inexpressible, what might the men who did not survive have accomplished? Children of war veterans have a clear and ongoing sense of what might have been lost had just one more soldier failed to return whole.

To offer just one example: the record left behind by Prime Minister Asquith's first son, Raymond, was widely considered brilliant. Had he survived, perhaps held high office, what might have been different? What might have been better, or, to complete the possibilities, what might have been worse? One cannot count such a cost; one may only lament its loss. Liddell Hart's book contains this simple but profound phrase: "...the vacant places in our midst."[57]

If every war has an incalculable cost, it also has a footprint in literature which survives time. As it involved so many individuals over so long, it is not a surprise that the Great War added a great deal to the world treasury of poetry. Whole volumes of it are published. In this study there is opportunity for just a sample of its breadth and macabre beauty as written by BEF personnel:

> Now, he will spend a few sick years in institutes
> And do what things the rules consider wise,
> And take whatever pity they may dole.
> Tonight he noticed how the woman's eyes
> Passed from him to the strong men that were whole
> How cold and late it is! Why don't they come
> And put him into bed? Why don't they come?

—Wilfred Owen, *Disabled* (1917).[58]

Amid longer works, there are grandly powerful lines such as Edmund Blunden's "The terror of the waiting night outlived" or Siegfried Sassoon's

"The rank stench of those bodies haunts me still, and I remember things I'd best forget." [59] The poetry of Sassoon is extraordinarily powerful as, "...the gossamer veils of rhetoric and sentiment (are) pierced. In his world, nothing was beautiful." [60] Referring to those who dug the tunnels to set mines under German trenches, Edmund Blunden wrote:

> While men in the tunnels below Larch Wood
> Were kicking men to death. [61]

The last line of one Charles Sorley poem is: "Great Death he made us all his for evermore." [62] The less well known Hugh Freston was just twenty-four when he wrote:

> After I am dead,
> And have become a part of the soil of France,
> This much remember of me:
> I was a great sinner, a great lover, and
> Life puzzled me very much. [63]

Ivor Gurney found the same theme:

> Leave them buried, hidden until the slow, inevitable
> Change should make them service of France alone. [64]

The more famous Rupert Brooke treatment of the same topic:

> Blow out, you bugles, over the rich Dead!
> There's none of these so lonely and poor of old,
> But, dying, has made us rarer gifts than gold. [65]

There is more than a trace of bitterness in these poets. Few are as blunt as the words of this famous father who lost his son in the battle of Loos in 1915:

> If any question why we died,
> Tell them, because our fathers lied. [66]

Wilfred Owen's work includes this first stanza from "Futility":

> Move him into the sun—
> Gently its touch awoke him once,
> At home, whispering of fields unsown.

One last illustration of the mood in which the nation found itself inexorably entrenched is again from Edmund Blunden:

> I have been young, and now am not too old;
> And I have seen the righteous forsaken,
> His health, his honor and his quality taken.
> This is not what we were formerly told.[67]

The citizen soldiers wrote of the war they experienced. But more remained after the guns grew cold. In the modern town of Leper is the "In Flanders Field" museum. In 2010, just before a remodeling project was begun, there was an exhibit of a badly damaged piece of sculpture close to the exit. Its descriptive card asked the observer to remember all those who survived the war, but survived it with wounds. Not all wounds are visible. After all, for many years after the armistice, millions of people continued to suffer from personal physical and mental injuries, from loved ones' disability or disfigurement, from destruction of belongings. Suffering lasted long after the guns fell silent.

These hideous injuries can be reduced to numbers. British records indicate half a million soldiers were seriously disabled. There were 240,000 "major amputees", 60,000 shell shock victims, and 10,000 blind.[68]

Just such case was Captain Mickey Chater. His face was about as disfigured as it is possible to be and yet survive. After the original injury, when the period of maximum swelling had been reached, his face was terribly deformed, bright red, distorted, unnatural. His face looked like a very large tumor. Only his eyes were unaffected. It was quite difficult to perceive how he could be helped. It was his great good fortune, if such may be said of him, to pass under the care of Major A. C. Valadier, a pioneer in the specialty later termed maxillofacial reconstructive surgery. In a series of operations, the surgeon was able to reshape the facial tissues in such a way as to give Captain Chater back his face: scarred, yes, but no longer hideously deformed. Post-healing photographs show a man with scars but a man whose appearance would not send children fleeing from a monster. The before and after photos, as well as some intervening stages, formed an article in the British surgeon's professional magazine, the *British Journal of Surgery*. In a small but poignant irony, this surgeon expressed his professional preference against the brass wire commonly in use among his colleagues in favor of the German silver wire.[69]

Captain Chater got his life back, so to speak. Others, many many others, were not so fortunate. Long after the war, the Government maintained what were termed hospitals for the grossly deformed. Whole hospitals were devoted to limbless men, for example. People living near these special facilities understood the code system. Blue benches were open to men with catastrophic wounds, men whose appearance was socially unacceptable. Other people—self-proclaimed normal people—were welcome to all the others. A disfigured person would only sit on the blues benches, but all were welcome there. If an individual were willing to converse with a disfigured one, the disfigured would welcome the company—but they would not impose themselves on the "normals." Just when these hospitals and special facilities began to dwindle in numbers, the next war came along to repopulate them.

Within the "In Flanders Field" Museum there is a photograph of a man standing in the rubble of the Cloth Hall just after the war. It is evident that the individual is attempting to make a living by selling what may be guide books or pencils or what have you. On closer examination, it is clear that this man has lost both arms. This begs an eminently practical question: how does he urinate? If he were to visit a public restroom, he would have to ask someone there for some intimate assistance. If he were to go home each time he needed to void, he would still need assistance. Did providing that aid become a novel obligation for his wife or children or parents? He appears to be perhaps forty years of age. This new dependency on others will remain with him for the rest of his life, however long that may be. And how many men (and other war-injured persons) were in such a position?

One of the little known aspects of the Great War involves the efforts of tinsmiths, artists and engineers to fashion a mask for many whose faces were mutilated. Using as an anchor whatever tissues remained, such as an ear or most of a forehead, a mask was fashioned as close to the individual's natural features as possible. While the author has seen many photographs of these masks, he never saw one in the flesh, as it were. He found that quite a puzzle until his military expert pointed out the obvious: most of the individuals utilizing such a device were buried wearing it.

Along these same lines, there is a series of family portraits on the wall of one museum in Flanders. There is the grandfather, and the son, and the grandson. The first two appear hale and hearty. The third has the greater part of his head shrouded with permanent bandages, clearly a continuing part of his attire. Nearby is a portrait of three women dressing in mourning. They appear to be a mother, a wife, a daughter, silent testimony to the impact of just one of the deaths among so very many.

Many soldiers left military service for civilian life carrying wounds, large or small. Medical care for them out of the Army was still by experienced physicians: nearly one-half of the nation's doctors had served in the military. Often the individuals continued to suffer to greater or lesser extents, as in this case, exactly as the writer expressed it:

...I got shot through the face just missed my eyes and the roof of my mouth
the wound still runs every time I eat anything but then there are lots worse
off than me so I must thank God.... I don't think it will ever heal properly
for I have been under three operations and it is still the same....[70]

This letter illustrates two points. One is that no matter how willing, the fate
of the men often depended on the skill of the medical care received. It is an
obvious but overlooked truth that someone had to be last in his or her class
in medical school, and at least in combat situations, only the luck of the draw
decided who operated on whom.

That being said, no doubt the more wealthy veterans could afford to shop for
the most skilled practitioners in their field of need. But that leads to a second
point, an insight revealed in the letter to Lieutenant Worthington quoted above:
the letter-writer, Kennedy, was a common soldier, Worthington an officer. Yet
they maintained a limited correspondence for many years after the war. Kennedy
wrote an annual message to Worthington telling of his health and job and family
matters. Had there been no war, their social paths would probably never have
crossed. Yet as a result of this war, they maintained a social correspondence for
many years, well into old age. The war caused a realignment of the social classes
in Britain, a subject beyond the scope of this study.

There was also an effort to find employment for veterans who were unable to
live independently, but who did gain or retain the skills to work in a sheltered
workshop. In such an environment, men are given paid tasks they are able to
perform, and are thus able to earn a wage and feel productive. One example
of such workshops involved "Thermega" brand electric blankets. Even Earl
Haig, as the Field Marshal became in 1919, was photographed touring their
production facility. In the 1920's major stores carried these blankets, and those
who purchased them were deliberately made to feel that they were "helping."[71]

The health consequences of the war were not only physical. A number of
men cracked under the horrendous strain of what today would be termed
"shell shock." But to the men and Army medical personnel in the early days of
this war, shell shock and cowardice were indistinguishable. Who was faking,
who was the slacker? Since one could not be sure, arrest them both. As one
eyewitness put it:

At the front, in the 1914-1918 war, the psychiatric jargon was never used.
There was no such thing as shell shock in the face of the enemy: it was
cowardice and the offender was shot.[72]

But a turning point was reached when the situation was better understood.
Between April 1915 and April 1916, 1,300 officers and 10,000 men were

sent to special hospitals in Britain for shell shock.[73] As late as 1921, there were 65,000 men receiving pensions for "nervous complaints" which begs the question as to how many ought to have been receiving such a pension.[74] The bottom line remains, though, that:

> ...senior officers in the First World War did not have the luxury of almost 100 years of hindsight; a man who refused to fight—for whatever reason—was a serious problem.[75]

There were 3,000 courts-martial during the war. Common charges included drunkenness, desertion, and cowardice. At first, when a soldier was found guilty of a serious violation and shot, his family was told he was executed. Later, a little mercy entered the process, and the family was told their beloved had "died." While many of the convicted men were sentenced to death, after all the Army appeals processes were completed, the total executed was 322.[76]

Ten years after the Great War ended, 65,000 soldiers were in mental hospitals.[77] Fully twenty years after the war, of the more traditional afflictions, this "uniquely ghastly" war left disability pensions being paid to 11,600 men with amputated limbs, 10,000 pensions to blind men, and 3,200 still receiving pensions in mental asylums. As late as 1980, the Kingdom was still paying 27,000 pensions.[78]

A more pervasive health issue after the war could be termed a national malaise. This study has quoted from the papers of Rowland Myrddyn Luther. He did not write them until near the end of his life when he was aged 83. As he looked back over his life, his mood was somber. Mixing the profound and the mundane, he reflected:

> I plodded on through life and found some of the depressing years very difficult to live through. The "Land fit for heroes", as promised by Lloyd George, was just silly nonsense. The profiteers of the War had made their pile, and the gallant soldiers had been forgotten. The whole thing was now recognized as a ghastly mistake. The high-ranking generals had monuments built to their glorious victory and were given payments accordingly, but the rank and file were forgotten.[79]
>
> Soldiers were begging and playing instruments in the streets. One million British were dead, and two million had been wounded—and for what? We had served our country, and it was not for us to reason why.[80]

As war memorials were erected all around the nation, many took comfort in such ceremonies and remembrances. Not Luther:

The war had become a thing of the past, until the War Memorial was erected, and I stood and gazed at the names of so many of the men I knew—there were over 400, and I pictured my own name there—to what purpose, I do not know. Everything had changed much—everyone was miserable, food was dear and scarce, and I sold my army coat back to the army for 1 pound, payable at any railway station.[81]

The great national memorial in central London is a cenotaph, an ancient Greek word meaning hollow tomb. The large empty stone monument stands in the center of a busy street. One wonders what Roland Murddyn Luther might have made of that choice for the nation's principle memorial.

When he returned to his home on the outskirts of Oxford, Robert Graves had continuing experiences with former servicemen. He remembered that:

> Ex-servicemen were continually coming to the door selling boot-laces and asking for cast-off shirts and socks. We always gave them a cup of tea and money.[82]

Some of the men who came to Graves's door were not real veterans but were imposters, men posing as needy veterans to benefit from a nation's gratitude.[83]

These were not the only lasting reminders of the war for Graves. Like so many other veterans of the trenches, war-formed habits remained with him, including checking "conditions", long after he returned to civilian life: "Food, water supply, possible dangers, communications, sanitation, protection against the weather, fire and light—I ticked off each item as satisfactory."[84] But issues remained:

> Shells used to come bursting on my bed at midnight, even though Nancy shared it with me; strangers in daytime would assume the faces of friends who had been killed.[85]

Sixty years after the Great War, soldiers still held vivid memories. In his annual letter to Lieutenant Worthington, James Kennedy recalled:

> ...well Sir i [sic] never liked the army for you lived with a lot and denied with a lot and slept with a lot you had no privacy there are times when everyone wants to be alone if its only for an hour (no punctuation)[86]

In a letter from 2 January 1974, another soldier recalled a unique memory:

> We all remember the mud in the trenches and out, and stumbling over

obstacles on the way to the trenches. The railway cutting and the stench of dead bodies. I was always impressed by the calm of the mules under heavy fire.[87]

In an interview in 1984, Leslie Walkinton still recalled that the "Trenches were up to our knees in water sometimes" and that water was carried in a two gallon can. So was petrol. Often, he recalled, the water had a strong taste of gasoline or chloride of lime.[88]

Luther's diary closes with some poignant words:

The contemptible British Army which fought the First World War died in vain. We must let them sleep in those poppy fields of Flanders—only a memory to those who live on. Goodbye, gallant comrades.[89]

Pearson managed to pack a great deal of meaning into just a few words. Talking about the memories of the Great War, he aptly observed that "It does not live for those who were not actually involved in it."[90] He also asked the question: "...is the nation worthy of them and their sacrifice?"[91] Discussing the need for a remembrance ceremony, Pearson, who was then 83 years old, wrote the last line in his epilogue:

No, we do not need a yearly festival to remember those our friends of 1914/18—in our hearts we always do & shall remember them.[92]

The Great War profoundly affected Great Britain. It was so costly in so many ways that it caused a national miasma. Some thought the "Great" had been sucked out of "Great Britain." Certainly her world power was diminished. The impact was widespread. A new common culture emerged, a shared experience based on trench warfare and all that went with it. One historian wrote of a "...communal daze over the magnitude of the slaughter."[93] "For the ex-soldier, the war experience was a fully laden pack which he could not easily discard."[94] "The historian Gerhard Ritter, who experienced the carnage, called it '...monotonous mutual mass murder....'" [95]

To assemble that huge army meant that a high proportion of the men of the nation had to report for pre-conscription physicals. Just as the Doomsday Book presented a picture of the nation in the time of William the Conqueror, so too does that medical data give a snapshot of the national health at the time. In 1917, the Director-General of Recruiting found too many men were underweight, had poor chest measurements, or bad teeth.[96] The National Service Medical Boards found thirty-one or thirty-two percent of the examined men to be category "C3", which meant they had either "marked physical

disabilities" or "evidence of past disease."[97] Nearly one-third of the nation's
men were unfit for service? What a remarkable finding for a supposedly highly
civilized and "modern" nation.

The contemporary historian Gerald DeGroote has brilliantly summarized so
much of this brutal history in pithy phrases. He pointed out that "...cemeteries
occupy more ground than was won in battle" and "Little happened, but
millions died."[98] He also concluded:

> Flanders means endless human endurance. Flanders means blood and scraps
> of human bodies. Flanders means heroic courage and faithfulness unto
> death.[99]

Another gifted historian put it quite simply: "Flanders had become sacred
ground."[100]

Winston Churchill penned his tribute:

> Merciful oblivion draws its veils; the crippled limp away; the mourners fall
> back into the sad twilight of memory.[101]

For the soldiers of the BEF, the end of the war also brought a sense of wonder
and bewilderment. One wondered why he was spared and his neighbor not?
What they had endured—was it worth it? War warps a man's world. It takes
him from family and friends and work and all he has known. It delivers him
to lost time with his loves, whomever and whatever they may be. War costs.
Opportunities, time, treasure, imponderables: war warps, war costs.

Proof? Just a few years later, a blustering Chancellor of a resurgent
Germany rattled his sword, and the political leadership of Britain caved. In
the 1930's, Prime Minister Neville Chamberlain desperately sought a way to
avoid another war, to avoid what he thought would be climbing back into the
trenches. He allowed Hitler to take Czechoslovakia despite the British treaty
obligation to defend that ally. In public life, Winston Churchill was nearly
alone as he thundered in his prophetic phrase: "Britain and France had to
choose between war or dishonor. They chose dishonor. They will have war."

Was Chamberlain wrong? Much of the nation saluted his policies, sharing
his dread of doing it all again. The British lion had become more of a kitten.
Much of its spunk lay fertilizing Flanders.

War had warped the British spirit. But when pushed far enough, this time
by a demonstrably evil man, the citizen soldiers would reluctantly once again
put away their peacetime pursuits and respond once again to the call of arms.
This time, Germany's defeat would be total. This "do-over" would cost the
British lion dearly, but the price would be paid. The lasting peace that the BEF

of Flanders did not purchase would be achieved by their sons. The price paid in blood and mud would have an ultimate achievement. The Great War ended with the nearly universal sentiment throughout the British Empire of "War no more", war never again.

All this treasure expended, what had changed? What was different in 1918 from 1914?

Certainly the Armies were different. Gone were the bright red pants, the flamboyant moustaches, the old fashioned rifles. Arrived were the camouflage uniform, the steel helmet, the rapid fire rifle. But did these changes really matter? Did they justify the cost to humanity? Just what was Private Joseph Valentine Strudwick's life worth? How would he answer the question: what's been accomplished?

There are some final things that may be said about this war. After all the struggle over shell shortages and shell production, by the end, the British had fired 170 million rounds of ammunition, five million tons.[102] They also left "...scores of maimed and blinded men in our hospitals."[103] It is also possible to report the later days of some of those included in this study. Field Marshal Haig left active service shortly after the war ended, became active in veteran's causes, and died suddenly of a heart attack at age sixty-six in 1928. He was given a state funeral. Sir Jonathan Peel went on to become a long-serving Chief Constable of Essex, retiring in 1962 and dying in 1974 at age 81. When he died, this comment appeared in the police department newspaper recalling his administration:

> Older members of the force will recall Sir Jonathan's memory for names and his ability to know all about the wife's operation, the kids, and how long constables had served at particular stations.[104]

Captain William Henry Bloor had a much shorter story: he was killed in action on 3 January 1918. Let him represent those mentioned in this study who gave their lives—and the millions unmentioned who did as well.

In his book published in 1930, Liddell Hart wrote that "We know nearly all that is to be known."[105] May the author disagree with respect. Each time an attic chest yields a previously undiscovered diary, each time a researcher opens a packet of 1914-1918 letters, a bit more light is shed on a very dark time. And each one of those documents reminds us of how much is owed the men who endured the carnage, who gave their blood in the mud of Flanders and France.

A very great deal is owed the Lost Generation.

Endnotes

Prelude

1. Winston Groome, *A Storm in Flanders: The Ypres Salient: 1914-1918: Tragedy and Triumph on the Western Front* (New York: Atlantic Monthly Press, 2002), p. 2.
2. Michael Howard, *The First World War* (Oxford: Oxford University Press, 2002), p. 8.
3. Groome, p. 2.
4. Howard, p. 9.
5. The King of the United Kingdom was also styled the Emperor of India.
6. Howard, p. 11.
7. Robert Wohl, *The Generation of 1914* (Cambridge: Harvard University Press, 1979), p. 93.
8. William Philpott, *Three Armies on the Somme: The First Battle of the Twentieth Century* (New York: Alfred A. Knopf, 2010), p. 5.
9. Colonel (and Doctor) Cyril Helm, Helm Papers, IWM, 99/13/1, p. 2.
10. Rowland Myrddyn Luther, "The Poppies are Blood Red." IWM, 87/8/1.

Chapter I

1. Archer Jones, *The Art of War in the Western World* (Oxford: Oxford University Press, 1987), p. 464.
2. Barbara Tuckman, *The Guns of August* (New York: Ballantine Books, 1994), p. 20.
3. Stephen Bull, "The Early Years of War" in Gary Sheffield, Ed., *War on the Western Front* (Oxford: Osprey Publishing, 2007), p. 175.
4. The same person who would lead Britain in the Second World War.
5. Churchill, *The World Crisis* (New York: Charles Scribner's Sons, 1923), p. 422.
6. *Ibid.*, p. 131.
7. *Ibid.*, p. 147.
8. John McIlwain Diary, 27 August 1914. IWM. 96/29/1.
9. His wife, whose picture he carried with him. T. H. Cubbon Diary, IWM, 78/4/1.

10. *Ibid.*, 29 September 1914.
11. McIlwain Diary, 17-21 September, 1914.
12. Cubbon Diary, 19 September 1914.
13. McIlwain Diary, 17 September 1914.
14. Cubbon Diary, 19 September 1914.
15. Henry T. Williams, "My Memories: True Stories of Incidents that Happened in the First World War." IWM, 02/4/1.
16. Helm Diary, 29 October 1914.
17. *Ibid.*, 28 October 1914.
18. *Ibid.*, p. 14.
19. Jones, p. 420.
20. *Ibid.*
21. Martin Pegler, "British Tommy" in Sheffield, p. 105.
22. *Ibid.*, p.107.
23. *Ibid.*
24. David Stevenson, *Cataclysm: The First World War as a Political Tragedy* (New York: Basic Books, 2004), p. 148.
25. Groom, p. 19
26. *Ibid.*, p.17.
27. Jones, p. 453.
28. There is a display of a stuffed pigeon in a parachute in the Imperial War Museum, London.
29. Martin Gilbert, *The Somme: Heroism and Horror in the First World War* (New York: Henry Holt and Company, 2006), p.19.
30. Gary Sheffield and John Bourne, Editors, *Douglas Haig: War Diaries and Letters 1914-1918* (London: Phoenix, 2005), 24 August 1914.
31. Helm Diary, p. 6.
32. McIlwain Diary, 16 September 1914.
33. Jones, p. 439.
34. Cubbon Diary, 19 September 1914.
35. Stephen Bull, "The Early Years of War" in Sheffield, p. 188.
36. Groom, p. 74.
37. Gerard DeGroot, *The First World War* (New York: Palgrave, 2001), p. 164.
38. Robert Graves, *Goodbye to All That* (New York: Random House, 1998), p. 99.
39. Churchill, p. 130.
40. Limbers were usually two-wheeled horse-drawn carts with slots for carrying shells; they were sometimes modified to carry water or other supplies.
41. Helm Diary, August, 1914, p. 5.
42. Bully beef is also known as corned beef.
43. Luther, p. 21.
44. Cubbon Diary, 3 October 1914.
45. *Ibid.*, 5 September 1914.
46. Cubbon Diary, 4 October 1914.
47. *Ibid.*, 15 September 1914.
48. *Ibid.*, 18 September 1914.
49. Helm Papers, p. 8.
50. Gilbert, p. 22.

51. 17 November 1914.

52. McIlwain Diary, 2 September 1914.

53. Americans would call these "crackers" or "saltines."

54. Cubbon Diary, 17 August 1914.

55. *Ibid.*, 19 September 1914.

56. H. T. Williams, "My Memories."

57. Graves, p. 138.

58. *Ibid.*, p. 193.

59. Victor Packer, quoted in Max Arthur, *Forgotten Voices of the Great War: A History of World War I in the Words of Men and Women Who Were There.* (Guilford, Connecticut; Lyons Press, 2002), p. 85.

60. Thomas McIndoe, Oral Interview, IWM, Dated 17 February 1983. No reference number attached.

61. Luther, p. 11.

62. Ralph Smith Papers, IWM, 86/36/1. p. 22.

63. A. S. Carter, "Account of Service", IWM, 01/48/1, p.5. The American soldiers would later call lice "seam squirrels."

64. Graves, p. 104.

65. Ralph Smith Papers, 1914.

66. John Ellis, *Eye Deep in Hell: Trench Warfare in World War I* (Baltimore: Johns Hopkins University Press, 1976), p. 57.

67. Private Clifford Lane, quoted in Arthur, p. 95.

68. Luther, p. 11.

69. Peel Diary, 12 December 1914.

70. McIlwain Diary.

71. Cubbon Diary, 17 September 1914.

72. *Ibid.*

73. McIlwain Diary.

74. H. T. Williams, "My Memories."

75. Cigarette.

76. Cubbon Diary, 30 September 1914.

77.   *Ibid.*, 19 September 1914.

78. Captain Maberly Esler, recorded interview, IWM, #378, 1974.

79. Helm Diary, Spring, 1915.

80. Graves, p. 131.

81. H. T. Williams, "My Memories."

82. Helm Diary, November, 1914.

83. McIlwain Diary, 1-5 October, 1914.

84. Cubbon Diary, 27 August 1914.

85. McIlwain Diary, 16 October 1914.

86. Cubbon Diary, 8 November 1914.

87. Clive Hughes, "The New Armies" in Ian Beckett and Keith Simpson, *A nation in arms: A social study of the British army in the First World War* [sic] (Manchester: Manchester University Press, 1985), p. 109.

88. The government postcard was a printed form where the soldier could check off statements to personalize the preprinted message, such as "I'm feeling better now, thanks."

89. Helm Diary, 21 October 1914.

90. McIlwain Diary, 2 September 1914.

91. *Ibid.*, entry dated "Sept. 17-20", 1914.

92. The very extensive war damage to these structures was fully repaired by the 1960s.

93. This is the correct local spelling. But many variations were used by the British, including "Passondale" and "Passendale."

94. Groom, p. 48.

95. Helm Diary, 22 October 1914.

96. 3 October 1914.

97. *Haig Diary*, 1 November 1914.

98. Cubbon Diary, 11 November 1914.

99. Helm Diary, 20 October 1914.

100. Ellis, p. 33.

101. *Ibid.*, p.48.

102. Martin Pegler, "British Tommy" in Sheffield, p. 101.

103. November, 1914.

104. Ralph Smith Papers, 1914.

105. One person who fought in Flanders that autumn and later became infamous: Adolph Hitler.

106. McIlwain Diary, 12 November 1914. These lines must have been edited after the date mentioned.

107. R. H. Mottram cited in Peter Simkins, "Soldiers and Civilians: billeting in Britain and France" [*sic*] in Beckett, p. 183.

108. Churchill, p. 853.

109. Stevenson, p. 76.

110. *Ibid.*, p.164.

111. *The Times*, 3 September 1914.

112. Wohl, p. 93.

113. Grooms, p. 20.

114. Jones, 421.

115. Jay Winter, "Army and society: the demographic context" [*sic*] in Beckett, p. 198.

116. Edward Spiers, "The regular army in 1914" [*sic*] in Beckett, p. 39.

117. Churchill, p. 134.

118. And yet as General Joffre reminded King George V of England: Napoleon was defeated at Waterloo—not at sea.

119. *King Richard II.*

120. Martin Pegler, "British Tommy", in Sheffield, p. 96.

121. Fred Dixon quoted in *Ibid.*, p. 98.

122. Peter Simkins, "Soldiers and civilians: billeting in Britain and France" [*sic*] in Beckett, p. 166.

123. *Ibid.*, p.170.

124. *Ibid.*, p. 171.

125. Churchill, p. 134.

126. Pegler, "British Tommy", in Sheffield, p. 95.

127. Lord Kitchener advised the army commanders to "practice economy" with shells. Groom, p. 50.

128. In the summer of 1971, the author briefly worked in a factory producing

rail cars and auto parts. Huge stamping machines bent a sheet of metal into a car's trunk lid, for example. The press performing the actual striking held two "dies" or molds composed of individual pieces called "steels", and each "steel" was crafted to very precise measurements on a smaller machine by a highly skilled individual. The more modern method employs lasers, robots and computers, none of which were available, of course, during the Great War.

129. DeGroote, p. 145.

130. Graves, p. 110.

131. War Diary of Captain William Henry Bloor, Royal Field Artillery, IWM 99/22/1. 2 December 1915.

132. Emphasis in the original. *Haig Diary.*

133. Post War Survey Form, Barclay Godfrey Buxton Papers, IWM, 78/60/1.

134. Cubbon Diary, 29 September 1914.

135. Victor Packer in Arthur, p. 83.

136. Groom, p. 67.

137. DeGroote, p. 174.

138. Ellis, p. 119.

139. Pegler, "British Tommy" in Sheffield, *War on the Western Front*, p. 115.

140. Ellis, p. 98.

141. Marmaduke Leslie Walkinton, Oral Interview # 8499, 1984. IWM.

142. Conversation between General Haig and King George V, *Haig Diary*, 4 December 1914.

143. Helm Diary, 21 October 1914.

144. *Ibid.*, 20 October 1914.

145. McIlwain Diary, 17-21 Sept. 1914.

146. Oral Interview, 1986, IWM.

147. Martin Pegler, "British Tommy" in Sheffield, p. 122.

148. McIlwain Diary, 5 October 1914.

149. Private Frank Sumpter in Arthur, p. 56.

150. Gilbert, p. 60.

151. Luther, p. 11.

152. Princess Mary was the sole daughter of the King and Queen.

153. Colonel Reginald Leonard Haine Interview, 1973, IWM, #33.

Chapter II.

1.   Letter, Arthur Edwards to "Will", 26 July 1915. Edwards Papers, IWM, 85/15/1.

2.   Cubbon Diary, 5 and 7 January 1915.

3.   Pearson Papers, p. 36.

4.   Lyn Macdonald, *1914: The Days of Hope*, cited in Groom, p. 77.

5.   Brooks Diary, IWM, 87/62/1. January, 1915.

6.   Grooms, p. 87.

7.   Stephen Bull, "The Early Years of War" in Sheffield, p. 196.

8.   Martin Pegler, "British Tommy" in *Ibid.*, p. 106.

9.   Helm Diary, 17 October 1914.

10. Pearson Papers, p. 32.

11. *Ibid.*, p. 35.

12. Interview, Victor Fagence, 1983. IWM, # 6615.

13. Pearson Papers, p. 32.
14. Letter, George A. Rose (eyewitness) to Captain J. B. L. Noel, 20 May 1974. This letter was in response to a published letter from Captain Noel asking for veterans to write to him about their experiences sixty years earlier. Noel Papers, IWM, 92/52/1.
15. *Ibid.*, 29 April 1915.
16. Pearson Papers, March, 1915.
17. Letter, Captain Noel to "My dear ones", 4 April 1915.
18. Luther, p. 18.
19. 17 August 1914.
20. Ralph Smith Papers, 1914.
21. Graves, p. 226.
22. Clive Hughes, "The New Armies" in Beckett, p. 103.
23. Jay Winter, "Army and society: the demographic context" [*sic*] in Beckett, p. 196.
24. *Ibid.*, p. 93.
25. *Ibid.*, p. 196.
26. *The Times*, 18 August 1914.
27. Jay Winter, "Army and Society: the demographic context [*sic*] in Beckett, p. 197.
28. Clive Hughes, "The New Armies" in Becket, p. 108.
29. After the war, the name "Ypres" was changed to "Iper."
30. The Boer War between the British and South African Boers was fought between 1899 and 1901 and was the last major action of the British army before this war. The quote is from Luther, p. 4.
31. *Ibid.*, p. 6
32. Brabyn Papers, IWM, 87/59/1, p. 9.
33. Luther, p. 6.
34. *Ibid.*, p. 9.
35. *Ibid.*, p. 7.
36. James Fillis, *Breaking and Riding*. (Lyons Press, 2005), p. 220. This was originally translated from the French and published in 1902.
37. Luther, p. 8.
38. Helm Diary, February-March, 1915.
39. March, 1915.
40. Luther, p. 28.
41. Bloor Diary, 13 December 1915.
42. *Ibid.*, 17 Dec. 17, 1915.
43. Photograph of "Shackling", #Q 36208, IWM.
44. Fillis, p. 232.
45. A tambour is a form of a drum. *Ibid.*, p. 228.
46. *Ibid.*, p. 214.
47. Luther, p. 7.
48. *Ibid.*, p.10.
49. *Ibid.*, p. 16.
50. Wrestling on horseback: photo #17355; tug of war, photo #17304. IWM.
51. Scots Greys were famously grey war horses, and thus not easily disguised. Graves, p. 243.

52. McIlwain Diary, 20 October 1914.
53. Barclay Diary, 2 June 1915.
54. Stephen Bull, "The Somme and Beyond" in Sheffield, *War on the Western Front*, pp. 237-238.
55. Gilbert, *The Somme*, p. 7.
56. Churchill, p. 298.
57. *Ibid.*, p. 853.
58. Ellis, p. 39.
59. *Ibid.*, p. 45.
60. Cubbon Diary, 14 January 1915.
61. Pearson Papers, p. 36.
62. Brooks Diary, 13 November 1915.
63. Ellis, p. 49.
64. IWM, recorded 14 February 1983.
65. Ellis, p. 114.
66. *Ibid.*, p. 24.
67. Private Alfred Bromfield in Arthur, p. 79.
68. Graves, p. 158.
69. *Ibid.*, p. 157-159.
70. Arthur, p. 105.
71. Corporal Edward Glendinning in *Ibid.*, p. 101.
72. May, 1915.
73. Barclay Diary, May 1915.
74. Graves, p. 235.
75. Luther, p. 13.
76. Pegler, "British Tommy", in Sheffield, p. 112.
77. Ellis, p. 127.
78. Barclay Diary, April, 1915.
79. Luther, p. 17.
80. Barclay Diary, 30 May 1915.
81. Pearson Paper, 28 March 1915.
82. *Haig Diary*, 20 January 1915.
83. Ellis, p. 156.
84. Bloor Diary, Dec. 7-11, 1915.
85. Barclay Interview, 1974, IWM, #299.
86. Ellis, p. 146.
87. Pegler, "British Tommy", in Sheffield, p. 115.
88. Ian Beckett, "The nation in arms: 1914-1918" [*sic*], in Beckett, p. 46.
89. Sergeant Alfred West in Arthur, p. 93.
90. Ralph Smith Papers, p. 55.
91. Graves, p. 122.
92. Barclay Diary, April 1915.
93. Graves, p. 114.
94. Pearson Papers, pp. 34-35.
95. Graves, p. 163.
96. Churchill, p. 460.
97. *Haig Diary*, 22 January 1915.
98. Robin Prior and Trevor Wilson, *The Somme* (New Haven: York University

Press, 2005), p. 7.

99.   Stephen Bull, "The Early Years of War" in Sheffield, p. 195.

100. *Haig Diary*, 11 February 1915.

101. *Ibid.*, 10 February 1915.

102. Prior, p. 261.

103. *Haig Diary*, 18 March 1915.

104. Prior, p. 307.

105. Groom, p. 80.

106. *Haig Diary*, 20 January 1915.

107. Barclay Papers, 23 April 1915.

108. *Ibid.*

109. *Ibid.*, April 1915.

110. *Ibid.*, 25 April 1915

111. Colonel Helm Diary, Easter Sunday (4 April), 1915.

112. Jones, p. 465.

113. Letter from "C Nation" to Captain Noel, Noel Papers, 17 May 1974.

114. Helm Diary, 23 April 1915.

115. Barclay Diary, 25 April 1915.

116. Stephen Bull. "The Early Years of War" in Sheffield, p. 211.

117. Ellis, p. 67.

118. H. T. Williams. "My Memories."

119. Howard, p. 62.

120. Jon Silkin, *The Penguin Book of First World War Poetry* (London:Penguin Books, 1996), p. 85.

121. Helm Diary, 1915, p. 31.

122. Graves, 28 May 1915, p.113.

123. *Ibid.*, p.115.

124. Groom, p. 117.

125. Barclay Diary, April 1915.

126. *Ibid.*, 23 April 1915.

127. B. H. Liddell Hart, *The Real War 1914-1918* (Boston: Little, Brown and Company, 1930), p. 185.

128. Gilbert, p. 28.

129. *New York Tribune*, 1 May 1915, p. 6.

130. 8 May 1915.

131. 10 May 1915.

132. Churchill, p. 425.

133. Paul Strong and Sanders Marble, *Artillery in the Great War* (Barnsley: Pen and Sword Military, 2011), p. 38.

134. Prior, p. 9.

135. Pearson Papers, p. 40.

136. *Haig Diary*, 16 September 1915. When reading the Haig diary, one must always kept in mind that he knew he had an audience for each line he wrote.

137. *Ibid.*, 20 September 1915.

138. *Haig Diary*, 19 August 1915.

139. Liddell Hart, p. 187.

140. *Ibid.*

141. Ellis, p. 93.

142. *Ibid.*
143. Letter, Arthur Cornfoot to "Winnie", 29 September 1915 IWM, #6409.
144. Liddell Hart, p. 195.
145. *Ibid.*, p. 198.
146. General Haig to King George V, 11 August 1914. *Haig Diary.*
147. Prior, p. 281.
148. This anti-poison gas sprayer, looking like a modern insect sprayer, could turn green if the copper parts were not kept dry. Graves, p. 217.
149. Stephen Bull, "The Early Years of War" in Sheffield, p. 194.
150. Ellis, p. 193.
151. Andy Simpson, *Hot Blood and Cold Steel: Life and Death in the Trenches of the First World War* (London: Tom Donovan, 1993), p. 109.
152. Ian Becket, "The nation in arms, 1914-18" [*sic*] in Beckett, p. 21.
153. Ellis, p. 138.
154. Pegler, "British Tommy", in Sheffield, p. 113
155. Ellis, p. 25.
156. Stephen Bull, "The Early Years of War", in Sheffield, p. 101.
157. Prior, p. 17
158. Stephen Bull, "The Early Years of War", p. 207.
159. Jones, 461.
160. Bloor Diary, 3-6 December 1915.
161. Ralph Smith papers.

Chapter III

1. Silkin, p. 193.
2. Prior, p. 31.
3. *Haig Diary*, 29 March 1916.
4. Stephen Bull, "The Somme and Beyond" in Sheffield, p. 263
5. IWM, # 8279.
6. Daniel John Sweeney Papers, IWM, 76/226/1. 23 June 1916.
7. Lt. Colonel Fredrick Packer, 22 March 1916. IWM, 1653.
8. Pearson Papers, p. 47.
9. Gilbert, p. 13.
10. Prior, p 32.
11. Philpott, p. 133.
12. Bloor Diary, 26 June 1916.
13. *Haig Diary*, 13 November 1916.
14. Groom, p. 3.
15. Philpott, p. 153.
16. Pannier: a form of luggage; similar to saddlebags. Sergeant Ernest Bryan in Arthur, p. 149.
17. Whiteman, *My Brief Memories,* 1 July 1916.
18. Jones, p. 422.
19. Philpott, 133.
20. Prior, p. 302.
21. *Ibid.*, p. 65.
22. Gilbert, p. 50.
23. Lieutenant Charles Carrington in Arthur, p. 147.

24. Luther, p. 26.
25. Jones, p. 457.
26. Stephen Bull, "The Early Years" in Sheffield, p. 195.
27. *Ibid.*
28. Grant Diary, 6 March 1916. IWM, 97/16/1.
29. Bloor Diary, 22 February 1916.
30. The Roneo machine used "stencils", which were a top sheet of what looked like white paper attached to a purple colored backing sheet. One could write with a pen, or print, or type on the white sheet, tear it off, pin it to the drum of the machine, and generate a limited number of copies. In the author's experience, teachers used them in American schools well into the 1980s. The quote is from Philpott, p. 137.
31. Martin Pegler, "British Tommy" in Sheffield, p. 105.
32. Luther, p. 26.
33. Prior, p. 64.
34. Stephen Bull, "The Somme and Beyond" in Sheffield, p. 243.
35. Bloor Diary, 9 June 1916.
36. Hoult Diary, 16 April 1916. IWM, 07/62/1.
37. Sweeney Papers, July 1916.
38. Pearson Papers, p. 41.
39. Luther, p. 21.
40. Bloor Papers, 31 May 1916.
41. Jay Winter, "Army and society: the demographic context" [*sic*] in Becket, p. 196.
42. *Ibid.*
43. Bloor Diary, 31 May 1915.
44. Harold Brooks Diary, 5 January 1916, IWM, 87/62/1.
45. W. J. Grant, Diary, 27 April 1916, IWM, 97/16/1.
46. Buxton Post War Survey.
47. Lachrymatory gas was designed to cause eye irritation.
48. Graves, p. 105.
50. Andy Simpson, p. 18.
51. Lieutenant Victor Hawkins in Arthur, p. 80.
52. Sweeney Papers, 16 May 1916.
53. Ounsworth Interview, #332, IWM.
54. Both, W. J. Grant Diary.
55. Luther, p. 27.
56. Bloor Papers, 22 June 1916.
57. Stephen Bull, "The Somme and Beyond" in Sheffield, p. 227.
58. *Ibid.*, p. 243.
59. Boor Diary, 25 June, 1916.
60. *Ibid.*, 29 June, 1916.
61. Stevenson, p. 150.
62. Prior, p. 65.
63. 1 July 1916.
64. Gilbert, p. 52.
65. Sweeney Papers, 29 June 1916.
66. Lieutenant Colonel Alfred Irwin in Arthur, p. 154.

67. *Ibid.*, p. 154.
68. Pearson Papers, p. 44.
69. Sweeney Papers, July 1916.
70. Grant Diary, 1 July 1916.
71. *Ibid.*
72. Prior, p. 74.
73. *Ibid.*, p. 78.
74. Arthur, p. 102.
75. Peel Diary.
76. Whiteman, 1 July 1916.
77. Pearson Papers, p. 45.
78. Bloor Diary, 3 July 1916.
79. *Ibid.*, 9 July 1916.
80. Trooper Walter Becklade in Arthur, p. 76.
81. Grant Diary, 7 July 1916.
82. Bloor Diary, 12 July 1916.
83. Strong, p. 38.
84. An insulting nickname for the Germans.
85. Bloor Diary, 12 July 1916.
86. *Ibid.*, 14 August 1916.
87. *Ibid.*
88. Peel Diary, 15 July 1916.
89. Bloor Diary, 15 August 1916.
90. *Ibid.*, 1 August 1916.
91. Grant Diary, 1 July 1916.
92. Bloor Diary, 31 July 1916.
93. *Ibid.*, 1 August 1916.
94. Pearson Papers, p. 45.
95. Luther, p. 24.
96. *Ibid.*, p. 24.
97. The Prince of Wales (later Edward VIII) to Captain Faussett, 14 September 1916. IWM, 1141.
98. Prior, p. 300. Another source gives the figure as 420,000 killed, wounded, prisoners or missing. J. P. Harris, *Douglas Haig and the First World War* (Cambridge: Cambridge University Press, 2008), p. 271.
99. Liddell Hart, p. 243.
100. Churchill, p. 745.
101. Dockworkers: 25 October; Hughes, 28 June; Canterbury, 21 May, all in 1916. *Haig Diary*.
102. Harris, p. 194.
103. *Ibid.*, p. 195.
104. Gage refers to the distance between the rails. Smaller gage is usually faster to construct and can be brought closer to the front line.
105. Harris, p. 255.
106. *Ibid.*, p. 186.
107. *Ibid.*, p. 275
108. Adjutant-General, a staff officer.
109. Liddell Hart, p. 245.

110. General Haig also urged that the Navy launch a tank attack from the North Sea. Diary, 18 September 1916.

111. Philpott, p. 6.

112. Churchill, p. 742 and 744.

113. DeGroote, p. 171.

114. The Germans employed a new armor piercing bullet that could penetrate the tank and wound or kill the crew, but this was in short supply, partly due to the naval blockade.

115. Philpott, p. 10.

116. *Ibid.*, p. 100.

117. Pegler, "British Tommy" in Sheffield, p. 125.

118. Prior, p. 32.

119. *Ibid.*, p. 115.

120. DeGroote, p. 29.

121. Prior, p. 270.

122. *Haig Diary*, 13 November 1917.

123. Philpott, p. 105.

124. Harris, pp. 272-273.

125. Prior, p. 302.

126. Letter, Haig to King George V, 5 October 1916. *Haig Diary*.

127. *Ibid.*, 8 November 1916.

128. Bloor Diary.

129. Sweeney Papers, 20 August 1916.

130. *Ibid.*, 11 August 1916.

131. Brabyn Diary, IWM, 85/15/1.

132. A detachable shoe covering which fits over the ankle and instep; today often worn by marching bands.

133. Buxton Papers.

134. H. T. Williams, "My Memories."

135. Peel's letters home were copied by his family into a notebook. The (?) notation is in that notebook.

136. Pearson Papers, p. 44.

137. *Ibid.*, p. 43.

138. Brabyn Papers, p. 16.

139. Laidlaw Papers, 25 October 1916.

140. Peel Papers, "On the Somme", October, 1916.

141. *Ibid.*, October 1916.

142. Pearson Papers, p. 57.

143. *Ibid.*, p. 56.

144. *Ibid.*, p. 60.

145. *Ibid.*, p. 50.

146. Luther, p. 26.

147. Letter, Frank Noel to Captain Noel (his brother), 10 September 1916. Noel Papers.

148. Luther, p. 29.

149. Harris, p. 273.

150. *Ibid.*, p. 267.

151. *Ibid.*, p. 268.

152. *Ibid.*, pp. 267-268.
153. *Ibid.*, p. 267.
154. Prior, p. 140.
155. *Ibid.*, p. 60.
156. Peel Diary, 9 October 1916.
157. 18 October 1916.
158. Bloor Diary, 13 August 1916.
159. Grant Diary, 9 December 1916.
160. Brooks Diary, p. 38.
161. Lieutenant Charles Carrington in Arthur, p. 135.
162. Groom, p. 76.
163. Silkin, p. 123.
164. *Ibid.*, p. 89.
165. http://www.edmundblunden.org/index.php?pageid=98. Accessed February 14, 2013.
166. Ellis, p. 80.
167. Harris, p. 271.
168. *Haig Diary.*
169. German planes had bombed London, which the British denounced as making war on civilians.
170. *Daily Telegraph*, 1 July 1916.
171. 1 July 1916.
172. Beanfeasters were groups of people who left London for a day's holiday in the country; the author is trivializing soldier's sacrifices, although with good intentions—not to frighten the populace.
173. *Daily Telegraph*, 5 July 1916.
174. Ellis, p. 178.
175. Noel Hoult, Letter to "Connie", Christmas Day, 1916. Hoult Papers, IWM, 07/62/1.
176. Noel Papers, 10 September 1916.

Chapter IV

1. Harris, p. 281.
2. Edward Spiers, "The regular army in 1914" [*sic*] in Beckett, p. 57.
3. Dennis Wheatley, <u>Officer and Temporary Gentleman: 1914-1919</u>. London: Hutchinson & Co., 1978. p. 197.
4. *Ibid.*, p. 157.
5. *Ibid.*, p. 156.
6. Q 1649, IWM, photo annex.
7. A "haybox" was a container designed to keep things hot or cold, using hay as insulation. Lt Ulrich Burke in Arthur, p. 242.
8. Brabyn Diary, p. 28.
9. *Ibid.*, p. 26.
10. Revd John Francis Bloxam Letter in the Noel Papers, IWM, 2249, 23 September 1917.
11. Haine Interview.
12. Pearson Papers, March, 1917, p. 85.
13. The Prince of Wales to Captain Foussett, 29 June 1917. IWM, 1141.

14. Harris, p. 287.
15. Footnote, *Haig Diary*, p. 270.
16. 28 January 1917.
17. Peel Diary, 21 December 1917.
18. Luther, January 1917, p. 30.
19. Pearson Papers, p. 37.
20. Ellis, p. 51.
21. Haine interview.
22. Letter to "My Dearest Father", 20 January 1917.
23. *Ibid.*, 6 February 1917.
24. Brabyn Papers, p. 32.
25. Pearson Papers, p. 66.
26. Luther, p. 32.
27. Ellis, p. 51.
28. Pegler, "British Tommy" in Sheffield, p. 123.
29. Ellis, p. 44.
30. Pearson Papers, p. 65.
31. Luther, p. 38.
32. Ellis, p. 41.
33. Keith Simpson, "The officers" [*sic*] in Beckett, p. 87.
34. Lieutenant Ulrich Burke in Arthur, p. 241.
35. Luther, p. 15.
36. A range of figures is offered in Alexander, p. 162; Ellis, p. 116; Stevenson, p. 169. They average 80%.
37. Groom, p. 175.
38. Captain Maberly Esler, Royal Army Medical Corps, in Arthur, p. 100.
39. Ellis, p. 58.
40. Pegler, "British Tommy" in Sheffield, p. 124.
41. Graves, p. 103.
42. Groom, p. 113.
43. Ellis, p. 117.
44. *Ibid.*, pp. 58-59.
45. Ralph Smith Papers.
46. Pegler, "British Tommy" in Sheffield, p. 123.
47. Ellis, p. 155.
48. Private Thomas McIndoe, Oral Interview, IWM, #6615.
49. Peter Simkins, "Soldiers and civilians: billeting in Britain and France" [*sic*] in Beckett, p. 186.
50. *Haig Diary*, 7 February 1917.
51. Gary Sheffield, *The Chief: Douglas Haig and the British Army* (London: Aurum Press, 2011), p. 201.
52. Sheffield, *The Chief*, p. 194.
53. Peel Diary, 28 February 1917.
54. Whiteman, February 1917.
55. Sheffield, *The Chief*, p. 211.
56. Jones, p. 474.
57. Sheffield, *The Chief*, p. 199.
58. Churchill, p. 754.

59. Jones, p. 475.
60. Pearson Papers, p. 69.
61. Groom, p.174.
62. *Ibid.*, p. 161.
63. Peter Baron, Peter Doyle and Johan Vandewalle, *Beneath Flanders Fields: The Tunnellers' War 1914-1918* (Staplehurst: Spellmount Limited, 2004), p. 269.
64. *Ibid.*
65. *Ibid.*, p. 268.
66. Stephen Bull, "The Somme and Beyond" in Sheffield, p. 260.
67. *Haig Diary*, 12 April 1917.
68. Groom, p. 155.
69. The day-to-day losses of men due to snipers, accidents, illness, etc.: the daily weakening of the army not caused by major battles.
70. *Haig Diary*, 3 May 1917.
71. Groom, p. 156.
72. Sheffield, *The Chief*, p. 148.
73. 20 June 1917.
74. Churchill, p. 612.
75. Stevenson, p. 266.
76. Ian Beckett, "The nation in arms, 1914-18" [*sic*] in Beckett, p. 25.
77. Howard, page 101.
78. *Haig Diary*.
79. *Ibid.*, 11 November 1917.
80. Churchill, p. 734.
81. *Pall Mall Gazette*, 6 and 12 November 1917.
82. Sheffield, *The Chief*, p. 219.
83. Harris, p. 336.
84. 19 April 1917, Harris, p. 334.
85. Sheffield, *The Chief*, p. 214.
86. Ellis, p. 119.
87. Harris, p. 349.
88. Churchill, p. 734-735.
89. *The Times*, 2 March 1917.
90. Harris, p. 352.
91. Buxton Papers, 6 February 1917.
92. *Ibid.*
93. Peel Diary, 28 January 1917.
94. *Ibid.*, 28 February 1917.
95. Grant Diary, 25 February 1917.
96. Pearson Papers, p. 68.
97. *Ibid.*, p. 67.
98. Whiteman, February, 1917.
99. Grant Diary, 4 March 1917.
100. Littlewood War Diary, IWM, 98/33/1, 8 March 1917.
101. Arthur, p. 86.
102. Barclay Diary, 17 April.
103. *Haig Diary*, 30 July 1917.
104. Grant Diary 27 May 191.

105. *Ibid.*, 2 December 1917.

106. Martello is a strong beer. Captain Noel letter, 25 April 1915.

107. Peel Papers, 30 August 1917.

108. *Haig Diary*, 7 June 1917.

109. Website, Firstworldwar.com/today/messinesmine.

110. Sheffield, *The Chief*, p. 228.

111. Groom, p. 174.

112. *Ibid.*, p. 184.

113. Captain J. C. Hill in Arthur, p. 217

114. Groom, p. 185.

115. Stephen Bull, "The Early Years of War" in Sheffield, p. 210.

116. *Ibid.*, p. 259.

117. Wheatley, pp. 209-210.

118. Luther, 31 July 1917.

119. Ellis, p. 45.

120. Grant Diary, 31 July–4 August, 1917.

121. Quoted in Arthur, p, 235.

122. *Haig Diary*, 17 August 1917.

123. *Ibid.*, 13 October 1917.

124. P. Smith Papers, 18 September 1917. IWM, #11412.

125. *Ibid.*, 17 September 1917.

126. *Ibid.*, 18 September 1917.

127. Buxton Papers, 22 July 1917.

128. *Ibid.*, 29 July 1918.

129. Grant Papers, 23 September 1917.

130. "Trail left"—aim the weapon more to the left.

131. This was not published until 1920. Depending on the source, there are slightly different versions of a few lines of this poem. Silkin, p. 193.

132. Groom, p. 209.

133. Whiteman, 1917.

134. *Ibid.*

135. Harris, p. 377.

136. Peel Diary, 5 August 1917.

137. *Ibid.*, 12 August 1917.

138. Stephen Bull, "The Somme and Beyond" in Sheffield, p. 241.

139. Quoted in Arthur, p. 249.

140. *Ibid.*, p. 214.

141. There is some controversy about this figure. See Groom, p. 229.

142. Churchill, pp. 737-738.

143. Italy was a minor ally of the British and was losing against Austria, Germany's ally.

144. Groom, p. 226.

145. Liddell Hart, p. 343.

146. Wheatley, p. 155.

147. Groom, p. 224.

148. Graves, p. 107.

149. Bloor Diary, 9 April 1916.

150. Jones, p. 456.

151. Groom, p. 201.
152. Field Marshall A. P. Wavell quoted in Keith Simpson, "The officers" [*sic*] in Beckett, p. 85.
153. Haine Interview.
154. Groom, p. 233.
155. Luther, p. 41.
156. Sheffield, *The Chief*, p. 256.
157. Stevenson, p. 277.
158. Stephen Bull, "The Somme and Beyond" in Sheffield, p. 261.
159. Grant Diary, 18 November 1917.
160. Ellis, p. 36.
161. Quoted in Arthur, p. 222.
162. Peel Diary, 23 August 1917.
163. *Ibid.*, 18 August 1917.
164. *Ibid.*, 14 September 1917.
165. *Ibid.*, 12 December 1917.
166. Buxton to his parents, 18 December 1917.
167. Harris, p. 384.
168. Grant Diary, 17 December 1917.
169. Churchill, p. 763.
170. Stevenson, p. 331.
171. *Haig Diary*, 7 December 1917.
172. *The Times*, 17 March 1917.

Chapter V

1. "Warbride" in Fiona Waters, *A Corner of a Foreign Field: The Illustrated Poetry of the First World War* (Hertfordshire: Transatlantic Press, 2007), p. 26.
2. Laidlaw Papers, 1 January 1918.
3. Cook papers, 10 January 1918.
4. Peel Diary, 10 January 1918.
5. F. S. Cooke Papers, 12 January 1918.
6. *Ibid.*, 20 February 1918.
7. F. S. Cook Papers, 13 March 1918.
8. A. S. Carter, 12 January 1918.
9. Peel Papers, 25 February 1918.
10. Pearson Papers, March 1918, p. 71.
11. Churchill, p. 764.
12. Pearson Papers, p. 83.
13. *Haig Diary*, 19 March 1918.
14. J. P. Harris, p. 436.
15. Sheffield, *The Chief*, p. 259.
16. Grant Diary, March, 1918.
17. Arthur, p. 259.
18. Pearson Papers, March 1918.
19. Harris, p. 434. Another source indicated 80,000 men were home on leave. DeGroote, p. 119.
20. *Ibid.*, p. 433.
21. Liddell Hart, p. 366.

22. Harris, p. 433.
23. Sheffield, *The Chief*, p. 261.
24. Harris, p. 423.
25. *Ibid.*, p. 435.
26. Stevenson, p. 332.
27. Letter to Sir Charles Cavanaugh, 3 March 1918. *Haig Diary*.
28. Harris, p. 447.
29. Stevenson, p. 333.
30. Jones, p. 475.
31. Grant Diary, 16 March 1918.
32. *Ibid.*, 21 March 1918.
33. Pearson Papers, March 1918, p. 89.
34. Jones, p. 479.
35. F. S. Cook, 26 March 1918.
36. Grant Diary, 28 March 1918.
37. Pearson Papers March 1918, p. 90.
38. Grant Diary, 27 March 1918.
39. Sergeant Major Richard Tobin in Arthur, p. 268.
40. Grooms, p. 236.
41. *Haig Diary*, 29 March 1918.
42. Stevenson, p. 336.
43. Churchill, p. 787.
44. Groom, p. 239.
45. *Ibid.*, p. 240.
46. Firstworldwar.com.
47. *Haig Diary*, 9 April 1918.
48. Churchill, p. 765.
49. Pearson Papers, March 1918, p. 80.
50. F. S. Cooke, 30 March 1918. "Mentioned in dispatches" refers to the practice of including the names of individuals and units for official praise in reports to higher headquarters. It was a point of honor to be included, and so a deeply felt slight to not be mentioned.
51. Grant Diary, 4 April 1918.
52. Diary, 18 April 1918.
53. Sheffield, *The Chief*, p. 287.
54. It took until November 1918 to reach this total. Stevenson, p. 331.
55. Pearson Diary, March, 1918, p. 76.
56. *Ibid.*
57. H. T. Williams. "My Memories."
58. Hardman Papers, IWM, 84/11/1.
59. Grant Papers, 27 April, 1918.
60. *Haig Diary*, 12 April, 1918.
61. F. S. Cooke, 3 May, 1918.
62. http://www.bbc.co.uk/insideout/eastmidlands/series2/blast_chilwell_somme.shtml. Accessed 2/9/2013.
63. 2 July 1918.
64. 13 July 1918.
65. Laidlaw Papers, 16 May 1918.

66. *Haig Diary*, 24 June 1918.
67. *Ibid.*, 19 July 1918.
68. Sheffield, *The Chief*, p. 295.
69. Bull, "The Somme and Beyond" in Sheffield, p. 256.
70. *Haig Diary*, 31 July 1918.
71. Bull, "The Somme and Beyond" in Sheffield, p. 256.
72. Andy Simpson, p. xviii.
73. *Haig Diary*, 8 August 1918.
74. *Ibid.*, 21 August 1918.
75. A phrase often used to describe U. S. strategy in the Pacific War of 1941-1945 against Japan. Major Japanese island bases were essentially ignored, rather than expending American lives to capture just another island.
76. *Haig Diary*, 19 August 1918.
77. *Ibid.*, 1 September 1918.
78. *Ibid.*
79. *Ibid.*, 7 September 1918.
80. *Ibid.*, 25 August 1918.
81. *Ibid.*, 15 September 1918.
82. *Ibid.*, 10 September 1918.
83. Luther Papers, Summer, 1918, no page number.
84. *Daily Mail*, 11 September 1918.
85. *Ibid.*
86. Grant Papers, 4 September 1918.
87. Harold Brooks Papers, 11 September 1918.
88. Cooke Diary, 21 September 1918.
89. Grant Papers, 27 September 1918.
90. Laidlaw to his wife, Bertha, Laidlaw Papers, 30 September 1918.
91. *Haig Diary*, 28 September 1918.
92. Haine Interview.
93. Jones, p. 473.
94. Sheffield, *The Chief*, p. 299.
95. Stevenson, p. 347.
96. Andy Simpson, xviii.
97. Cooke Diary, 10-11 October 1918.
98. Pearson Papers, p. 78.
99. *Haig Diary*.
100. Groom, p. 247.
101. Stevenson, p. 351.
102. *Haig Diary*, 12 October 1918.
103. Laidlaw Papers, 2 October 2 1918.
104. Grant Diary, 15 October 1918.
105. *Ibid.*, 23 October 1918.
106. F. S. Cooke, 31 October 1918.
107. Colonel Cordeaux to his wife, 7 November 1918. IWM, 16975.
108. *The Times*, 2 November 1918.
109. Private Hubert Trotman in Arthur, p. 309.
110. *Daily Mail*, 12 November 1918.
111. Letter from a Nurse describing the Death of a Soldier, IWM, Document

13657.

Chapter VI

1. Silkin, p. 201. Owen was just 24 years old when he wrote these lines.
2. Stevenson, p. 164.
3. T. D. Laidlaw, 12 March 1919. Laidlaw Papers.
4. 5 January 1919.
5. Keith Jeffrey , "The post-war army" [*sic*] in Beckett, p. 212.
6. 1 January 1919.
7. Pearson Papers, 29 January 1919.
8. *Ibid.*, p. 106-109.
9. Worthington Papers, IWM, 75/28/1. p. 96.
10. *Ibid.*, p. 89.
11. Jay Winter, "Army and society: the demographic context" [*sic*], in Beckett, p. 201.
12. *Haig Diary*, 11 November 1918.
13. Worthington Papers, p. 86.
14. Sheffield, *The Chief*, p. 293.
15. Stevenson, p. 348.
16. Keith Jeffrey, "The post-war army" [*sic*] in Beckett, p. 214.
17. *Ibid.*, p. 213.
18. Luther Papers.
19. Edward M. Spiers, "The regular army in 1914" [*sic*] in Becket, p. 43.
20. 5 February 1920.
21. Fiona Reid. *Broken Men: Shell Shock, Treatment and Recovery in Britain, 1914-1930* (London: Continuum, 2010), p. 29.
22. *Daily Mail*, 1 May 1919.
23. Cordeaux Papers, 3 May 1919.
24. Keith Jeffrey, "The post-war army" [*sic*] in Beckett, p. 215.
25. 9 January 1919.
26. Worthington Papers, p. 81.
27. In order: thanks, please, cheers and to your health. *Ibid*, p. 97.
28. Keith Jeffrey, "The post-war army" [*sic*] in Beckett, p. 214.
29. *Ibid.*, p. 221.
30. *Ibid.*, p. 214.
31. Buxton Oral Interview, IWM, #299, 1975.
32. Keith Jeffrey, "The post-war army" [*sic*] in Becket, p. 225.
33. *Daily Mail*, 3 May 1919.
34. Keith Jeffrey, "The post-war army" [*sic*] in Becket, p. 217.
35. Kathryn Hadley, "Remains of German Soldiers found in France", *History Today* website, accessed 1 August 2012.
36. Barton, p. 266.
37. Ian Beckett, "The nation in arms, 1914-1918" [*sic*] in Beckett, p. 27.
38. Barton, p. 267.
39. Groom, p. 259.
40. Barton, pp. 264-265.
41. *The Times*, 5 February 1920.
42. Oral History, IWM, 8517.

43. Groom, p. 262.
44. Commonwealth War Graves Commission Website.
45. Keith Jeffrey, "The post-war army" [*sic*] in Becket, p. 223.
46. Worthington Papers, p. 81.
47. *Ibid.*, p. 80.
48. Churchill, p. 745.
49. *Ibid.*, p. 299.
50. Wohl, p. 105.
51. Sheffield, *The Chief*, p. 4.
52. Reid, p. 19.
53. Gary Sheffield and John Bourne, *Haig Diary*, p. 28.
54. Ian Beckett, "The nation in arms: 1914-1918 [*sic*] in Beckett, p. 11.
55. Martin Pegler, "British Tommy" in Sheffield, p. 92.
56. Richard Van Emden & Victor Piuk, *Famous 1914-1918* (Barnsley: Pen & Sword Books, 2008).
57. p. 470.
58. Silkin, p. 195.
59. Blunden: Silkin, p. 106; Sassoon, Silkin, p. 124.
60. Wohl, p. 95.
61. Groom, p. 161.
62. Ellis, p. 197.
63. Gilbert, p. 17.
64. Silkin, p. 117.
65. http://www.oucs.ox.ac.uk/ww1lit/education/tutorials/intro/brooke#title.
66. Rudyard Kipling. Silkin, p. 136.
67. *Ibid.*, p.113.
68. Stevenson, p. 448.
69. Major A. C. Valadier, "A Few Suggestions for the Treatment of Fractured Jaw." *British Journal of Surgery*, Vol. IV, Bristol: John Wright and Sons, 1916.
70. James W. Kennedy to Lieutenant James Worthington, 16 July 1919. Worthington Papers.
71. Reid, p. 161.
72. Brabyn Papers, p. 9.
73. Reid, p. 13.
74. *Ibid.*, p. 10.
75. *Ibid.*, p. 100.
76. Ellis, p. 185
77. Groom, p.115
78. Andy Simpson, ix.
79. The politicians decided to honor various military leaders with titles and financial packages, and these were in some cases negotiated. For example, Field Marshal Haig was created an earl and given £100,000 to sustain a concomitant lifestyle.
80. Luther, p. 46.
81. *Ibid.*
82. Graves, p. 314.
83. *Ibid.*, p. 315.
84. *Ibid.*, p. 287.

85. Graves, p. 287.

86. James Kennedy to Lieutenant Worthington, 12 June 1974.Worthington Papers.

87. E. J. M. Eldridge to Captain Noel, Noel Papers.

88. Walkinton Interview, IWM.

89. Luther Papers, p. 48.

90. Pearson Papers, p. 2 A.

91. *Ibid.*, p. 113

92. Pearson Papers, p. 23.

93. Sheffield, *The Chief*, p. 359.

94. DeGroote, p. 200.

95. *Ibid.*, p. 42.

96. Keith Jeffrey, "The post-war army" [*sic*] in Beckett, p. 200.

97. Reim, p. 91.

98. DeGroote, p. 23.

99. *Ibid.*, 175.

100. Groom, p. 246.

101. Churchill, p. 849.

102. Ellis, P. 63.

103. H. T. Williams, "My Memories."

104. *The Law: The Newspaper of the Essex Police.* December, 1979, No. 121.

105. Liddell Hart, p. 471.

Primary Sources, Imperial War Museum Collection

Barclay Papers. 06/55/1.

Bloor, Captain William Henry. "War Diary", 99/22/1.

Brabyn, Reverend F. J. 87/59/1.

Brooks, Harold. Diary, 87/62/1.

Buxton, Godfrey Buxton. Papers, 78/60/1.

Carter, A. S. "Account of Service", 01/48/1.

Chater, Captain A. D. "Mickey." Medical Records. 87/56/1.

Cooke, Fredrick Stuart. 87/13/1.

Cubbon, Sergeant T. H. Diary. 78/4/1.

Edwards, Arthur. 85/15/1.

Grant, W. J. 97/16/1.

Haine, Colonel Reginald Leonard. Oral History. 33.

Hamilton, Major E. S. Burt. War Diary. 87/33/1.

Hardiman, T. 84/1/1.

Helm, Colonel (and Doctor) Cyril. 99/13/1.

Hoult Papers. 07/62/1

Kitwood, Colonel R. T. S. 3176.

Laidlaw, T. Douglas. 09/76/1.

Littlewood, Captain Martin W. War Diary. 98/33/1.

Luther, Rowland Myrddyn. "The Poppies are Red", 87/8/1.

McIlwain, John. 96/29/1.

McIndoe, Thomas Walter. Oral Interview 568.

Noel, John Baptist Lucius "Bert." 92/52/1.

Oldham, Thomas. 08/38/1.

Pearson, R. 87/51/1/

Peel, Captain Sir Jonathan. 80/34/1.

Smith, P. 11412.

Smith, Ralph I . 86/36/1.

Spence, H. V. 03/31/1.

Sweeney, Daniel John. Extracts from the Letters of. 76/226/1

Valadier, Major A. C. "A Few Suggestions for the Treatment of Fractured Jaw." *British Journal of Surgery*, Vol. IV, Bristol: John Wright and Sons, 1916.

Whiteman, Rev. Henry. "My Brief Memories." 80/23/1.

Williams, Henry Thomas. "My Memories: True Stories of Incidents that happened in the First World War", 02/4/1

Worthington, Lieutenant James. Papers. 75/28/

Selected Bibliography

There are entire volumes of bibliographies of the Great War. Here are just a few of the most useful for this particular study.

Arthur, Max, *Forgotten Voices of the Great War: A History of World War I in the Words of the Men and Women Who Were There* (Guilford, Connecticut: Lyons Press: 2002).

Barton, Peter; Peter Doyle, Johan Vandewalle, *Beneath Flanders Fields: The Tunnellers' War, 1914-1918* (Staplehurst, Kent: Spellmount, 2004).

Beckett, Jan and Keith Simpson, *A nation in arms: a social study of the British army in the First World War* [sic] (Manchester: Manchester University Press, 1985).

Churchill, Winston, *The World Crisis* (New York: Charles Scribner's Sons, 1923).

Cross, Tim, *The Lost Voices of World War I: An International Anthology of Writers, Poets and Playwrights* (Iowa City: University of Iowa, 1988).

DeGroot, Gerald J, *The First World War* (New York: Palgrave, 2001).

Ellis, John, *Eye Deep in Hell: Trench Warfare in World War I* (Baltimore: Johns Hopkins University Press, 1976).

Fillis, James, *Breaking and Riding: With Military Commentaries*. Translated by M. H. Hayes (Gilford, Connecticut: Lyons Press, 2005. (Originally published in 1902).

Gilbert, Martin, *The Somme: Heroism and Horror in the First World War* (New York: Henry Holt and Company, 2006).

Groome, Winston, *A Storm in Flanders: 1914-1918: Tragedy and Triumph on the Western Front* (New York: Atlantic Monthly Press, 2002).

Harris, J. P., *Douglas Haig and the First World War* (Cambridge: Cambridge University Press, 2008).

Holt, Tonie and Valmai, *Major and Mrs. Holt's Pocket Battlefield Guide: Ypres and*

Passchendaele (Barnsley, South Yorkshire: Pen and Sword Military, 2006).

Howard, Michael, *The First World War* (Oxford: Oxford University Press, 2002).

Jones, Archer, *The Art of War in the Western World* (Oxford: Oxford University Press, 1987).

Liddell Hart, B. H. *The Real War: 1914-1918* (Boston: Little, Brown and Company, 1938).

Philpott, William, *Three Armies on the Somme: The First Battle of the Twentieth Century* (New York: Alfred A. Knopf, 2010).

Prior, Robin and Trevor Wilson, *The Somme* (New Haven: Yale University Press, 2005).

Reid, Fiona, *Broken Men: Shell Shock, Treatment and Recovery in Britain, 1914-1930* (London: Continuum, 2010).

Sheffield, Gary, Editor, *War on the Western Front* (Oxford: Osprey Publishing, 2007).

Sheffield, Gary and John Brown, Editors, *Douglas Haig: War Diaries and Letters, 1914-1918* (London: Weidenfeld and Nicholson, 2005).

Silkin, Jon, *The Penguin Book of First World War Poetry* (London: Penguin Books, 1996).

Simpson, Andy, Editor, *Hot Blood and Cold Steel: Life and Death in the Trenches of the First World War* (London: Tom Donovan, 1993).

Stevenson, David, *CATACLYSM: The First World War as a Political Tragedy* (New York: Basic Books, 2004).

Strong, Paul and Sanders Marble, *Artillery in the Great War* (Barnsley: Pen and Sword Military, 2011).

Tuckman, Barbara, *The Guns of August* (New York: Ballantine Books, 1994).

Van Emden, Richard and Victor Piuk, *Famous: 1914-1918* (Barnsley: Pen and Sword Books, 2008).

Waters, Fiona, *A Corner of a Foreign Field: The Illustrated Poetry of the First World War* (Hertfordshire: Transatlantic Press, 2007).

Wheatly, Dennis, *Officer and Temporary Gentleman 1914-1919* (London: Hutchinson and Co., 1978).

Whiteman, Cedric, *Patriot, Padre and Priest: A Life of Henry Whiteman* (Worthing, West Sussex, 1985).

Wohl, Robert, *The Generations of 1914* (Cambridge: Harvard University Press, 1979).